# Rediscoveries

*Books by the same author*

FICTION
The Shadow Knows
Cassandra Singing
The Beautiful Greed

NONFICTION
American Dreams, American Nightmares (Editor)
James M. Cain
The Poetic Image in Six Genres
Proletarian Writers of the Thirties (Editor)
Tough Guy Writers of the Thirties (Editor)
Wright Morris

# Rediscoveries

*Informal Essays in Which Well-Known Novelists
Rediscover Neglected Works of Fiction
by One of Their Favorite Authors*

EDITED AND WITH AN INTRODUCTION BY

# DAVID MADDEN

CROWN PUBLISHERS, INC.     NEW YORK

© 1971 BY CROWN PUBLISHERS, INC.
LIBRARY OF CONGRESS CATALOG CARD NUMBER: 79–147337
MANUFACTURED IN THE UNITED STATES OF AMERICA
PUBLISHED SIMULTANEOUSLY IN CANADA BY
GENERAL PUBLISHING COMPANY LIMITED

All the essays in REDISCOVERIES were written expressly for that volume, although the following appeared in periodicals prior to their publication in book form.

KAY BOYLE, "Wolfgang Borchert's THE MAN OUTSIDE," Introduction to the New Directions edition.

BRAINARD CHENEY, "Caroline Gordon's THE MALEFACTORS," *The Sewanee Review.*

EVAN S. CONNELL, JR., "Janet Lewis's THE WIFE OF MARTIN GUERRE," *Atlantic,* under the title "Genius Unobserved."

JAMES B. HALL, "Mario Puzo's THE DARK ARENA," *West Coast Review.*

JOYCE CAROL OATES, "Harriette Arnow's THE DOLLMAKER," *The New York Times Book Review.*

WALKER PERCY, "Walter M. Miller, Jr.'s A CANTICLE FOR LEIBOWITZ," *The Southern Review.*

WALLACE STEGNER, "Glenway Wescott's GOOD-BYE WISCONSIN," *The Southern Review.*

HARVEY SWADOS, "Boris Pilnyak's THE VOLGA FALLS TO THE CASPIAN SEA," *Dissent.*

ROBERT PENN WARREN, "Andrew Lytle's THE LONG NIGHT,"
*The Southern Review.*

Quotations from Wolfgang Borchert, THE MAN OUTSIDE,
translated by David Porter and Copyright 1949 by Rowohlt
Verlag GMBH, are reprinted by permission of New Directions
Publishing Corporation.

To Walter Van Tilburg Clark,
a fine writer
and one of the greatest teachers
in the country

## ACKNOWLEDGMENTS

For this volume no editor could have been more appropriate than David McDowell. As a publisher (McDowell, Obolensky), he built up a distinguished list, including James Agee's *A Death in the Family;* as an editor with various houses and magazines, he has discovered an impressive number of writers. *Rediscoveries* was conceived in conversations with Robie Macauley and George Lanning in 1965. I want to thank E. R. Hagemann for his suggestions in the early stages of this project. Margaret Myers, Marie Jones, Elie Ward, and, above all, and always, my wife, Robbie, were helpful in the preparation of the manuscript.

# CONTENTS

# Contents

# Contents

# Rediscoveries

# INTRODUCTION

Everyone has a favorite little-known novel that he is fond of urging upon his friends. The novelists whose essays are assembled here were asked to rediscover their own favorite neglected work of fiction. Although as it happened, the books discussed are of many types, periods, and nationalities, there has been no attempt to be representative. That I had neither heard of nor read some of the books chosen by the contributors illustrates the purpose of *Rediscoveries;* I have now read practically all of them, inspired less by editorial obligation than by the essays themselves. In a couple of cases, I have been unable so far to beg, borrow, or steal copies anywhere.

The purpose of *Rediscoveries* is to pay attention, and tribute, to works that are not known, even to many discriminating readers. Listening to writers talk about some of their favorite reading is in itself enjoyable, and these essays will have special appeal for readers who want to discover writing that current literary fashions neglect. The contributors would argue that the works discussed here are as "relevant" as better-known novels because they have retained their value as literature in every lasting sense of the term.

In his preface to Vanguard's reissue of Ford Madox Ford's *The Fifth Queen,* Graham Greene says of *The Good Soldier,* "I don't know how many times in nearly forty years I have come back to this novel of Ford's, every time to discover a new aspect to admire." To the person who champions it, every neglected work of the imagination is—to echo that memorable first line of Ford's novel—"the saddest story I have ever heard."

1

Sometimes a neglected writer's methods bring fame to many other writers who may never have even heard the innovator's name. Caroline Gordon tells about Ford's visit to her creative writing class in 1938. He observed that his Impressionistic technique was being used in a *Saturday Evening Post* serial that happened to be lying on the table. Miss Gordon, who has called Ford the best craftsman of his day, found it easier to understand the neglect of his novels in his own day than in ours, "for he would seem, in these times, to have a special claim on our attention." Since Ford himself had hardly been recognized in America, Miss Gordon thought it "highly suitable" that the "brilliant" preface to Knopf's 1950 reissue edition of *Parade's End* (1925) should be written by a young writer, Robie Macauley, "whose own work will doubtless be better known later on." Caroline Gordon herself is well known to critics but to too few readers; as Brainard Cheney points out in his essay on Miss Gordon's *The Malefactors,* all eight of her novels are out of print.

James Joyce was one of those writers who refined the technique of an obscure author and became, after prolonged struggle, a famous writer himself. He rescued from oblivion the man who originated the interior monologue technique that Joyce made famous—Édouard Dujardin. Neglected writers aren't always sympathetic to other neglected writers. But while Ford, Pound, and many others were creating interest in his own works, Joyce was encouraging Italo Svevo, who had published two novels. "There is no unanimity so perfect as the unanimity of silence," Svevo said. "I could come to only one conclusion, that I was not a writer." Joyce read the two novels, and said, "Do you know that you are a neglected writer?" Joyce's biographer, Richard Ellmann, tells us that partly because of Joyce's praise, Svevo "began to write again more seriously than he had for some years." The result was *The Confessions of Zeno* (1923). When this one was poorly received, Svevo felt, at sixty, that he had done a foolish thing. But Joyce had the novel sent to friends, calling Svevo the "only modern Italian writer who interested him," and their encouragement made a great difference in Svevo's life.

Writers have always enjoyed helping other writers. Some indirectly: with a comment in his preface to his own *Major Barbara,* Shaw aroused interest in Samuel Butler's *The Way of All Flesh* (1903). Ezra Pound, Ford Madox Ford, William Carlos Williams, and Gertrude Stein made direct, sometimes massive, efforts to help writers, a kind of work done today by authors like Allen Tate, Anaïs Nin, Granville Hicks, R. V. Cassill, and George Garrett.

In "An Unread Book," his introduction to Holt's 1965 reissue of Christina Stead's *The Man Who Loved Children* (1940), Randall Jarrell lucidly expressed the rediscovery spirit. "When we think of the masterpieces that nobody praised and nobody read, back there in the past, we feel an impatient superiority to the readers of the past. If we had been there, we can't help feeling, *we'd* have known that *Moby Dick* was a good book—why, how could anyone help knowing?" When Stead's novel first appeared, Jarrell bought two copies, "one to read and the other to lend." Having lost both to borrowers, he had to use a library copy to write his introduction. Readers returned to him unread the copies of *Crime and Punishment* and *Remembrance of Things Past* that he lent.

> There is no book you can lend people that all of them will like. But *The Man Who Loved Children* has been a queer exception. I have lent it to many writers and more readers, and all of them thought it good and original, a book different from any other. They could see that there were things wrong with it—a novel is a prose narrative of some length that has something wrong with it—but they felt that, somehow, the things didn't matter.

This strange experience made Jarrell see that Stead's novel was one of those books that "their own age neither reads nor praises, but that the next age thinks a masterpiece." Stead is better known now, but still neglected.

Some novels are never widely read even though critics and writers repeatedly refer to them as classics. As if in anticipation of the problem, Harcourt, Brace in 1937 asked T. S. Eliot to introduce Djuna Barnes's *Nightwood:*

> I am conscious of impertinence in introducing the book at all; and to have read a book a good many times does not necessarily put one in the right knowledge of what to say to those who have not yet read it. . . . I can justify this preface only in the following way. One is liable to expect other people to see, on their first reading of a book, all that one has come to perceive in the course of a developing intimacy with it. . . . What one can do for other readers . . . is trace the more significant phases of one's own appreciation of it. For it took me, with this book, some time to come to an appreciation of its meaning as a whole.

Asked to rediscover the novel for New Directions' 1949 reprint, Eliot replied only that his admiration had not "diminished." In 1962 Farrar, Straus & Giroux published the *Selected Works of Djuna Barnes.*

But even for books that are originally well received by both critics and public the future is by no means assured. In his introduction to Viking's 1963 reissue of Elizabeth Madox Roberts's *The Time of Man* (1926), Robert Penn Warren observed that Ford Madox Ford, T. S. Stribling, and Glenway Wescott were among many who praised Miss Roberts's genius. The novel was a best seller and a Book-of-the-Month Club selection. When she died in 1941, Miss Roberts had "lived past her reputation and her popularity. Now she is remembered only by those who read her in their youth when she was new, and news." Warren wonders how a novel so good could disappear so soon, without a trace. "We may remember, however, that this is not the first good book, or writer, to go underground. There is, for one thing, what we may call the natural history of literary reputation. When a writer dies, we find, immediately after the respectful obsequies, the ritual of 'reassessment'—which is another word for 'cutting-down-to-size.' "

The social-problem-solving thirties found her irrelevant, and the wartime forties forgot her. Robert Penn Warren's essay for this volume deals with one of the most strangely neglected writers of our time, Andrew Lytle, whose four novels are out of print.

Writers' judgments about other writers are not always to be trusted, and sometimes they are rather odd. There is the famous instance of John O'Hara's claim, on the publication of *Across the River and into the Trees,* Hemingway's worst novel, that Hemingway was the greatest writer since Shakespeare. And when a writer of Faulkner's achievement puts Thomas Wolfe above himself, we can only wonder what his criteria are.

I suppose even our most famous contributors have at least one work that needs rediscovery. In correspondence, several prospective contributors expressed an urge to rediscover one of their own novels. Commenting on one's own work is risky. In *Advertisements for Myself,* Norman Mailer showed his usual eagerness to run risks: he described the ordeal of revising and publishing one of his least successful works, *The Deer Park.* Withdrawn in proof stage by its original publisher, it went to eight more houses before Putnam picked it up. Taking another, last look at proof, Mailer discovered that after "three years of living with the book, I could at last admit the style was wrong, that it had been wrong from the time I started, that I had been strangling the life of my novel." It was a "style which came out of nothing so much as my determination to prove I could muster a fine style." But he had never enjoyed work so much before and he felt that he was finally "learning how to write." *The Deer Park* was well advertised, fairly well reviewed, and made the best-seller list for a while. But Mailer wanted its success to soar beyond *The Naked and the Dead.* "Having reshaped my words with an intensity of feeling I had not known before, I could not understand why others were not overcome with my sense of life. . . . I no longer gave a sick dog's drop for the wisdom, the reliability, and the authority of the public's literary mind, those creeps and old ladies of vested reviewing."

In "News for the Mineshaft," an essay reprinted, along with Mailer's, in *Afterwords: Novelists on Their Novels* (1969), Reynolds Price (blessed with a fine publisher from the start) reminds his readers of their obligations. They failed the test art exacts. The year his novel appeared, Price could offer his readers "nothing more helpful than that the fault was theirs, not the book's or mine. And now at a distance . . . I can offer little more: they were found lacking. *A Generous Man,* however imperfect (and I'm sure that I am the chief authority on its imperfections) . . . discovered holes in a number of its readers—in their appreciative ability." One objection was to Price's difficult style, his "refusal to contract with readers-on-horseback, racing by." The race in which they entered his novel was not the one Price had entered. They failed to judge his "performance over his own course." "I trusted the wit of the audience. I may not again."

In talking about the works themselves, most of the contributors are moved by the rediscovery experience to comment on the ironies, paradoxes, and mysteries of neglect.

There are many instances, of course, of immediate and sustained critical and popular success on the American literary scene: Irwin Shaw, Walker Percy, Robert Penn Warren, Norman Mailer, and Reynolds Price. But first novels have a way of fading from view even when the author later becomes famous. Gertrude Stein herself, says Jane Mayhall, claims to have "forgotten" her first novel, *Things As They Are* (written in 1903), and it was not until 1950 that a small press published it—posthumously. Suffering the fate of many experimental writers whose experiments have been assimilated by other writers into the mainstream, Gertrude Stein is not read much today. Ironically, *Things As They Are,* the least experimental of her novels, is read much less than *Three Lives.*

Some first novels become *only* novels. Warren Eyster expresses the melancholy of finding a yellowed copy of his rediscovery, Humphrey Cobb's *Paths of Glory* (1935), in a college library. "I am the only person ever to have read it." The red and blue of its cover now suggests "dried blood and faded loyalty." Like Cobb himself, who wrote no more novels, Eyster is pessimistic: Did Cobb "discover that the reading public accords books the same bored, predetermined, and unheeding pretense of attention that a military court-martial offers to its victims?" Even selection by the Book-of-the-Month Club couldn't "break through public apathy. . . . Poor fools who believe in rediscoveries!" And yet Eyster believes in them enough to make one himself—and to inspire for Cobb who knows how many young readers, more reluctant now than ever to be led by the nose down paths of glory.

Humphrey Cobb's novel was perhaps more acceptable in 1935 than Mario Puzo's first novel, *The Dark Arena,* was in 1955, but the prophetic visions of both remain unheeded. Although hindsight isn't always sharper, we are often wrong, says James B. Hall, about what is important in fiction. "The 'important' fiction and nonfiction of America in the mid-fifties is like some gray, inflated apparition disappearing across the flat fields of memory." He laments the influence of the best-seller list in the fifties as a recommendation of "quality" for people who buy books. Some of the best were neglected also by critics who "worked not so much for a new vital literature" as for a New Criticism. Many of the novels taken seriously in the fifties can be seen now, Hall argues, as more profound versions of the sentimentality, evasiveness, and false optimism of Norman Vincent Peale. Mario Puzo's *The Dark Arena* offered no compromise; in this novel, one may discover a stark reflection of the nature of the American occupation of Germany and perhaps reach some understanding of our Vietnam tragedy.

Many good novels start inauspiciously. Janet Lewis's *The Wife of Martin Guerre* (and her other novels) was published by the distinguished small press, Alan Swallow. "I dislike historical novels," says Evan Connell, "and will go several steps out of my way to avoid anybody who is promoting one." As often happens, he cannot now imagine who directed him to Lewis. Sometimes we don't need to reread or rediscover, because some of our favorite books "print themselves permanently on the mind."

It was one of the contributors who suggested that volumes of short stories be rediscovered. There was, characteristically, little response to that plea, but Glenway Wescott, Marianne Hauser, and Wolfgang Borchert represent the form well. The problem of neglect is, of course, much more complex for volumes of stories. Philip Roth and Joyce Carol Oates are rare in first winning recognition with stories. Even established writers put out collections at their publisher's loss. In the twenties, Glenway Wescott earned "many readers, universal critical praise," and was considered a major young writer; but Wallace Stegner admits that Wescott's reputation has "sagged." After *Good-Bye Wisconsin* (1928), a collection of stories, Wescott's last important work was *The Pilgrim Hawk* (1940).

A volume of stories that must depend upon the limited advertising and distributing facilities of a university press gets off to a doubly damned bad start; a blessing, however, is that it will stay in print, usually, long after collections of stories by established writers published by trade houses have been remaindered. Marianne Hauser's *A Lesson in Music* (1964), rediscovered by Anaïs Nin, was published by the University of Texas Press. Recently, university presses have made a special effort to take this unwanted child of mass publishing and guide it patiently over the congested terrain of modern bookselling.

Some contributors describe their relationship with the book they discuss as if they were characters in a Jamesian novel, tracking down clues about the mystery of a person who is a puzzle with key pieces missing. George Lanning's essay is the most obvious example, as he retraces his investigations relating to "Elizabeth," Countess Russell. Her *Mr. Skeffington* is known in the United States (Bette Davis in the movie was unforgettable, at least), but Lanning prefers to discuss *The Pastor's Wife* (1914), her least typical and most neglected novel. Literary detective work is a normal preoccupation for those who, like Jack Matthews, "read liberally in that strange, seemingly incestuous type of literature called 'Books About Books,' in which collectors give expression to their enthusiasms." These bookmen, "for all their expertise and all their love for literature, had it within them to be monumentally wrong"— overpraising, for instance, Christopher Morley at a time when Faulkner had not been rediscovered. Their judgments were universally sound, however, Matthews insists, about Norman Douglas's *South Wind*. Matthews found a copy in an old junk store, and his rereading even corroborated the dust-jacket rhetoric.

The works of unfashionable foreign writers face especially unpredictable futures. George P. Elliott sums up the problem of the foreign novel that is presented to the public under the best circumstances—respected author, reputable publisher, excellent translation, decent reviews—but still sinks into obscurity. Ramón Sender's *A Man's Place* (1940) and Jean Giono's *The Horseman on the Roof* (1954) published almost fourteen years apart, suffered similar neglect. Elliott's theory is that these novels were shrugged off for failing to "do homage to the great god Zeitgeist."

Writers are not the only readers who lament, "I can't understand why this novel was so poorly received!" The same groups of readers—reviewers, writers, critics, teachers, scholars, the public, and, lest we forget, publishers—who neglect one book are the ones who discover and rediscover others. It is easy to blame these groups, separately or collectively, for the decline of books, even careers; so easy that it's done quite often. The guilt is not entirely off-target, of course; but the process is almost as mysterious, gratuitous, and chance-ridden, as the creative process itself.

In William Gaddis's *The Recognitions,* a "big, unshaven

man" (who some of the characters suspect is Ernest Hemingway) says: "What I get a kick out of is these serious writers who write a book where they say money gives a false significance to art, and then they raise hell when their book doesn't make any money." Some writers become embittered to incapacitation by the abuse or neglect of reviewers and readers. Gore Vidal says of John Horne Burns's *The Gallery* (1947), "the best book of the Second War," that "extreme circumstances made him write a book which was better than his talent, an unbearable fate for an ambitious artist." All his later work "is overshadowed by the splendid accident of a moment's genius." Burns "detested all other writers, and wanted to be great," says Vidal. "Night after night, he would stand at the Excelsior Hotel bar in Florence . . . insulting imagined enemies and imagined friends, and all the while complaining of what had been done to him by book reviewers." He died in self-imposed exile in Italy at the age of thirty-seven.

In a recent issue of the *New Republic,* Reed Whittemore, the literary editor (who is a poet as well), discussed the nature of reviewing today. Even his own magazine must, to survive, keep up with the latest and the loudest. "Their neglect would hurt *us.*" He would like to revive a practice of Malcolm Cowley's when he was literary editor in the thirties: Cowley wrote to prominent literary critics asking them to discover recent books that had not received appropriate attention. Whittemore decided, however, that "the obligation to ferret out the best being written—and see that it gets impartially, intelligently . . . , thoroughly and beautifully reviewed—is a joke when surrounded by thousands and thousands of titles. How does one push such incredible publishing quantities through a sound, all-purpose, aesthetic, intellectual, socially responsible, and maybe even honest filter?" If he reviews "quiet books of merit," his voice, too, will be drowned out. On the other hand, there's the problem of a scarcity of good books. Whittemore argues that a policy of reviewing only good—often unfashionable—books would result in his judgment being impugned: "Judgment in literature is impugned to the extent that it is exercised."

Although some writers are justified, at least partly, in attacking individual critics, the general contempt for criticism itself, voiced by some writers, is not justified. If one gang of critics stomps a writer to death, another may come along and resurrect him. Indifference by critics now may turn to passionate advocacy later. John Aldridge can be a very caustic critic, but he was one of the first to publish a book of essays on contemporary writers (*After the Lost Generation,* 1951). Now many students of literature are writing about current writers. *Rediscoveries* will suggest more possibilities; for we must not only study new writers for their relevance, but rediscover writers of the distant and recent past to fill the gaps that oversight has left.

Revivals of critical admiration do not necessarily create a steady following of general readers for a particular work, but there are enough instances of belated success to make the effort not just worthwhile, duty done, but exciting: Kurt Vonnegut, Jr., Saul Bellow, Bernard Malamud, William Golding, Vladimir Nabokov. Her first novel having appeared in 1911, Ivy Compton-Burnett achieved sudden fame in 1945. Irony is an occupational hazard for writers. While many great novels sold well from the start, others—Nathanael West's *The Day of the Locust* (1939), for example—sold under one thousand copies. West is very highly placed today. Who to thank? Don't overlook the critic. There are some standout instances of rediscoveries by critics: Melville, Henry James, Fitzgerald. One of the most famous examples is Malcolm Cowley's stimulus to a reexamination of Faulkner. In his introduction to the Viking Portable (1946), Cowley said: "No author has a higher standing among his fellow novelists." But "his early novels were overpraised, usually for the wrong reasons; his later and in many ways better novels have been obstinately condemned or simply neglected; and in 1945 all his seventeen books were out of print, with some of them unobtainable in the second-hand bookshops."

The fate of a novel is very unpredictable; a resurgence of interest can come at any time; sometimes it comes from a publisher. Horace McCoy was never as popular as his contemporary James M. Cain, although the French read him seriously in the forties. But in 1966, Avon reprinted *They Shoot Horses, Don't They?* (1935), and a movie version appeared a few years later (one of many instances in which the movies have revived interest in a novel). It is hoped that the fifteen out-of-print works discussed in *Rediscoveries* will be reprinted, at least in paperback, and made available to those readers who are persuaded by the personal testimonies of the contributors. Readers themselves can persuade publishers to reprint.

Anthony Burgess offered an essay on G. V. Desani's *All About H. Hatterr* (1948) to *Rediscoveries,* but it was to appear too soon as an introduction to a new edition of the novel. He recounts a familiar story: T. S. Eliot praised the novel in the highest terms and "other distinguished critics were equally laudatory, and Desani's name should have been made for ever. But, inexplicably [the book] went underground and became a coterie pleasure." Burgess insists that "it is the public that counts, and the public ought to have a chance to read it." That chance would be denied the public were it not for novelist-critics like Burgess himself and publishers like Farrar, Straus & Giroux. Among celebrated reprinting ventures are the Grove editions of D. H. Lawrence's *Lady Chatterley's Lover* and Henry Miller's *Tropic of Capricorn* and *Tropic of Cancer* (in the introduction to which Karl Shapiro contradicted O'Hara: "I call Henry Miller the greatest living author"). Recently, Avon has reprinted Roth's *Call It Sleep* and Michael Gold's *Jews Without Money* among many other neglected works; Delacorte has risked offering Robert Musil's *Five Women;* Harper & Row has had the audacity to chance a Wright Morris reader. Among the small presses, Alan Swallow keeps Allen Tate's *The Fathers* in print. Southern Illinois University Press is performing one of the functions we ought to expect of university presses; it is reprinting the early novels of Kay Boyle, D. H. Lawrence, Richard Aldington, H. G. Wells, and others, including the only novel of Zelda Fitzgerald, *Save Me the Waltz*. *Rediscoveries* is Crown's contribution to the always unfinished business of seeing belated acts of justice done.

While they assume the lasting relevance of art, many of the contributors also take pains to indicate the renewed relevance today of the work they discuss. Boris Pilnyak's work suffered for political reasons, even though he wrote in sympathy with Soviet experiments. Hailed at one time as "one of the giants of the modern novel," Pilnyak is seldom read now, and Harvey Swados, author of a new novel, *Standing Fast* (which analyzes the behavior of radicals over four decades), is interested in the problem of the thesis novel for an equivocating, "unheroic" author like Pilnyak for whom "degradation was followed by extinction." Swados could not have chosen a less fashionable sort of writer in whom to arouse our interest. The benefit of that risk is our own if we read *The Volga Falls to the Caspian Sea* (1931). Knut Hamsun's political stance—he welcomed the Germans to Norway—seriously constricted his circle of admirers. Jesse Hill Ford writes about *Growth of the Soil* (1917), recently reprinted, along with Hamsun's *Hunger*. For Ford, Hamsun's works, all of which he read while living in Norway as a Fulbright scholar in 1961, provide a larger humanitarian vision in our time of specific social issues and apocalyptic careenings.

Judson Jerome, who is participating in an experimental university venture, rereads Mariano Azuela's *Los de Abajo* (1915) as a counterrevolutionary novel that depicts revolution without sentimentality. Ironically, when he first read this journalistic exposé novel in 1949, it "radicalized" him "in an uncanny way; I have not recovered." Kay Boyle is another writer who testifies to having lived—seventeen years in her case—"intimately and passionately with one particular book. . . . There are days . . . when I have been unable to start writing without first opening Borchert's book and reading a page of it. . . . I have been startled awake at night by the terrifying conviction that the book is lost. . . . Fear of losing it is absurd, for even if it were to disappear, I have carried so much of it in me for so long a time that it could never be forgotten." She feels dependent upon the book, "almost as if it were an actual person." It becomes part of the lives of her creative writing students, too, for she talks about it in class; she teaches at San Francisco State College, where the book's political relevance, its exhortation to say "No" to social evil, became particularly acute several years ago, as she recounts in her new book, *The Long Walk at San Francisco State.*

Some of the contributors are even more personal in describing their affection for the work of their choice. "There are certainly greater novels than *The Dollmaker,*" says Joyce Carol Oates, "but I can think of none that have moved me more, personally, terrifyingly." (This description is true of the effect of Oates's own novels on many of her readers.) For R. V. Cassill, to rediscover Benjamin Constant's *Adolphe* (1816) is to reexperience a great deal more than a work of the imagination. "I first read *Adolphe* in French in a year when I had run off to Europe with a woman who had left her husband to go with me."

There are writers who are successful by virtue of sales or reputation, or both, who want to help other writers, and there are those who don't. Even some unsuccessful writers are too immobilized by neglect to care very much about somebody else's situation. Nearly every writer of consequence in America (and some in other countries) was invited to contribute to *Rediscoveries.* Some wanted very much to contribute but were understandably too intensely at work on new fiction of their own. Many replied with encouragement: Eudora Welty, Herman Wouk, Norman Mailer, Leslie Fiedler, John Barth, Thomas Berger, Andrew Lytle, Walter Van Tilburg Clark, Caroline Gordon, J. F. Powers, Max Steele, Bruce Jay Friedman, Elizabeth Hardwick, Mario Puzo, James Dickey, Philip Roth, Peter Taylor; others, who came very close to contributing, wished the venture well: Frederick Buechner, Thomas Williams, Louis Auchincloss, Vance Bourjaily, Anthony Burgess, Reynolds Price, Josephine Herbst, John Aldridge, Norman Corwin, R. H. W. Dillard, Herbert Gold, William Gibson, Louis Rubin, David Slavitt, Robie Macauley, Mark Schorer, Ralph Ellison, Richard Yates, Mark Harris. One hundred-fifty writers were invited; only two were unfriendly to the proposal that they write essays, boasting that they neither read nor write criticism; no one was hostile to the idea itself. Several writers cited some odd examples of neglect, from Uncle Remus and *Middlemarch* to *Sister Carrie* and *Native Son*. Reynolds Price replied that the writers he rereads don't need a general rediscovery: Tolstoy, Hardy, Eudora Welty.

Rereading is, of course, the test of a good book. Some potential contributors reread the works they wanted to write about, but discovered them not stimulating enough to warrant an essay. Rediscovery can be a risky business for author and reader alike.

Some of the contributors are better known than others. Many qualify for rediscovery themselves; it seemed appropriate that they rediscover other neglected writers. A restrained sampling of many other undeservedly neglected works, recommended by various writers and critics, are listed in an annotated bibliography.

Sometimes, as Katherine Anne Porter discovered, one's experience in recommending a book can be frustrating and bewildering. "A number of persons, some of them good friends, all of them well disposed to my work, have confessed that they simply (simply!) could not be interested in *The Itching Parrot*" (1816) by Fernández de Lizardi. "Some of them don't like the picaresque novels in any language." To offer one's favorite neglected novel is then, first of all, an act of personality, not only judgment. These essays should be read as expressions of the artist-person who wrote them—not as literary criticism in a usual sense. The concept of this book is part of the message of each essay.

The title, *Rediscoveries,* refers mainly to the contributors; for most readers the book will offer *discoveries.* Harvey Swados ends his essay by saying that the final word should belong to the author himself, for whom, in Pilnyak's own words, "every book is a convulsion of thought cheating death." The primary aim of *this* book is to persuade readers to reach for *other* books, to pick up, for instance, Richard Yates's *Revolutionary Road* and begin to read words too few eyes have beheld: "The final dying sounds of their dress rehearsal left the Laurel Players with nothing to do but stand there, silent and helpless, blinking out over the footlights of an empty auditorium. . . ."

David  Madden

# ROBERT PENN WARREN

## ON

## ANDREW LYTLE'S

# The Long Night

### ROBERT PENN WARREN

ROBERT PENN WARREN *was born in Guthrie, Kentucky, in 1905. With Cleanth Brooks he is co-founder of the* Southern Review. *He has taught at Yale and other universities. He has published stories, poems, essays, and reviews in too many magazines to list here. Among his nine volumes of poetry are* Brother to Dragons (*1953*), Selected Poems New and Old 1923–1966 (*1966*), Incarnations (*1968*), *and* Audubon: A Vision (*1969*). *Among his most notable novels are* All the King's Men (*1946*), World Enough and Time (*1950*), *and* Flood: A Romance of Our Time (*1964*). *A volume of short stories,* The Circus in the Attic, *appeared in 1948. Among Mr. Warren's many honors are two Pulitzer Prizes, a National Book Award, the Bollingen Prize for poetry, and, most recently, the 1970 National Medal for Literature. He is a member of The American Academy of Arts and Letters. His* Homage to Dreiser, *a critical study marking the centenary of Theodore Dreiser's birth, will be published this year.*

∽

### ANDREW LYTLE

ANDREW LYTLE *was born in Murfreesboro, Tennessee, in 1902. A graduate of Sewanee Military Academy, Mr. Lytle studied at Vanderbilt and at the Yale Drama School. For several years, he earned his living as an actor. His first book was* Bedford Forrest and His Critter Company (*1931*), *a biography. He contributed to the Agrarian manifesto* I'll Take My Stand (*1930*) *and to* Who Owns America? (*1936*); *he is the author*

17

*of numerous critical essays and has taught and lectured at the
University of Iowa, the University of Florida, the University
of the South, and at many writers' workshops and conferences.
His first novel,* The Long Night, *appeared in 1936. His other
works of fiction are* At the Moon's End *(1941),* A Name for
Evil *(1947),* The Velvet Horn *(1957), and* A Novel, Novella,
and Four Stories *(1958). He has received three Guggenheim
grants and the* Kenyon Review *Fellowship for Fiction; he
chaired the International Seminar on the Humanities at Harvard
in 1955. Editor of the* Sewanee Review, *Mr. Lytle lives in
Monteagle, Tennessee.*

---

One evening, back in the 1930s, in a camp on a bluff over-
looking the Cumberland River, my old friend, the historian Frank Owsley, launched into a story of his youth—or
rather, into a story that he had learned in his youth, back
about 1910, as well as I can now calculate it. Away from
home, at college, he received a letter from a kinsman whom he
had never seen, a great-uncle, an eccentric who had long since
withdrawn from the world and was remembered in the family
as only a dim legend. The letter commanded—and it was a
command uttered with, apparently, perfect certainty of obedience—that the young Frank come to the kinsman's house on a
certain day, and gave careful directions. The matter, the letter
declared, was one of the greatest urgency.

Frank, impelled by curiosity and family loyalty, obeyed,
and found his way to the remote spot in Alabama where the
old man lived in a solid old-fashioned prosperity, in a sealed-
off valley that in all particulars seemed to belong to the middle
of the preceding century. The uncle, a powerful and handsome
old man (the power and handsomeness easily believed, for
Frank had those qualities), received the guest with affection
but, also, with antique formality, and after dinner began a
nightlong tale that left the auditor shaken and sweating, in the
first cold dawn light.

The tale went back to the late 1850s, when the father of the old man, the great-grandfather of Frank, who had lately come to Alabama from Georgia, was shot to death in his bed, while his wife and youngest son looked on, by a gang of men who had burst into the house. The victim had fallen foul of a gang somewhat like the organization of Murrell, the great outlaw who earlier had terrorized the old Natchez Trace, and who, in his bloodlust and ambition, was reported to have dreamed an empire. This gang, as that of the prototype Murrell was reputed to do, operated in the guise of decent and respectable men, men who had, over some years, been corrupted and blackmailed or gradually sucked into the power of the mastermind, and the murdered man had had the ill fortune to stumble upon the fatal secret. The gang had framed the victim as a slave-stealer (and, I think, an abolitionist), and had made the murder appear as the act of an outraged citizenry; and since the gang's tentacles reached into places of influence and power, any real legal investigation was blocked.

The murderers, however, had reckoned without the young boy who had watched the deed and who was able to penetrate beneath some of the perfunctory masks and disguises. The boy became obsessed with vengeance. His life was one long act of execution. So the young Frank, sitting by the dying fire of that remote farmhouse, heard the avenger, now an old man, tell how over the years, he had sought out, one by one, the members of the gang. He had lived his strange, withdrawn life, and even in his later years had raised a family, but in his isolation and eccentricity, his goings and comings had long since ceased to arouse comment. He might be gone for a year or two on the trail of some victim concerning whom he had gleaned word in his indefatigable search; and when he had his satisfaction he would come home to his valley. His family knew nothing of his mission and mania. They knew only that "Poppa" had "business."

The old man had not summoned Frank because, at last,

he had to tell somebody, had to confess to clear his soul or to make his boast. Far from it. He was getting old. He could no longer trust his thews or his cunning, and two or three of the murderers yet remained alive. He had traced them—one to some town in Kansas, one to San Francisco. Frank was the male kin next in line for the mission of vengeance. As dawn came on in the room where the ashes had long since gone gray on the hearth, the great-uncle declared the obligation. He had all necessary data about the intended victims—very old men now forgetting or perhaps not even believing their own old deed of blood that cried out for vengeance.

Needless to say, Frank did not accept the mission offered by the bloodthirsty old loon, went on with college (punctuated, I think, with some stints of school teaching), and on to a Ph.D. at the University of Chicago. As for the story told so long after, it delighted me, but it was only one in a long line of stories from the old times that not infrequently were strange and bloody, this one different from others only in being somewhat stranger and bloodier. But a little later—or perhaps a little before Frank told the tale to me—he told it, sitting on the porch of a plantation in Alabama, to the perfect listener—to Andrew Lytle.

Andrew was always the perfect listener to tales, for the simple reason that he himself was the perfect teller of tales. I have heard a few great tale-tellers—Stark Young, Katherine Anne Porter, Brooks Hays, Lyle Saxon, and Roark Bradford; and Andrew was second to none—unless his own father. But if he was capable of listening in appreciation, he was also capable, on occasion, of listening for appropriation. This act, too, might be peculiarly selfless. The ill-formed tale needed to be set right, the ill-telling of the tale needed to be set right, to have pace, tone, or gesture amended. But out of a deeper reason yet, Andrew might appropriate a tale—because it touched something in his nature, in the way a subject "chooses" the writer. And the tale that Frank told him touched, I have al-

ways believed, that kind of "something" in the listener's nature.

The tale also sprang from the world that always most
stirred Andrew's imagination and humor. He knew the world
of the plantation and of the deeper backcountry in the hills
beyond the plantations. He knew the language, every shade of
it by tone and phrase, every inflection, every hint of pain or
poetry, the humor, the bawdiness, every expression of face. He
knew the objects and practices of the old times, and of the
backcountry, how meat was dressed, how food was cooked,
how meal was ground or hominy made, what people—men or
women or children—wore, how wool was carded, how shakes
were split and whiskey run. He knew such things because he
had the keenest of eyes, the shrewdest of ears, insatiable curiosity, and an elephantine memory; but most of all because he
had a natural generosity and simplicity of heart and could stop
a stranger on the road or lounge on the steps at the most deso-
late crossroads store and in ten minutes be swapping crop-talk
or tales with the local whittlers, in perfect ease and pleasure
and with devoted attention. He was soaked in history, as a
youth had lived in France and loved French literature, and
was not only a natural-born actor but a trained one who had
done a little stint on Broadway. But such things as travel and
education had merely sharpened his appetite for, and appreciation of, the world from which he had sprung.

In any case, Andrew was the perfect listener to the tale,
and Frank, sensing this, finally "gave" it to him, lock, stock,
and barrel. It became a novel, *The Long Night,* published in
1936.

"His voice stopped suddenly, as a clock might stop"—that is
the first sentence of *The Long Night.* Dawn has come, the
voice of the bloodthirsty old loon stops, the tale is over, and
the "I"—who corresponds to the young Frank Owsley—says,
in the next sentence: "I remember the room for a moment

seemed to hang in a hiatus of time, in such a hiatus as only the body can know when the heart's last stroke sounds down the blood stream." We know that we are in good hands. This teller knows the craft of telling, and we are ready to turn back in years to the moment when all had begun.

The tale unfolds, uncoils, thrusts forward, hesitates, lingers luxuriously in a sunlit moment, lifts, again thrusts forward. Like all good tales, it has its own life and will, and works its will on us. We forget the teller of the tale—the tellers in fact, for there is the old man, now Pleasant McIvor by name, and the young man who, there in the firelit room, had been "spitted" by the obsessed glare of the old man's gaze, held hour on hour while the fire dies, and whose voice now interfuses with that of old Pleasant McIvor: "From what he told me that night and from what I was able to learn from other sources, I was able to piece the story together, and of course you must understand that, at this late date, I cannot tell which words are his and which are mine . . ." But there is another voice behind these voices. It is the voice that, in the art of the telling, we forget—except in those few moments when the artistry flags. It is the voice of Andrew Lytle.

The tale had already been told twice—really "told"— once in the camp on the Cumberland bluff and once on Cornsilk Plantation. But, inevitably, the shape, pace, and "feel" of an oral tale is never twice the same. The hour of the day, the state of the weather or of the teller's digestion, the season, the attitude of the auditors, the kind of drink in the hand—a thousand things modify the tale. But when, in the cold light of morning, the teller faces the blank, white page, alone, with no friend present and no glass in the hand, all is different. The greatest difference is that now he is to freeze the tale in the act of telling. That is the terrible fact.

What does Andrew Lytle do *to, for, with,* the tale that had lived in voices? What, that is, beyond his own special narrative élan?

First, he gives it a world. In the other tellings the tale had not needed a world. The world had been solidly there in the consciousness, in the blood, even, of the listeners. But once a tale gets frozen on paper, what the reader knows or does not know about the world of the tale, in consciousness or bloodstream, is no longer relevant. In a sense, the reader is now an abstraction. He is not there when the telling—i.e., the writing—takes place. The tale must now "be" its own world as well as what happens in that world, and the "being" of this world is not mere information about geography, sociology, and history, but, ultimately, an aspect of form. Form is merely a complex of dynamic relations, and the relations between scene (world) on one hand and action and character on the other, are fundamental and germinal.

Effortlessly, as naturally as breath is drawn, as secretly as Pleasant McIvor ever stalked the appointed victim, the author of *The Long Night* creates his world. He never "describes" the world, he is merely aware of it. This is not to say that description does not appear. It does. At a summer dawn the sky "snapped open like a colored fan." At a moment of tension, when the outlaw chief instinctively asserts his authority over his gang, he let his gaze "slide across their faces like a plane." The avenger watches the "first bodiless flame" lick the wood of a house he has fired to burn the body of a victim. Or when a deputy reports the finding of the body of Judge Wilton, another victim, who had presumably died of an accidental fall from the balcony of an inn to the stones of the riverbank and has lain there all night, with one hand in the water, the deputy says: "The water had washed it plumb white. It was wrinkled like a old woman's hand."

Ordinarily, however, description appears in terms special to that world, opening some fuller or deeper glimpse into the world. On the first page, as the simplest kind of example, dawn light lies upon the "puncheon floor"—because the floor is of puncheons. In the next sentence, the fire curls over the "back stick into the dark suck of the chimney's mouth." True, the "dark suck of the chimney's mouth" is description, vivid with the word "suck," but the key to the world is in the innocent phrase "back stick"—instead of "back log." Or take the picture of exhausted hounds that "let their tongues hang dripping in the dust and trash." This is nothing, worse than nothing, until the word "trash," the only word the speaker of that world could have used. Or take the biscuits on Sheriff Botterall's table, "large as saucers and puffed out on top like feather pillows"—the kind of biscuits to be found on a Botterall table but not on that of the gentry like the Harrisons, however come down. Or take the remark about the close friendship from girlhood of two women now old: they "had set up housekeeping at the same time and had boiled water for each other when the children came." Or the remark of one of these old women to a young girl who can preen herself that her husband has not changed since the birth of their child: but "you're eaten yore white bread now"—not the bread of bran and tailings near the bottom of the barrel. Here is the glimpse of a world—the hard world for women in that country just two jumps and a spit this side of the frontier.

It is such glimpses, casual but profound, that give the texture of the world in which the action occurs, but the author has used more radical measures to create a human context for the action. Bit by bit, the reader's attention is shifted from the story of the avenger, Pleasant McIvor, to the common, daylight life of the community, the life that the secret members of the gang must live with their families and friends. Again and again, we enter that common life. It is a life of affection, pathos, and humor intertwined with the secret evil, but rendered with full fidelity to those normal interests and values.

For example, take the sequence of the shrouding of Brother Macon, the lone Campbellite in the region, slain as a member of the posse chasing Pleasant. In the kitchen the neighbor women preparing food for the wake discuss the

recipe for jugged pigeons, or discuss, as we have already remarked, the woman's world. Outside, in the dark, two lovers
meet. In the "laying-out room," the men, under the command
of Brother Abner Buchanan, pass the jug and brace themselves for the doleful duty:

"All right, men," he said, wiping his chin and setting the
empty jug by his chair, "I'm ready for Brother Macon."
Beatty and Simmons drew back the sheet.
"Where do you want him, Ab?"
Abner stepped back unsteadily and looked at the body.
"Well, now, you've got me stumped. I'm new to this kind
of a trade."
"Somebody git the wash tub," growled Botterall.
"You ain't figgering for me to set him in the tub, Lem?"
"Hell, no. But what's to keep you from standen him up in
it?"
"That's an idey. I deputize you to hold, sheriff."
"You can't deshutize the sheriff."
"That's a fact. Well, Joe, you hold him."
Joe looked at the corpse.
"He'll lean ag'in the wall," he said.
The tub was brought, and the corpse of Brother Macon,
after the clothes had been clumsily stripped, was lifted in. At this
moment Damon returned with another bucket of water. He saw
the grayish-brown figure leaning grotesquely against the mantel-
piece. The body was thin and drawn, and it had the cold shine
of death. The icy eyes stared into the room, and the beard hung
softly down. From the hole in the stomach a black stream of
dried blood had spread down the inside of a thigh, streaking the
calf, to the twisted toes. The hands were clenched, and at the
corner of the mouth dark stains turned down like tusks. A look
of fear and horror spread over Damon's smooth features. He
felt his scalp tingle, and when he spoke, there was hatred and
disgust in his voice.
"Here's the other bucket of water. Be enough?"
"A bucket of water? Dump it in the tub, my boy," Abner
said gaily, rolling up his sleeves.
Damon's face lost its color and he hesitated; but, looking
down, he did as he was told. He could not help but see the water

splash around the still, ashen legs. As soon as he had emptied
the pail, he picked up the other one and left the room.

"The boy's got weak guts," said Beatty pleasantly.

"That's a sight to turn stronger guts to jelly," answered
Botterall.

The assistants began to look a little grim.

"You boys ain't white-eyed on me?" Abner asked cheer-
fully.

"Hell, no," said Beatty. "He won't bite."

"Pitch the soap in that ar bucket and swing out the pot."

It was done in silence, and Buchanan picked up the broom.
He dipped it in the kettle and swung the scalding water on the
corpse.

"Ain't you a-goen to mix the water?"

"If it's too hot fer'm, he'll holler."

He ran the broom into the water, over the soap, then over
the legs of the corpse.

" 'Y God," he said, "but I believe the dirt's set on him."

In that world of common life, the members of the gang
wait for the moment when the avenger will again emerge from
his shadows. And our knowledge and suspense gives an image
of, and empathy for, the growing dread of the guilty as they
realize, death by death, the doom hanging over them. In a sense,
they are not, after all, villains. They are merely men, certainly
no better than they should be, but trapped somehow in their
destiny. Whose side are we on? This doubleness of view, and
the irony it entails, is a fundamental fact of the story as it appears in the novel.

If the novelist has undertaken to create a world and a
human context for the deeds of vengeance, the main change
from the original tale is in the nature of the avenger. In the
tale, once he is in the grip of his obsession, he becomes, simply,
his "role." This is all the tale demands, and from the avenger's
side of the action, the only variety possible will lie in the
method and circumstances of the killing. If, in the tale, he
ceases his pursuit of the guilty, it is only because he has grown
old. The novelist, however, cannot settle for this. He wants a

deeper drama. So he lets the Civil War fall across the action.

It is the outlaw chief, Lovell, who gives Pleasant the news of the coming of war—this in a dark room where Pleasant has surprised him and is ready to exact the penalty. But Lovell doesn't care now. His life is over, for his maniacal ambition to found an empire is cut off. His own scheme dwindles to nothing in the great convulsion of history. So Pleasant, to compound his vengeance, spares Lovell to let him taste the frustration of his dream and await, over years if necessary, the death stroke.

Meanwhile, for Pleasant the war provides the perfect cover for his operations, for as a soldier in the vast namelessness of the army, he can stalk his prey with impunity. But bit by bit, the great public bloodletting drains him of his private thirst for blood, the great public mania undermines his private mania. He finds that he can no longer sink himself in his role, even if he conceives of himself as merely God's hand exacting justice. He finds that he is human, after all. He is capable of friendship, and in the end he finds that friendship is a trap; in pursuing his private war he causes the death of his friend in the public war. He is caught up in human loyalties—to his friend and to the men with whom he marches. He has, however, discovered his humanity too late. The long night will never end.

Then suddenly he knew what he had done, what no man in this world may do. Twice he had loved—once the dead, once the living, and each by each was consumed and he was doomed. In the partial darkness he raised his eyes to the river. Stone's River, icy-cold and black, turned between the town and the cedar thickets across the Nashville pike, broke over the shallow rocks at McFadden's Ford, fell again into deep chasms, flowing north, silently flowing through the long night.

Pleasant straightened his body, looked once about him. The camps were still asleep, only the sentries walked their posts, frozen shadows in the darkening world. He looked to the south. Far to the south the hills of Winston rose close and stubborn out of the lowlands. The hills of Winston. It was no long jour-

ney to a man who knew the way, who had lost every other way.
There he would go. There, in the secret coves, far away from
the world and vengeance, a deserter might hide forever. . . .

The solution is the proper one for the novel. Where else
could Pleasant go except to the hills of Winston? But in working it out, the novelist involves himself, it must be put on the
record, in certain technical difficulties. In the sequence leading
up to the Battle of Shiloh, we lose Pleasant, the focus of interest shifts, becomes generalized and diffuse, and when we rediscover him in the battle, something has been lost and is never,
perhaps, completely recovered. No, that is not true. It is recovered, but only at the last minute, in the splendid conclusion.

This technical defect does not, in one sense, matter—nor
do certain more minor ones. The conception of the story is
firm, but the real reason such a defect does not matter is the
spirit of the work. We are not reading a realistic novel. The
work is full of realistic effects, the details of a real world and
real people, but the whole is more like a ballad than a novel—
a quintessential poetry of action, pathos, humor, and doom,
to be read innocently, in its own terms, in its perspective of
distance and a climate of feeling. It is strangely like a dream,
springing from a certain society, from a certain historical moment—not a record, but a dream, the paradoxical dream of
that society's, that historical moment's, view of itself.

There is no book quite like *The Long Night,* and there
will never be another quite like it. It says something about the
world of the South not said elsewhere, and something that is
true. But more importantly, it offers its own special fascination
and its own special pleasure. At least, that is what I always find
when I come back to it, the fascination, the pleasure.

# EVAN S. CONNELL, JR.

## ON

## JANET LEWIS'S

## The Wife of Martin Guerre

*EVAN S. CONNELL, JR.*

EVAN S. CONNELL, JR., *is former editor of* Contact. *He has received Eugene Saxton and Guggenheim fellowships. Born in Kansas City, Missouri, in 1924, he lives now in San Francisco. Among his publications are* The Anatomy Lesson (*1957*); Mrs. Bridge (*1959*) *and* Mr. Bridge (*1969*); The Patriot (*1960*); Notes from a Bottle Found on the Beach at Carmel (*1963*), *a narrative poem;* At the Crossroads (*1965*), *a volume of stories; and* The Diary of a Rapist (*1966*). *He is now working on* Notes 2, *a continuation of* Notes from a Bottle.

∽

*JANET LEWIS*

JANET LEWIS *was born in Chicago, in 1899, the daughter of novelist Edwin Herbert Lewis. After earning a Ph.B. at the University of Chicago in 1920, Miss Lewis worked for the American Consulate in Paris.* The Indian in the Woods, *her first volume of poems, appeared in 1922. Her first novel,* The Wife of Martin Guerre, *was published in 1941; an operatic adaptation of the story was produced in 1956. She has lectured at many writers' conferences and has taught writing at Stanford. Her work has appeared in the* New Yorker, *the* New Republic, Poetry, *and* Revue de Paris, *among other magazines.* Poems: 1924–1944 *was published in 1950. Her other novels are* Against a Darkening Sky (*1943*), The Trial of Sören Qvist (*1947*), *and* The Ghost of Monsieur Scarron (*1959*). *She has also written a book for children,* Keito's Bubble (*1961*). *Miss Lewis lives now in Los Altos, California.*

Janet Lewis has stated that she first came upon the story of the wife of Martin Guerre in a book called *Famous Cases of Circumstantial Evidence*. Later she found a discussion of Martin Guerre's trial in a recondite legal encyclopedia titled *Les Recherches de la France* by Estienne Pasquier, who was a celebrated jurist of the sixteenth century. It is said, too, that Montaigne refers in one of his essays to the curious case of Martin Guerre. So among Montaigne, Pasquier, and the anonymous anthologist of *Famous Cases* we can be fairly sure of the existence of a man called Martin Guerre and of the extraordinary events that have perpetuated his name.

The *Wife of Martin Guerre* is, therefore, a historical novel. I first read it years ago, some years after it was published by a small press in 1941. I dislike historical novels and will go several steps out of my way to avoid anybody who is promoting one, so that I cannot now imagine who or what directed me to this one. Furthermore, I did not at the time know anything about Janet Lewis as a writer; I knew her only as the wife of the poet and critic Yvor Winters. However, after reading this short novel I read every other novel she has written. They are not many. Next to *Martin Guerre,* I think the most important is *The Trial of Sören Qvist,* concerning the execution of a Danish parson in the eighteenth century. Then there is *The Ghost of Monsieur Scarron,* which is about a bookbinder during the reign of Louis XIV. All three, if I am not mistaken, derive from *Famous Cases of Circumstantial Evidence.* The intensity pervading them makes it clear that Miss Lewis is obsessed both by the possibility and by the actuality of injustice. She investigates this theme repeatedly, with the knowledge and the cold skill of a laboratory technician. In addition to these books, she has written a generally praised novel about the relationship between Indians and whites in the Northwest Territory, called *The Invasion;* I wanted to like it, too, but I did not.

Recently I reread *Martin Guerre* for the first time, although I have been mentioning it and handing out copies for quite a while. I had no interest in reading it again because some books, like certain scenes, print themselves permanently on the mind. However, it is not tedious to read a second time, and it remains for me one of the most significant short novels in English. I doubt that I shall forget the dignity of the concluding lines, or the opening.

Here is how it begins:

One morning in January, 1539, a wedding was celebrated in the village of Artigues. That night the two children who had been espoused to one another lay in bed in the house of the groom's father. They were Bertrande de Rols, aged eleven years, and Martin Guerre, who was no older, both offspring of rich peasant families as ancient, as feudal and as proud as any of the great seignorial houses of Gascony. The room was cold. Outside the snow lay thinly over the stony ground, or, gathered into long shallow drifts at the corners of houses, left the earth bare. But higher, it extended upward in great sheets and dunes, mantling the ridges and choking the wooded valleys, toward the peak of La Bacanère and the long ridge of Le Burat, and to the south, beyond the long valley of Luchon, the granite Maladetta stood sheathed in ice and snow. The passes to Spain were buried under whiteness. The Pyrenees had become for the winter season an impassable wall. Those Spaniards who were in French territory after the first heavy snowfall in September, remained there, and those Frenchmen, smugglers or soldiers or simple travelers who found themselves on the wrong side of the Port de Venasque were doomed to remain there until spring. Sheep in fold, cattle in the grange, faggots heaped high against the wall of the farm, the mountain villages were closed in enforced idleness and isolation. It was a season of leisure in which weddings might well be celebrated.

Bertrande had never spoken to Martin until that morning, although she had often seen him; she had not known until the previous evening that she was to be married. But she had knelt beside the boy in front of his father, they had then walked together across the snow, heralded by the sound of violins, to the church of Artigues where the ceremony was accomplished. She found her marriage quite as solemn an affair as her First Communion.

Afterwards, still to the music of the violins, which sounded thin and sharp in the cold air, she had returned to the house of her husband where a huge fire of oak logs garnished with vine-trimmings roared in the big fireplace, and where the kitchen, the principal room of the house, was set with improvised tables, long boards laid over trestles. The stone floor had been freshly strewn with broken boughs of evergreen. The sides and bottoms of the copper pans flashed redly with the reflection of the flames, and the air was rich with the good smell of roasting meat and of freshly poured wine. Underfoot the snow from the sabots melted and sank beneath the trodden evergreens.

So Bertrande de Rols is married in the year 1539, as clearly as if it happened this morning, as brightly as in a painting by old Breughel. The description of the wedding feast becomes an invitation to the senses—the smoky meat, the warmed wine and boiled chestnuts, the hard bread dipped in grease, the snow melting through the evergreen branches, the shrill music. It is a wedding to be remembered.

The groom, however, has not much liked being married. As soon as they are alone he hits her, yanks her hair, and scratches her face. That night they are put to bed together, and he, turning his back to her, remarks, "I am tired of all this business," and goes to sleep.

Despite this less than cordial honeymoon they grow together amicably enough, and after a few years Bertrande feels a softening of her distaste for Martin. She works beside her mother-in-law at their chores while the men work in the fields; in time she has a child, Sanxi; and she begins to experience a deep fulfillment. She feels satisfied with her husband, and the majestic figure of her father-in-law is comforting: his existence testifies that the animals on the farm are safe, the grain is safe, and neither the wolves whose voices can be heard on winter nights, nor marauding mercenaries whose presence occasionally is reported, will threaten her security.

The motion of this life appealed powerfully to Janet Lewis. Seasons alter, work is done yet never finished, children are born, old people die. Birds, beasts, and humans form a stately procession across a sixteenth-century tapestry of Languedoc. One easily can distinguish the figure of a youthful peasant in rough clothing on the day he leaves the farm, telling his young wife that he will come back in a week. He has taken some seed wheat from the granary without his father's permission in order to plant a field. It is for the good of the farm, but he knows his father will be angered by such presumption, so he will go away for a week. By then his father will have realized what a sensible idea it was to plant another field.

However, a week goes by and Martin Guerre does not return. Winter comes, Artigues is isolated. Finally the snow begins to melt. Bertrande waits for her husband. She waits through the summer. Winter comes again. Only then does she say to herself that he has left her. He has found liberty so sweet that he will not come home.

Gradually she forgets her husband. Yet each time she learns of strangers in Artigues she sends for them, feeds them, and asks if they ever have heard of Martin Guerre. She instructs them to tell him, if they should meet, that his father has died and now he may safely return.

Eight years after Martin's disappearance "a bearded man dressed in leather and steel" arrives at the farm. The old housekeeper cries: "It is he, Madame!"

He is heavier than the youth who went away, and to Bertrande it seems that even his voice has changed; yet the eyes, the countenance, and the demeanor are those of her husband. He greets each member of the household with authority, inquires about those who have died during his absence, praises the servants for their fidelity, and without hesitation assumes his place.

He is capable and just, and life on the farm continues as

though he had never gone away. Everybody is content, except
Bertrande, who is troubled by a conviction that he is not her
husband. She accepts him because everybody else, including
his sisters, his uncle, and his oldest friends, have accepted him,
and she again becomes pregnant, but she cannot forget her
suspicion. Finally she denounces him as an impostor. He is arrested and taken in irons to be held for trial in the village of
Rieux, because Artigues is too small to have a court of its own.

This—the denunciation—is as vitally shocking as any
idea in the book. It seems inconceivable, particularly to men,
that a woman would denounce a man who had treated her
kindly and with honor; and many women of our century must
feel that the accusation was, if not shocking, at least rather
foolish. Things were going well. Why did Bertrande insist on
questioning her good fortune?

At the trial some witnesses swear that the prisoner is Martin Guerre, others claim that he is not, while others cannot
make up their minds. The judges decide that the man is an
impostor and they condemn him to death; but the case is appealed to the parliament of Toulouse. A new trial is ordered.

Relatives and servants plead with Bertrande to withdraw
the accusation, for nothing has gone right at the farm since she
denounced her husband. She refuses.

On a September evening as she is returning from church
she comes upon the housekeeper seated beside the doorway
killing doves. The old woman asks if she has made her prayers.
Bertrande replies that she has. The housekeeper suggests that
she might have made them for a better cause. The scene that
follows this exchange is one of the most subtly murderous alle-
gories in fiction:

> She sighed, leaning forward, holding the dove head down
> between her hands, the smooth wings folded close to the smooth
> soft body, while the dark blood dripped slowly from a cut in the
> throat into an earthen dish. The dish, already filled with blood,
> darker than that which was falling into it, spilled over slightly,

and a barred gray cat, creeping cautiously near, elongated, its belly close to the ground, put out a rasping pale tongue and licked the blood. The housekeeper, after a little, pushed it away with the side of her foot. A pile of soft gray-feathered bodies already lay beside her on the bench. The living dove turned its head this way and that, struggled a little, clasping a pale cold claw over the hand that held it, and relaxed, although still turning its head. The blood seemed to be clotting too soon, the wound was shrunken, and the old woman enlarged it with the point of the knife which she had in her lap. The dove made no cry. Bertrande watched with pity and comprehension the dying bird, feeling the blood drop by drop leave the weakening body, feeling her own strength drop slowly away like the blood of the dove.

"What would you have me do?" she asked at length. "The truth is only the truth. I cannot change it, if I would."

"Ah," said the housekeeper, turning once more to the dove which now lay still in her hands, "Madame, I would have you still be deceived. We were all happy then." She laid the dead dove with the others, and stooped to pick up the dish of blood.

These words recur to Bertrande on the journey to Toulouse; and when, before the parliament in the Château Narbonnais, the time comes for her to confront the man she has accused, she is unable to look at him. She is puzzled that he does not seem to return her hatred with hatred; nor can she understand why he did not leave the farm when she first denounced him, when he could have escaped.

The witnesses are summoned again. Again they are divided. The shoemaker of Artigues testifies that the foot of the accused is slightly larger than the foot of Martin Guerre. It is established that the accused is stockier and somewhat shorter than Martin Guerre. But yet, Martin Guerre had two broken teeth in the lower left jaw, so has the accused; Martin Guerre had a drop of extravasated blood in the left eye, so has the accused; the nail of his left forefinger was missing and he had three warts on the left hand, two of which were on the little finger, exactly as does the accused. The judges, greatly perturbed, decide that the prisoner must be, in fact, Martin Guerre. But while this verdict is being written, a one-legged soldier enters the council chambers and announces that he, himself, is Martin Guerre.

The two men are ordered to stand side by side. There can no longer be any doubt. Martin Guerre has at last returned, minus a leg lost in the battle at Saint Quentin. The prisoner is therefore an impostor, who, in his subsequent confession, states that he had been tempted to it by the frequency with which he had been mistaken for Martin Guerre. He had not meant at first to assume the place of his double in the household, he had planned to stay just long enough to pick up a little gold or silver; but the sight of Bertrande had caused him to remain, even after he understood that his life was in danger.

This is the severely classic situation: a man who gambled his life in the hope of winning a woman. She, for her part, looked upon him with hate and contempt. Four centuries have not diminished the strength of their relationship.

The court at Toulouse decreed that the man, whose name was Arnaud du Tilh, had been guilty of the crimes of imposture, falsehood, substitution of name and person, adultery, rape, sacrilege, plagiat, which is the detention of a person who belongs to someone else, and of larceny. He was ordered to do penance before the church of Artigues "on his knees, in his shirt, with head and feet bare, a halter around his neck and a burning taper in his hand, asking pardon of God and of the king, of Martin Guerre and of Bertrande de Rols, his wife; the court then condemned him to be handed over to the common executioner, who should conduct him by the most public ways to the house of Martin Guerre, in front of which, upon a scaffold previously prepared, he should be hanged and his body burned."

That is the story of Martin Guerre and of his wife, and the impostor, Arnaud du Tilh. It did, as we know, happen; the record of this decree exists, dated the twelfth of September, the year 1560, in the city of Toulouse. That a factual case is always a precarious base for fiction is demonstrated by the general mediocrity of historical fiction, and the usual novelist would have written a melodramatic, implausible book from such melodramatic, implausible history. Janet Lewis wrote something else.

If there is one characteristic of this book that distinguishes it, I would call it dignity. This quality cannot be manufactured, as certain qualities can; it emanates from the author. And it is here as plentifully and as unmistakably as grain in the fields of Languedoc. Out of a few documents Miss Lewis created a man named Martin Guerre who returned from the wars, arrogant and unforgiving, without one of his legs, to demand his rightful place; Arnaud du Tilh, obliged by his respect for Bertrande to become a finer man than he ever had been, or expected to be; and Bertrande, who could not live with suspicion. All of them are aware of themselves, which is the true definition and the prerogative of dignity. I think it is because of this uncommon self-knowledge that they continue to live.

I do not much like extravagant praise, either to hear it or to employ it, and I am reluctant to use the term "masterpiece," which is used indiscriminately. I am not sure if *The Wife of Martin Guerre* qualifies; but I approach it with respect, as I approach ten or fifteen other books.

Concerning Martin Guerre himself, the author says that nothing more is recorded, whether he returned to the wars or whether he remained in Artigues, nor is there any further record of Bertrande; but when hate and love together have exhausted the soul, the body seldom endures for long.

# R. V. CASSILL

## ON

## BENJAMIN CONSTANT'S

# Adolphe

*R. V. CASSILL*

R. V. CASSILL *has been a painter, an editor, a critic, a reviewer, also a teacher of creative writing at the Writers Workshop of the University of Iowa and writer-in-residence at Purdue. He is presently teaching at Brown University. He is founder and director of the Associated Writing Programs.* The Eagle on the Coin (*1950*), Dormitory Women (*1954*)—*not as well known as it deserves to be*—Clem Anderson (*1961*), Pretty Leslie (*1963*), The President (*1964*), La Vie Passionnée of Rodney Buckthorne (*1968*), *and* Doctor Cobb's Game (*1970*) *are his major novels. Several of his short stories are prize winners and three volumes of his stories have been published. R. V. Cassill was born in Cedar Falls, Iowa, in 1919.*

〜৩

*BENJAMIN CONSTANT*

BENJAMIN CONSTANT *was born in Lausanne, Switzerland, in 1767. As soon as he reached his maturity, he plunged himself into the turbulent politics of France. His strong support for a liberal monarchy and freedom of the press resulted in his being exiled from France by Napoleon in 1802. During the next year, Constant wandered around Germany mixing with the Goethe-Schiller circle in Weimar. But he soon returned to France to immerse himself once again in the political turmoil of the times. After the Revolution of 1830, he found himself on the right side of the regime and was appointed president of the Council of State. He retained this office until his death later that year.*

38

Adolphe (*1815*) *is Constant's only novel. His two other major works are a five-volume treatise on religion and an edited collection of his numerous political tracts.*

---

Whether we like it or not—whether it is just conformable to the best aesthetic and critical prescriptions of how we *ought* to ingest the substance and the form of fiction or not—novels have a way of entering untidily into our systems of memory and merging fictive passions with those which were, in another sense, real. I first read *Adolphe* in French in a year when I had run off to Europe with a woman who had left her husband to go with me, and all this was working out as badly as ancient writers, the even older stars—or *Adolphe*—had foretold.

From that year I remember a hotel room in London, as cold as only London hotel rooms can be in December, and a voice calling through the dark from the other bed, "I didn't make it, did I?" And the hiss of the blue and orange flame that didn't even pretend to warm our room but only to bring in the idea of fire to intensify the immortal chill in which I huddled and had no reply to give. From reading *Adolphe* that year while we were in Paris I remember the scene of the snow field in Poland and the birdless air, the frozen grass crunching under the feet of Adolphe and Ellenore as they walk out in her last illness. And her complaint—"Pourquoi vous acharnez-vous sur moi?" *Acharner* . . . a term used in the training of hunting dogs, meaning "to blood."

It is a sentimental novel and a period piece. The emotions and the situation are unmistakably those of the very early part of the nineteenth century—and that for most of us is a brandy that has aged too long and lost flavor and sting. Subject to psychological analysis it yields fluently—and rather trivially. Adolphe is lazy, insecure, oversubtle, and equivocal in his intents. Ellenore is compulsive and self-deluding. There is hostility as well as love in the feelings of each for the other. All this has been much more deeply explored since Benjamin Constant wrote.

A very young man of good family falls in love with an older woman. She is the mistress, not wife, of a "man of forty whose family was connected with mine," Adolphe tells us. Her anomalous position inclines her more to rectitude than profligacy. All the more challenging a goal for conquest. "I looked upon her as a sacred being and my love was closely allied to religion." It is easier to believe that this young man of another century meant what he said than to translate his vocabulary into terms we can use in the privacy of our own passion. We know about everything now except the sweetness and fire of religious exaltation and the way it transfigures libidinal impulse.

Adolphe persuades Ellenore to "yield" and to give up the connection which has been at least comfortable, supportable, and reasonable. Abandoning her children, as so many heroines of nineteenth- and twentieth-century fiction were to do, she places her whole life at the disposal of the infatuated, importunate boy. It is more than he guessed he would get, more than he bargained for, to have the magnitude of her sorrows and sacrifices come along in the package with her tenderness and beauty. Unwillingly but helplessly he participates in her destruction. She dies in a fury of disillusion and recrimination that destroys the sense of Adolphe's life.

Thus, clearly, in the turning of the plot to make a statement about the nature and fate of the human pair, it is a prototype for *Anna Karenina, Madame Bovary,* and very many other stories of the century in which much of the question of human freedom was found in the riddles of adultery. But since it is so stripped, compact and epigrammatic, so lacking in furniture, scene, and complication compared to the novels of Flaubert and Tolstoy, why does *Adolphe* seem so necessary when we have *them?* I don't mean necessary to a literary historian, but to the all-out reader who, like James Dickey's owl king, says, "I swore to myself I would see . . . my sight going slowly out/ Inch by inch as into stone."

For my part, it seems all the more necessary and moving *because* we have those other, larger—more *novelistic*—expansions of a story essentially the same. It is as true to say that *Anna Karenina* prepares us to read *Adolphe* as to put the proposition the other way around. A straight chronological approach to the "development" of literary genres has its drastic limitations as well as its uses. And in any case, as Malraux said of Goya's early and late paintings, "Genius goes to the aid of its earliest productions."

It does not matter how we rank *Adolphe* or *Anna Karenina* as long as we perceive that the former, by its epigrammatic voice and a structure honed, worn, and fitted to an epigrammatic simplicity, holds the timeless quandaries about love and responsibility, liberty and choice, up to a different light. It may be that the epigrammatic novel reminds us that not all the soul's truth is rendered by representations of the visible world or by psychic response. There are agonies and exaltations more plainly revealed by and to the rational intellect than to the dumb, suffering body or the yearnings of emotion. There are existential contradictions in the human condition as well as the contradictions of intent dear to psychological therapists. *Le vautour est doux à Promèthe.* And it may be we seek purposely for emotional torments and the sexual disequilibriums guaranteed to provoke them in order to be diverted from the agony of the soul confronting its mortal condition. The pain and nobility of the contradictions perceptible to the intellect alone are the signal substance Constant isolates within the appearances of his sentimental tale. For this task the stark and epigrammatic manner is exactly suited. It is the weapon of choice for the ironic mind in its war with the ironies of the Creator.

And the most gallant submission. For irony is an assurance against victory. It armors the spirit, and makes it doubly vulnerable; offers intellectual haven from the shocks of contradiction and contingency—and exposes the primal flaw of contradiction in our mortality. It reconciles us to the equivocation of heaven by surrendering our deep hunger for simplicity and assurance.

O man, what will you have? Different kinds of irony? Fine. There are different kinds, and they *war* in this novel.

Adolphe's disapproving father writes to him: "I can only feel pity that with your spirit of independence you invariably do what you do not want to do." Plainly this is the voice of irony in its mocking aspect. In what we generally call its classic aspect. The experienced man wishes to warn and instruct his errant son by a satirical appropriation of irony. In age, in abnegation, irony is indeed a disciplining and consoling solvent. The *aqua regia* of despair. Pluck out thine eye and be whole, urges the classic spirit of satire. Lie on the Procrustean bed. "Keep it in your pants."

This is not, we feel, necessarily superior wisdom; nor is it the theme of *Adolphe,* which, though it is certainly a didactic novel, is not facile in its prescription. Nietzsche observed that nowhere are we closer to the spirit of the ancients than in the work of those French moralists La Rochefoucauld, Vauvenargues, and Chamfort. Constant is of the same temper. He would not have bothered with Adolphe only to let him be outsmarted by a satirical older party.

From the beginning Adolphe is quite as aware as his father that the affair with Ellenore is equivocal. "My long drawn-out battle against my own character, the irritation I felt at not having been able to overcome it, and my doubts about the chances of success all combined to tinge my letter with an emotional colour scarcely distinguishable from love," he says of his first declaration to the woman he aspires to win.

*Scarcely distinguishable from love. . . .* ("If the truth be beneficial, its semblance is even more mischievous," said La

Rochefoucauld, meaning the same thing.) The emotion is not love and the mischievous counterfeit will not be annealed even by the blood sacrifice of the woman at the end of the affair. Having accepted the bad coin, the impassioned young man cannot renounce it. The falsehood, the enacted lie, has been the inalienable signature of his "spirit of independence," his refusal to submit to the admonitory mockeries of his father or of the heavens. It is stamped on the liberty he gains by Ellenore's death. "I was free, truly, for I was no longer loved. I was a stranger to the whole world." Poor Prometheus, his vulture has died. Now he has no company but his thoughts. . . .

Adolphe's thoughts cannot contain the memory of a single moment, in his possession of the woman, which was unequivocally simple and true. "We lavished caresses upon each other and talked of love, but we talked of love for fear of talking about something else." "Her giving herself to me thus unreservedly meant that she concealed none of her changes of mood, so that when I came back into her room, resentful at being back earlier than I would have liked, it would be to find her upset and annoyed." "We embraced but a first blow had been struck, a first frontier crossed. We had both said irreparable things; we might be able to stop talking but not to forget. There are things which are not said for a very long time, but once they are said they are constantly repeated."

The novel offers no period or moment of relief in this sexual agony. The pacing of the story (which is often confused by indifferent readers with a question of whether something gaudy happens on each page, but which truly has to do with the way interest is compounded in the central issue) is like the tightening of a bowstring when the bow is drawn. It is, literally, awful. Searching for one touch of redemption or remission from this progress, my mind stumbles after something like the remissive lines in George Meredith's "Modern Love."

> Love, that robbed us of immortal things,
> This little moment mercifully gave.

There is no such mercy in Constant's novel. Only the icy geometry of fate, exacting anguish at every moment as the price of youthful persistence in the face of impossibility. No English tolerance. Only the braying of desire in the stony vessel of the law.

The psychology of the main character is lucid enough— even rather trivially schematic, as I said before—until one locks with the mystery of why one who understands so well that he is headed for despair nevertheless persists on his course. Against common sense and then against the mocking that succeeds it, he goes on, deeper and deeper. It is not an inferior wisdom that makes him persist. He hopes, however ingenuously, that the contradictions which he recognizes so sharply can be traversed. Hold fast an hour longer, drive an inch or a mile farther, and daylight will appear. Equivocation and contradiction cannot be denied or overcome by the unvanquished spirit, but perhaps, just perhaps, they can be transfigured. Hope as well as satiric mockery is an ironic response to the conditions of mortality. Hope is irony in its tragic aspect.

Novels, I heard a novelist say the other night, are great conglomerate globs of often shoddy writing mingled with a few moments of penetration and illumination that stick to the passing reader like burrs picked up on a walk through a grassy field. There is no way of holding them intact and single in the mind, he felt, and if this is so of the things themselves—novels —then the way they are read compounds the difficulty in talking among ourselves about them to a degree that should make the thoughtful person renounce comment.

And yet—ironically—the opposite is also true. The novels that stick in our minds and seem, as I have called this one, necessary, go on and on as part of memory because the encounter with them has left a persisting note in our minds, a note so crystalline and impenetrable that it can no more be analyzed than the whistle of a bird. Magically the unwieldy conglomerate becomes a unity so nearly indivisible that our best attempts to reckon its meaning do not come from efforts to take it apart but from an infinitude of comparisons and associations with things outside itself. If it is a note that has signaled to something persistent and profound in us, the process of comparison and association goes on involuntarily. We don't have to try to retain the signal, like a grade-school arithmetic problem, until such time as superior learning permits us to solve and have done with it, once and for all. The mysterious signal stays with us, riddles through us, moves through our lives like a needle embedded in the flesh.

I read *Adolphe* first in a foreign language, guilty and unlucky in love and far from home. I hear the clear, crystalline signal again and again, penetrating what might be called purely intellectual concentrations as well as those that might seem the farthest from the realm of the intellect. I have wondered, not quite voluntarily—perhaps even subverbally among those operations of cognition where words and things are not perfectly distinguishable from each other—if the paradigmatic form of *Adolphe* is not simply that of the common genital sexual act. Is this unsynchronizable exchange of stimulations not so deeply embedded in the biological forms of male and female that it must always show itself in long, short, and intermediate intercourse? And if this is so, does it not mean that fate is flesh and all act is thought?

I review a contemporary novel and—not quite voluntarily—transpose its scenes and dramatic development into epigrammatic patterns and syllogisms like those which show so plainly on the surface of *Adolphe*. It is not quite certain that the art of the novel, or of reading novels, is a constant engagement with concreteness, or with things *realized,* in the Jamesian phrase. Our grasp of the kind of realities fiction has to deal with can never be accomplished without the kind of generalization Constant handled so brilliantly.

I wonder why Nietzsche, that subtlest listener to the bird

calls of literature, did not and would not hear Pascal among those Frenchmen who sang like the ancients, and to whose names Constant makes such a natural addition. I think I know. There is no robustness of desire in Pascal to counter the grim candor. He's not with us. He's from the other party. Almost glad to see Prometheus chained on the rock. And Constant is not. In his view, the hopes of Adolphe ought to govern destiny though they cannot.

Yeats writes: "Man is in love and loves what vanishes." The incredible balance of that line, I reflect, is like the note of *Adolphe*. It would be such a different matter if it only said, "Man loves what vanishes." To be "in love" is an affirmation that balances the deception of loving what must flee and fade.

I think about *Adolphe* and *Don Quixote*. The note and the values in *Quixote*, essentially Christian, are close enough for comparison, but not the same. The knight's mortal defeat is, in itself, transfigured. In renunciation he claims. By yielding affirms. There is a transfiguration in *Adolphe*, but it has nothing to do with the outcome of the story. Spirit and flesh, and their destiny, are more nearly integrated. There is no "otherworldliness" about it. The heights and the depths are closer home.

I remember being in love and wanting to be adequate to it. That is a way of thinking about *Adolphe*—as the novel in turn, with all its associations in literature and memory, is a way of thinking about this necessarily hopeful, necessarily desperate condition.

# WALLACE STEGNER

## ON

## GLENWAY WESCOTT'S

# Good-Bye Wisconsin

## WALLACE STEGNER

WALLACE STEGNER *has for many years directed the famous Stanford University creative writing program.* He was born in Lake Mills, Iowa, in 1909 and is an active conservationist; he has written and edited many books of nonfiction about the West and is former editor-in-chief of American West *magazine. Among his many awards and honors are three Guggenheims and a Rockefeller Foundation grant.* Remembering Laughter (1937), On a Darkling Plain (1940), Fire and Ice (1941), The Big Rock Candy Mountain (1943), The Women on the Wall (1950), A Shooting Star (1961), *and* All the Little Live Things (1967) *are only a few of his works of fiction.* Sound of Mountain Water (1969) *and* Angle of Repose (1971) *are his most recent works. He is a member of the National Institute of Arts and Letters and the American Academy of Arts and Sciences.*

∼৹

## GLENWAY WESCOTT

GLENWAY WESCOTT *was born in Kewaskum, Wisconsin, in 1901. His first novel,* The Apple of the Eye, *was published in 1924. He won the Harper Prize for* The Grandmothers *in 1927.* The Bitterns (1920) *and* Natives of the Rock (1925) *are volumes of poetry. His short stories are collected in two volumes,* Like a Lover (1926) *and* Good-Bye Wisconsin (1928). *His other works of fiction are* The Babe's Bed (1930), The Pilgrim Hawk (1940), *and* Apartment in Athens (1945). Images of Truth (1962), *criticism, is his most recent book. Mr. Wescott*

47

*attended the University of Chicago for two years; he lived in
New Mexico, Germany, and New York before settling for eight
years in France during the twenties and thirties. Since 1934 he
has lived on the family farm at Haymeadows, in Rosemont, New
Jersey. Mr. Wescott has served as president of the National Institute of Arts and Letters and was elected to the American
Academy of Arts and Letters.*

----

When *Good-Bye Wisconsin* appeared in 1928, Glenway
Wescott was twenty-seven years old and already a prod-
igy. He had published his first volume of poems, *The Bitterns,*
at nineteen; his first novel, *The Apple of the Eye,* at twenty-
three. The year before the publication of *Good-Bye Wisconsin,*
his novel *The Grandmothers* had won him the Harper Prize,
many readers, and universal critical praise, and had established him as a major name among the gifted and aggrieved
who were turning the twenties into an American renaissance.
Now these short stories, prefaced by a lyrical essay on the
themes of exile and return, added to his already formidable
reputation.

The reputation, buttressed by other and very different
achievements, has lasted, but the vogue has passed; and in particular *Good-Bye Wisconsin* is a book known by name—and
sometimes confused with a short novel by Philip Roth—but
not much read. Though exile and return are main roads
through the twenties, and indeed through the whole modern
period from *Dubliners* onward, this book of stories is not com-
monly listed among the landmarks.

Much of the literature of the twenties grew out of the
Midwest, which, Wescott tells us, "is a certain climate, a certain landscape; and beyond that, a state of mind of people
born where they do not like to live." Of that state of mind
*Good-Bye Wisconsin* is a quintessential expression, but you
will not often find it on the reading lists of college classes in

American literature, you will not see it on the paperback shelves, and its stories do not crop up in the pages of the collections that incessantly winnow and sift short stories, and so harden the tradition. It is a rare student who could name the title of a single one of Wescott's stories, and for every one who knows *Good-Bye Wisconsin* even vaguely, ten thousand know Winesburg and Spoon River and Main Street in detail, hundreds know the Nebraska novels of Willa Cather, dozens know the Cedar Rapids repudiations of Carl Van Vechten.

A partial explanation is simple timing. By the time literary historians have sifted the evidence, it is the innovators who get the headlines, and Wescott was an intelligent and eclectic learner from others' innovations rather than an innovator himself. He learned from the Imagists, from Joyce, from the Chicago School: he was of their party but not quite of their company. Born in 1901, he was part of the second wave of modernism, a little behind the World War I generation, and well behind the true pioneers. *Good-Bye Wisconsin* appeared a good forty-five years after Ed Howe's *Story of a Country Town,* to which it is vastly superior but of which it is a sort of spiritual descendant. It appeared nineteen years after *Dubliners,* to which it owes a good deal, nine years after *Winesburg, Ohio,* to which it likewise owes a good deal, and eight years after *Main Street,* to which it owes practically nothing, but with which it must inevitably be associated. Wescott's stories are actually one of the last major expressions of what we too glibly call the revolt from the village.

Moreover, they mark the end of Wescott's personal preoccupation with the themes and subject matters of that literary fashion. He was finishing up what others had begun, making use of it as an apprentice ground. Many of the stories were published in magazines before the appearance of *The Grandmothers,* which represents a refinement upon them in technique and subtlety as they represent a refinement upon *The Apple of the Eye.* Gathered together and sent off under the

wing of the title essay like a crowd of children in care of the
hired girl, they cleared the house for other things. The book is
literally a good-bye. The heart is already in Villefranche, not
in Kewaskum. Any future use of the Wisconsin materials, as in
*The Pilgrim Hawk,* will be only a faint and silvery echo, the
half-heard memory of a country carefully forgotten.

Nevertheless, Wescott's farewell to the climate, landscape, and state of mind of the Midwest is not a book that
deserves to be lost. Its stories survive the time and impulse that
produced them, and the title essay, one of the first of those
personal and lyrical statements that Wescott made into a form
peculiarly his own, is a brilliant evocation of the ambivalent
emotions of being born in, bound by, and attached to, a place
where one cannot bear to live.

There are ten stories in *Good-Bye Wisconsin.* They are
not uniformly successful, but they are illuminating even when
they are not, for they not only isolate and stain the village
virus, they suggest the exile which is its presumable cure. They
begin the exploration of the double, uneasy, two-civilization
life that *The Grandmothers* and *The Pilgrim Hawk* continue,
and that is surely one of the major themes of our literature. In
some, such as "The Sailor," "The Whistling Swan," and "The
Dove Came Down," America and Europe already coexist.
New and old, the half-formed and the civilized, the deprived
and the emancipated, America's ambiguous innocence and
Europe's ambiguous corruption, live within a single sensibility
or situation.

The merest glance reveals the gross symptoms of the village virus. "The Runaways" are a lumpish couple who escape
a worn-out farm to the sad and vulgar freedom of a carnival.
"Adolescence," one of the very best of the stories, shows us a
young boy dressed as a girl for a masked party, and bewil-
dered, angered, eventually changed by what the masquerade
has done to his sense of himself. In "A Guilty Woman" a spin-

ster who has murdered the man who married and abused her seizes a wry second chance at happiness by taking away her best friend's man. The young protagonist of "The Dove Came Down" refuses Communion in the town church, and by his act sets off in the girl he is to marry a turmoil of convulsed religious memories and repressed doubts. In "Like a Lover," a woman who has first married and then fled a psychopath must sit as silent as a doll under glass and watch him lure and destroy another. The admirable and Andersonian "In a Thicket" gives us a young girl who watches breathlessly, numb with something almost longing, something nearly fear, while an escaped black murderer lurks outside her father's isolated house, and in a muted and symbolic moment slits with his knife the symbolic screen. "Prohibition," a chronicle of brutal drunkenness, has a sequel, "The Sailor," in which one son who has found his way to the dubious romance of foreign ports comes back home and tries to explain to his envious farmbound brother what he has learned. The bridegroom of "The Wedding March" stands at the altar with one woman and thinks of the older woman who has taught and relinquished him. The musician of "The Whistling Swan," having had and failed his chance abroad, returns to the soul-shrinking limitations of a town like Kewaskum and the affectionate inadequacy of the girl he left behind him.

Familiar themes, known stories, voices we have heard before, characters who though subtler and more inward as a rule, are not so different from the characters of an earlier Wisconsin writer, Hamlin Garland. But something has happened to Garland's strenuous victims of rural hardship. They have been brutalized, like the drunken Rileys, or they have been squeezed and distorted into grotesques—less likable grotesques on the whole than Anderson's, bleaker, sadder.

These are, again like Anderson's, stories of whole lives (the continuing influence of Spoon River?) and their method is narrative. They do not focus narrowly on moments of crisis as Hemingway's, for example, do. They carry a burden of duration. Though with hardly an exception they begin dramatically ("The mist thinned and broke like a cobweb in the May sunshine," "One day in midsummer Evelyn Crowe, the murderess, left the state penitentiary," "Terence or Terrie Riley, back from sea, leaned on the edge of the water-trough in the barnyard") they do not continue that way, but break down almost at once into retrospection or outright summary, to return to dramatic scene again only when the author has finished his job of filling in the past, labeling motives, analyzing character, and telescoping time. In the stories where Europe and America, or present and past, have a reciprocating function, brief scenes from one are likely to alternate with scenes from the other, as in "The Wedding March," where the bridegroom goes through the motions of being married while scenes of his old love pass through his head.

In collections of stories laid in a single place, especially in collections written from exile, one half expects some figure of the artist, frank or disguised, who serves to unify the collection emotionally, objectify the artist's anger and rejection, or dramatize the conflicts that sent him into exile. The "I" of the first three stories of *Dubliners* establishes a sensibility that provides a constant if unemphasized commentary on Dublin's paralysis. The Kezia of Katherine Mansfield, the Miranda of Katherine Anne Porter, the George Willard of *Winesburg, Ohio,* are uneradicated traces of the artist's personal presence. But in *Good-Bye Wisconsin,* aside from the opening essay in which Wescott speaks in his own voice, there are no such clear representatives of the author's feeling, and when they do occur they have an air of being left over from an imperfect revision, something the author would have eliminated if he had fully accomplished his intention.

There is no I, but there are Wescott-like figures. By all odds the plainest is Philip in the story "Adolescence." He is an early version of Alwyn Tower, who will be Wescott's mask and mouthpiece in *The Grandmothers* and *The Pilgrim Hawk*. Sensitive, nearly epicene, nonresident, an outsider, he has such a shattering experience of loneliness and separateness when he dresses in girls' clothes that he passionately wants that evening to be an end to everything he has been: the shock that shatters him opens a door, such a door as Wescott himself escaped through. At the end of the story he stands at that place which has fascinated so many writers: the moment when the bird is about to fly, the girl to become a woman, the boy a man, the prisoner free.

The other story in which one may if he chooses read elements of Wescott's personal experience is "The Whistling Swan," whose musician protagonist has, like Wescott, fled Wisconsin to live and study in France, but who has let the excitement of Paris interfere with his music, has alienated his patron, and has been forced to return home. His mother's kindness, his fiancée's understanding and decency, smother him. Taking a long walk with a shotgun in an effort to clear his soul, he shoots a whistling swan which, dying and beating the water with its great wings, symbolizes for him the death of talent, grace, pride, everything that he went away to develop. For modern tastes, the symbolic swan is perhaps a little obvious—though it is no more obvious, say, than Chekhov's cherry orchard. Later, especially in *The Pilgrim Hawk,* Wescott learned to pile up symbolism in complex interlocking structures. Here, he presents us with one clear image to serve us, and possibly himself, as warning. This is what can happen if one weakens and returns. That is why the book has a good-bye in its title.

Apart from those two, the stories of *Good-Bye Wisconsin* have an exceptional objectivity. The omniscient author who does not hesitate to intrude and comment is disinterested and impersonal; he is in no sense Glenway Wescott speaking spitefully or in hatred against Wisconsin, or displaying the wounds he received in Kewaskum. Except perhaps in the tender and lyrical "In a Thicket," there is none of the warmth that some-

how oozes from Sherwood Anderson and fills all his characters, however grotesque, and all the space between them.

Bleak as they often are, these stories have a certain thin-
ness and distance, a minor key of elegy and regret, as if the
lives of their characters had never been quite real enough to
their author to hurt him, or as if they were known so long ago
that they have acquired the quality of legend. It is a quality
that persists in *The Grandmothers,* where it is counteracted by
our constant awareness of Alwyn Tower's sensibility ruminating and brooding upon the past. In the stories, or some of
them, such aloof impartiality makes for a certain indifference.
One feels that Wescott has known and understood these people
but never much sympathized with them, and perhaps never
even hated them heartily enough. Some, as he says of the Rileys, "have no hearts to break." The man who created or remembered them could not quite feel them as people.

It is otherwise with those who do have hearts to break,
though the artist may be just as far off, and just as indifferently
paring his fingernails. The murderess Evelyn Crowe in "A
Guilty Woman" is a complex portrait of a Winesburg spinster
carried not only to the point of passion and violence, but past
it, and back to life. Here, as also in the dark and compulsive
"Like a Lover," decency and generosity and kindness are ad-
mitted to exist even in Wisconsin. This is no Menckenesque
assault on the northern Bible Belt but a thoughtful and dispas-
sionate community portrait. The Midwest has all landscapes
but the noblest, Wescott tells us. That one feels the need of
Alps is no reason not to admit the beauty of hills.

Having served an apprenticeship to the Imagists, Wescott
came to fiction with a self-conscious preoccupation with style.
For some, his writing has always been slightly tainted with
artiness and preciosity. Certainly he does not belong with the
Twains and Andersons and Frosts, the champions of the
spoken and idiomatic. But he was too good an artist to impose

an intricate or jeweled or highly personal style upon stories whose intention was to maintain a tone so strictly impersonal. He understood that objective fiction is not the place to practice prose; it is a place to practice dramatic propriety. The personal style, the variable and illuminating gift, the carefully carpentered sentences, the verbal felicity, are apparent in the title essay rather than in the stories, and they emerge at full strength in *The Grandmothers* and *The Pilgrim Hawk,* where the voice of Alwyn Tower can be virtually synchronous with that of his creator. In *Good-Bye Wisconsin* the style is marked by a deliberate matter-of-factness in passages of reporting, a low-keyed epigrammatic terseness in passages of comment.

Thus when Evelyn Crowe takes away the suitor of her generous friend Martha, who has sheltered her after her release from prison, the meaning of their lives is stated as rueful paradox:

> Indeed, there was no choice at this parting of the ways. The unfortunate one of the two could not choose more misfortune, nor the fortunate one happiness. Evelyn could not expiate the evil she had done; Martha could not profit by her noble lifetime.
> It was late and growing colder. The two aging women kissed one another. The scenery of their hearts was exactly like that of nature in the dusk. Their cheeks were very cold because they had been wet.

Restraint and control are primary weapons in such a style, precise observation and precision of language are of the essence. Without affecting, like Joyce, a scrupulous meanness, Wescott clearly tried to curb his personal and idiosyncratic voice, just as he resisted the intrusion of his own personality and the expression of his own feelings. Those could have their expression elsewhere, in essays or in another kind of fiction, when he had freed himself from Wisconsin.

He yearned for purity, he aspired to make himself into an instrument, a lens without a flaw, and he aspired to focus himself on forms of life less crude and troubling than Wisconsin's.

"I should like to write a book about ideal people under ideal circumstances," he says toward the end of the title essay. "No sort of under-nourishment, no under-education, nothing partial or frustrated . . . no lack of anything which, according to its children, Wisconsin denies." And a little later, remembering the sailors who signaled each other with little flags in the harbor of Villefranche, he says, "For another book I should like to learn to write in a style like those gestures: without slang, with precise equivalents instead of idioms, a style of rapid grace for the eye rather than sonority for the ear, in accordance with the ebb and flow of sensation rather than with intellectual habits, and out of which myself, with my origins and my prejudices and my Wisconsin, will seem to have disappeared."

It is the statement of a very knowing writer, and a program which I for one am glad he never fully realized. At the time when he said good-bye to Wisconsin and tried to erase it from his soul and his language, he was headed toward something dangerously close to effete—airless, bloodless, dirtless, refined out of existence. I am glad that Wisconsin is still here in these stories, for it is the tension between Wisconsin and Europe, village philistinism and artistic aspiration, crude hurtful stories and a controlled and subtle telling, that gives this book —or should give it—a high place in the record of imperfections which is our literature.

# JOYCE CAROL OATES

## ON

## HARRIETTE ARNOW'S

# The Dollmaker

## *JOYCE CAROL OATES*

JOYCE CAROL OATES's *short stories have been reprinted in* Best American Short Stories *almost every year since 1963 and frequently in the O. Henry Prize Story collections; they have been gathered into three volumes,* By the North Gate (*1963*), Upon the Sweeping Flood (*1966*), *and* The Wheel of Love (*1970*). *Two of her novels,* A Garden of Earthly Delights (*1967*) *and* Expensive People (*1968*), *were nominated for the National Book Award, and a third,* Them (*1969*), *received the prize. One of her plays,* Sunday Dinner, *was produced at the American Place Theatre. She has also written two volumes of poetry,* Anonymous Sins (*1969*) *and* Love and Its Derangements (*1970*), *and received a Guggenheim fellowship and a Rosenthal award from the National Academy of Arts and Letters. She teaches at the University of Windsor, Ontario, Canada. Joyce Carol Oates was born near Lockport, New York, in 1938.*

こ╱◦

## *HARRIETTE SIMPSON ARNOW*

HARRIETTE SIMPSON ARNOW *was born in Wayne County, Kentucky, in 1908. Educated at Berea College and the University of Louisville, she taught for six years in the public schools of Pulaski County. Her first novel,* Mountain Path, *appeared under her maiden name, Simpson, in 1936. After* Hunter's Horn (*1949*) *came* The Dollmaker, *a 1954 best seller and winner of several awards. She has written articles and reviews for the* New Republic *and other magazines, and several of her stories have*

57

*been reprinted in the O. Henry annuals.* Seedtime on the Cumberland (*1960*) *and* Flowering of the Cumberland (*1963*) *are historical works, highly regarded among scholars. Her most recent novel is* The Weed-killer's Daughter (*1970*). *Mrs. Arnow lives in Ann Arbor, Michigan.*

---

This brutal, beautiful novel has a permanent effect upon the reader: long after one has put it aside, he is still in the presence of its people, absorbed in their trivial and tragic dilemma, sorting out their mistakes, rearranging their possibilities, pondering upon the fate that makes certain people live certain lives, suffer certain atrocities, while other people merely read about them. Because Harriette Arnow's people are not articulate, we are anxious to give their confusion a recognizable order, to contribute to their reality, to complete them with language. They are assimilated into us, and we into them. *The Dollmaker* deals with human beings to whom language is not a means of changing or even expressing reality, but a means of pitifully recording its effect upon the nerves. It is a legitimate tragedy, our most unpretentious American masterpiece.

First published in 1954, *The Dollmaker* tells the story of a dislocated Kentucky family during the closing years of World War II. The Nevels family comes to Detroit, so that the father can contribute to the "war effort" by working in a factory. The war is always a reality, though at a distance: real to the Kentucky women who wait anxiously for mail, dreading the arrival of telegrams, real to the workers of Detroit who dread its ending. But the "war" itself becomes abstracted from common experience as the Nevels family gradually is accommodated to Detroit and its culture of machines, the radio being the means by which war news is always heard, and also the primary means of entertainment. In the foreground is a life of distracting, uprooted particulars, everything dependent upon everything else, tied together magically in the complex economic knot of a modern industrial society. How can the human imagination resist a violent assimilation into such a culture? In Kentucky, the Nevels are themselves a kind of domestic factory, producing their own food; in Detroit they are the exploited base of a vast capitalistic pyramid, utterly helpless, anonymous cogs in a factory that extends beyond the brutal city of Detroit to take in the entire nation. They are truly American, as they become dehumanized—Gertie Nevels is encouraged to make cheap dolls, in place of her beautiful hand-carved figures, and her children are enthusiastic about selling themselves in various clever ways, knowing that one must be sold, one must therefore work to *sell oneself*. A pity they can't put up a sign over their door, they say, declaring this three-bedroom apartment to be the "Nevels' Woodworking Plant Number 1!" The enthusiasm of the children's acquiescence to the values of a capitalistic society is one of the most depressing aspects of this novel.

It is a depressing work, like most extraordinary works. Its power lies in its insistence upon the barrenness of life, even a life lived in intimacy with other human beings, bound together by ties of real love and suffering. Tragedy does not seem to me to be cathartic, but to deepen our sense of the mystery and sanctity of the human predicament. The beauty of *The Dollmaker* is its author's absolute commitment to a vision of life as cyclical tragedy—as constant struggle. No sooner is one war declared over than the impoverished, overworked citizens of Detroit anticipate the start of another war, the war against "communists," particularly those in Detroit!—no sooner is one domestic horror concluded, one child mutilated and killed, than another horror begins to take shape. The process of life demands total absorption of one's energies, there is no time to think, no time to arrange fate, no time to express the spiritual life. Life is killing, a killing of other people or of oneself, a killing of one's soul. When the war is over, concluded by the drama of the atomic bombs, "Gertie could hear no rejoicing, no lifting of the heart that all the planned killing and wounding of men was finished. Rather it was as if the people had lived on blood, and now that the bleeding was ended, they were worried about their future food."

It is a fact of life that one must always worry, not about the "planned" killing and wounding of men, but about his own future food.

*The Dollmaker* begins magnificently on a Kentucky road, with Gertie in her own world, knowing her strength, having faith in her audacity—a big, ungainly, ugly woman astride a mule, ready to force any car that comes along to stop for her. She is carrying her son Amos, who is dangerously ill, and she must get a ride to town in order to take him to a doctor. Her sheer animal will, her stubbornness, guarantee the survival of her son; she is not afraid to cut into his flesh with a knife in order to release pus. She succeeds in stopping a car with an army officer in it and she succeeds in overwhelming this man by the determination of her will. But it is her last real success: after the novel's beginning, everything goes downhill for Gertie.

Basic to her psychological predicament is a conflict that has been an obsession in the American imagination, particularly the imagination of the nineteenth century—the twin and competitive visions of God, God as love and God as vengeance, a God of music and dollmaking and domestic simplicity, and a God whose hell quivers with murderous heat. The God of hell is the God worshiped by Gertie's mother, who is responsible for the tragedy of the novel. If the God of this hell rules the world also, and it is Gertie's deepest, helpless conviction that He does, then all of life is forecast, determined; and the fires of Detroit's steel mills are accurate symbols for Gertie to mull over. Gertie, like Judas, is foreordained to sin against such a God. The novel resolves itself in a bitter irony as Gertie betrays herself, giving up her unique art in order to make herself over into a kind of free-lance factory worker, turning out dolls or foxes or Christ, on order; she is determined to be Judas, to betray the Christly figure in the piece of wood she never has enough time to carve out, and the Christly figure is at once her own and that of the millions of people, Americans like herself, who might have been models for Christ. They do not emerge out of the wood, they do not become incarnated in time, they are not given a face or a voice. They remain mute, unborn. Man is both Christ and Judas, the sacred, divine self and the secular, betraying, human self, the self that must sell itself for "future food" because this is the foreordained lot of man.

"She thought she was going to cry. . . . So many times she'd thought of that other woman, and now she was that woman: 'She considereth a field and buyeth it; with the fruit of her own hands she planteth a vineyard.' A whole vineyard she didn't need, only six vines maybe. So much to plant her own vines, set her own trees, and know that come thirty years from now she'd gather fruit from the trees and grapes from the vines. . . ." Gertie's only ambition is to own a small farm of her own. In order to live she must own land, work the land herself. The owning of property has nothing to do with setting up boundaries (there are no near neighbors); it is a declaration of personality, an expression of the profound human need for self-sufficiency and permanence. Wendell Berry's *A Place on Earth,* also set during the closing months of World War II but dealing exclusively with those Kentuckians who did not leave home, is a long, slow, ponderous, memorable novel of praise for a life lived close to the earth, to one's own earth, a "place on earth" which is our only hope; the earth and human relationships are our only hope. In the government housing project in Detroit this desire is expressed feebly and pathetically in the tenants' planting of flowers, which are naturally trampled and destroyed, though a few somehow survive—the tragedy is that this desire lies beyond the reach of nearly everyone, and therefore identity, personality, the necessary permanence of life itself are denied. To be "saved" in this culture one must remake oneself entirely, one must sell oneself as shrewdly as possible. One's fate depends not upon his sacred relationship with the land, but his secular, deceptive relationship with society.

There are great works that deal with the soul in isolation, untouched importantly by history. Sartre's *Nausea,* which concerns the salvation of a historian, is an ahistorical work, a work of allegory; Dostoyevsky's *Notes from the Underground,* neurotic and witty and totally subjective, is nevertheless a historical work. It seems to me that the greatest works of literature deal with the human soul caught in the stampede of time, unable to gauge the profundity of what passes over it, like the characters in certain plays of Yeats's who live through terrifying events but who cannot understand them; in this way history passes over most of us. Society is caught in a convulsion, whether of growth or of death, and ordinary people are destroyed. They do not, however, understand that they are "destroyed."

There is a means of salvation: love, particularly of children. But the children of *The Dollmaker* are stunted, doomed adults, destroyed either literally by the admonition "Adjust!" or destroyed emotionally, turned into citizens of a demonic factory-world. There is another means: art. But art is luxury, it has no place in the world of intense, daily, bitter struggle, though this world of struggle is itself the main object of art. Living, one cannot be saved; suffering, one cannot express the phenomenon of "suffering." Gertie Nevels is inarticulate throughout most of this novel, unable to do battle effectively with the immense hallucination of her new life, and her only means of expression—her carving—must finally be sacrificed, so that her family can eat. So the social dislocation of these Kentucky "hillbillies" is an expression of the general doom of most of mankind, and their defeat, the corruption of their personalities, is more basic to our American experience than the

failure of those whom James thought of as "freed" from economic necessity, and therefore free to create their own souls.
Evil is inherent in the human heart, as good is inherent in it;
but the violence of economic suffering stifles the good, stimu-
lates the evil, so that the ceaseless struggle with the fabric of the
universe is reduced to a constant, daily heartbreaking struggle
over money, waged against every other antlike inhabitant of
the city, the stakes indefinable beyond next month's payment
of rent or payment on the car.

If the dream of a small farm is Gertie's dream of Eden,
the real "Paradise Valley" (a Negro slum section of Detroit) is
an ironic hell, and the "Merry Hill" to which she and her
family come to live is, though segregated "by law," no different. Detroit is terrifying as seen through the eyes of this Kentucky farm woman. The machines—the hurrying people—the
automobiles—the initial sounding of that ugly word "Hill-
billy!"—everything works to establish a demonic world, the
antithesis of the Kentucky hills. There, man can have privacy
and dignity though he may be poor; in the housing development money appears and is lost, there is no privacy, everyone
intrudes upon everyone else, the alley is "one churning, wrig-
gling mass of children." The impact of this dislocation upon
children is most terrible: Reuben, the oldest boy, becomes
bitter and runs away from home, unable to "adjust"; Cassie,
deprived of her invisible playmate Callie Lou, is killed by a
train in the trainyards near her home. I can think of no other
work except Christina Stead's *The Man Who Loved Children*
that deals so brilliantly and movingly with the lives of children,
and Mrs. Arnow has chosen not to penetrate the minds of the
Nevels children at all but simply to show us their development
or deterioration from the outside. It is a fact of slum life that
children dominate in sheer numbers. The more impoverished
the neighborhood, the more children to run wild in its streets
and on its sidewalks, both powerful and helpless. The fear of
anarchy, shared by all of us who have been children, material-

izes in the constant struggle of children to maintain their identities, striking and recoiling from one another: in miniature
they live out tragic scenarios, the pressure upon the human
soul in our age, the overcrowding of life, the suffocation of the
personality under the weight of sheer numbers, noise, confusion. Yet no dream of wealth, no dream of a fine home in
"Grosse Pointe" is too fantastic for these people to have;
corrupted by movies, by the radio, by the mystery of the dollar,
they succumb happily to their own degradation, alternating between a kind of community and a disorganized, hateful mass
that cannot live in peace. Neighbors cannot live in peace with
neighbors, nor parents with their own families, nor children
with children. The basic split in the American imagination between an honoring of the individual and a vicious demand for
"adjustment" and conformity is dramatized by the gradual
metamorphosis of the surviving Nevels children. Gertie is still
Gertie, though profoundly shaken by the loss of Reuben and
Cassie, but her other children have come a long way, by the
end of the novel, when they can laugh at a cartoon of a woman
with a mule, having learned the proper contempt for a "hill-
billy."

    Gertie's husband, Clovis, with his liking for machines,
adapts himself easily to the new culture. He takes pride in buying his wife an Icy Heart refrigerator (on time) and a car for
himself (on time) and in "hunting Christmas" for his family in
smelly department-store basements. It is part of the moral confusion of life in Detroit that Clovis, essentially a good, "natural" man, should become a murderer, revenging himself upon
a young man hired to beat him up because of his union activi-
ties. There is no time to assess properly Clovis's act of murder
—Gertie has no time to comprehend it, except to recoil from
what she senses has happened. But the struggle continues;
nothing is changed by the murder; another thug will be hired
to take that man's place, by the mysterious powers with money
enough to "hire" other men; at the novel's conclusion Clovis,

like millions of other men, is out of work and we can envision his gradual disintegration, forced to look desperately for jobs and to live off his wife and children.

It is part of the industrial society that people of widely varying backgrounds should be thrown together, like animals competing for a small, fixed amount of food, forced to hate one another. Telling an amiable anecdote about factory life, Clovis mentions a Ukrainian: "He hates everything, niggers, hillbillies, Jews, Germans, but worse'n anything he hates Poles an that Polack foreman. An he is a good-hearted guy. . . ." Catholics hate and fear non-Catholics, spurred on by their famous radio priest "Father Moneyhan," but Irish Catholics hate Polish Catholics. However, the hatreds seethe and subside, especially in the face of common human predicaments of drunkenness and trouble; at any rate they can be easily united into a solid hatred of Negroes, should that need arise. Living in fear more or less constantly, being forced to think only of their "future food," these people have no choice but to hate the "Other," the constant threat. What a picture of America's promises *The Dollmaker* gives, and how unforgettable this "melting-pot" of economic democracy!

Mrs. Arnow writes so well, with so little apparent effort, that critical examination seems almost irrelevant. It is a tribute to her talent that one is convinced, partway through the book, that it is a masterpiece; if everything goes wrong, if an entirely unsuitable ending is tacked on, the book will remain inviolate. The ending of *The Dollmaker* is by no means a disappointment, however. After months of struggle and a near-succumbing to madness, Gertie questions the basis of her own existence; inarticulate as she is, given to working with her hands, in silence, she is nevertheless lyrically aware of the horror of the world in which she now lives. Behind her, now unattainable, is the farm in Kentucky which her mother talked her out of buying; all around her is the unpredictable confusion of Detroit. What is the point of having children? "What was the good of trying to keep your own [children] if when they grew up their days were like your own—changeovers and ugly painted dolls?" Throughout the novel Gertie has been dreaming of the proper face for the Christ she wants to carve. She never locates the proper face: instead she takes the fine block of wood to be split into smaller pieces, for easily made dolls.

The drama of naturalism has always been the subjecting of ordinary people to the corrosive and killing facts of society, usually an industrial one. *The Grapes of Wrath,* so much more famous than Mrs. Arnow's novel, and yet not superior to it, is far more faithful to the naturalistic tradition than is *The Doll-maker:* one learns a great deal about the poetic vulgarities and obscenities of life from Steinbeck, and this aspect of life has its own kind of immortality. *The Dollmaker,* however, is not truly naturalistic; a total world is suggested but not expressed. Mrs. Arnow, like Gertie Nevels, flinches from a confrontation with sexual realities. The frantic naturalism of such a work as the recent *Last Exit to Brooklyn,* superimposed upon this little Detroit epic, would give us, probably, a more truthful vision of Detroit, then and now; but such naturalism, totally absorbed in an analysis of bodily existence, is perhaps equally unfaithful to the spiritual and imaginative demands that some people, at least, still make. So Gertie is an "artist," but a primitive, untheorizing, inarticulate artist; she whittles out figures that are dolls or Christs, figures of human beings not quite human, but expressive of old human dreams. She is both an ordinary human being and an extraordinary human being, a memorable creation, so real that one cannot question her existence. There are certainly greater novels than *The Dollmaker,* but I can think of none that have moved me more, personally, terrifyingly, involving me in the solid fact of life's criminal exploitation of those who live it—not hard, not sentimental, not at all intellectually ambitious, *The Dollmaker* is one of those excellent American works that have yet to be properly assessed.

# IRWIN SHAW

## ON

## DANIEL FUCHS'S

# Homage to Blenholt

---

### *IRWIN SHAW*

IRWIN SHAW *is well known as a playwright, screenwriter, and, above all, as a novelist and master of the short story.* Sailor Off the Bremen (*1939*), Welcome to the City (*1942*), Act of Faith (*1946*), Mixed Company (*1950*), Tip on a Dead Jockey (*1958*), *and* Love on a Dark Street (*1965*) *are collections of his stories. His first novel,* The Young Lions (*1948*), *was followed by* The Troubled Air (*1951*), Lucy Crown (*1956*), Two Weeks in Another Town (*1960*), Voices of a Summer Day (*1965*), *and, most recently,* Rich Man, Poor Man (*1970*). *He was born in New York City in 1913, and now lives most of the time in Switzerland.*

⌒〜

### *DANIEL FUCHS*

DANIEL FUCHS *was born in New York City in 1909, and was educated at City College there. His short stories have appeared in the* New Yorker. *His Williamsburg trilogy—*Summer in Williamsburg (*1934*), Homage to Blenholt (*1936*), *and* Low Company (*1937*)*—was praised by critics but had a very small sale. Mr. Fuchs has written numerous screenplays; he won the Academy Award in 1955 for* Love Me or Leave Me. *He lives in Beverly Hills, California.*

67

An entire group of characters who have contributed much to American literature has just been finished off in a wild burst of hilarity—the first- and second-generation urban Jewish family. After Portnoy, where can a man go? When will a writer again dare to use for comic effect the domineering mother, the pathetic, hardworking, henpecked father, the husband-hunting sister, the bright, bookish, rebellious son?

All honor to the novel that has laid these useful and heroic figures to rest. But amid present laughter, remember Portnoy's ancestors. Chief among them are the inhabitants of Williamsburg of whom Daniel Fuchs wrote in *Homage to Blenholt,* his second novel, first published in 1936 and republished in a single volume some years ago along with his other two novels, *Summer in Williamsburg* and *Low Company.*

If Roth has reaped the harvest, a good case could be made that Fuchs had sown the seed.

"Nu, nu, Columbus," says the old Jewish actor, in gentle reproach to America, when once again his hopes are dashed, his peace disturbed, his dignity affronted, and "Nu, nu, Columbus" might be the catchall phrase, the underlying theme, of a whole school of Jewish-American writing, from Odets to Roth.

The old actor, who once played Hamlet in Yiddish in Melbourne, now works as a sandwich man, advertising Madame Blanche's Beauty Shop, walking the hot streets of Williamsburg, streets that he had dreamed of as being paved with gold when he was a boy in Russia, where he was born. His dreams are dead now, but his son, Max Balkan, the central figure of the novel, has not yet been defeated. He rises early most mornings "to walk the streets, for then he felt as though he were eight feet tall and weighed three hundred pounds. There were, in America, it was true, the proud and the meek, and in the mornings, alone in the mist, he too was with the mighty. . . . At seven o'clock the streets of Williamsburg were barely awake, there was no humiliation, no indignity, and it was possible for him to feel a man, living in great times, with grandeur and significance."

Portnoy, too, dreams of grandeur and significance, but where Portnoy is brought to earth by lust and knows himself guilty, Max Balkan is stricken by the world's refusal to understand him and knows himself innocent. Roth looks at his hero with a glaring and merciless eye and the laughter is violent and cruel. Fuchs's eye is compassionate, his laughter gentle. Portnoy is capable of slapstick but not tragedy; Balkan is capable of both at the same time. Portnoy conspires against himself; the whole world conspires against Balkan. Portnoy is the product of the Affluent Society, in which, if a man seeks pain, he must seek it within himself. Balkan is caught in the Depression, when pain was on every street corner, and for a man of feeling, unavoidable. Balkan dreams of no *shicksas,* no blonde beauties. His world is absolutely circumscribed, Jewish to its outer limits. He wishes to overcome it not by conquests in bed but by becoming rich and powerful. Meek, timid, poor, nearsighted, he admires the movers and shakers, the ruthless, the men who impose their will on others, the easeful rich, cleareyed enough to know that if you have money in the bank it makes no difference what you did to put it there.

The American dream, complex and optimistic, bears Max Balkan along from day to day on its powerful tide. Opportunity is just around the corner, one ingenious idea is enough to set up a man for life. Regard Ford, Edison, powers in the land, poor boys who made it with genius and luck. Williamsburg, too, is a wilderness that can be tamed by spirit and persistence. Who would work day in and day out at demeaning jobs, pushing handcarts on Seventh Avenue, when a single telephone call at any moment might lift you forever from the squalor in which you live?

So Balkan bombards the ramparts of Business with the

splendid ideas with which his mind teems—a proposal to the
Telephone Company for a central office which tells its sub-
scribers what is playing in the neighborhood movie; a plan for
individual paper covers for toilet seats; a suggestion to the
marketers of onions for putting onion juice in bottles, odorless,
tearless; a modest invitation to the citrus industry to can orange juice, to save the trouble of squeezing. He does not have
his head in the clouds, Balkan, he knows the practical nature
of greatness in the society in which he lives. Inspiration must
pay off in dollars and cents, sales and dividends.

Balkan is fed by literature—Tamburlaine is his model
and he recites Marlowe's mighty lines—but he knows that in
this era there is no riding across the plains of Asia leading
victorious horsemen. Today Tamburlaine rides to Wall Street
in a limousine. Or like the late, lamented Blenholt, the Commissioner of Sewers, whom Balkan has never met but whose
funeral he is going to attend in well-deserved tribute, he rides
in large black automobiles to Labor Union headquarters, to
Democratic Clubs, to subcontractors' offices, to synagogues
and Italian weddings, surrounded by henchmen who are not
averse to throwing unwilling vassals into the East River if they
refuse to pay the tax levied on them by the Great Man for the
privilege of setting up pushcarts on the streets over which he
presides. Different ages, different weapons. Only the ruling
character remains unchanged through the centuries—ambitious, farseeing, without pity, unswervingly oriented toward
domination.

Naturally the women in Balkan's life do not see eye to
eye with him, although he does his best to explain himself to
Ruth, who lives in the same tenement, whose breast he has
once touched in Prospect Park, and who has been, theoreti-
cally, his fiancée for the last five years. Balkan says:

> See, this play, Tamburlaine, it's about a peasant boy, a shep-
> herd. That's his name. He didn't want to stay a shepherd all his
> life. He wanted to be a great man, a king, a ruler of kings. The
> idea of power and importance. Of course, that's only the bare

idea. Telling it this way it kills the whole effect, it ruins the entire impression. But he wants to be a king and he tries and he
conquers everyone. . . . See, the idea is—listen, I don't want
to give you the idea that I think I'm Tamburlaine—but the same
urge for power, for significance, for importance—I've got that
too. In a way I am Tamburlaine, only in Williamsburg, now, not
a shepherd in the olden days. I can't win out by conquering
kings the way he did. I've got to get ahead by making money.
That's the difference, but behind it it's all the same thing.

"Well?" Ruth asks. "You want to make money? Then why
don't you look for a job?"

Go talk to women.

His mother calls him Mr. Fumfotch the Second. The title
of Mr. Fumfotch the First is reserved for his father.

Returning to the world of men, Balkan has little more
success. He has extracted promises from two friends of his in
the same building, Coblenz and Munves, to accompany him to
Blenholt's funeral. But Coblenz, horseplayer, drinker, aspiring
writer, is bathing a sore tooth with whiskey and madly pound-
ing on the ceiling of his room with a broom handle to show his
disapproval of the two children who roller-skate all day over
his head in the apartment above (not even with ball bearings,
Coblenz screams in agony) and cannot be budged to do homage to the fallen giant, who, like all tragic heroes, had his fatal
flaw. A diabetic, forbidden to touch sugar, Blenholt had accepted candy smuggled into his hospital room by favor seekers
and had died for his one weakness.

Instead of saluting the cortege, Coblenz muses drunkenly
in his room. "God," he says, "what a lousy world it is. I ought
to commit suicide." Some day, the way he felt, he would write
a great bitter work of literature that would immediately shame
the race into wholesale self-slaughter. Epitaphs and Epitaphs,
he would call it:

CHAPTER I: Life's a Bowl of Cherries—All Rotten.
CHAPTER II: Ninety-nine out of a Hundred People Are Lice, The
  Hundredth, The Fattest Louse of All Because He Gets Away
  with It.

CHAPTER III: Go Fight City Hall.
CHAPTER IV: Fellow Passengers—To the Grave.
CHAPTER V: Any Guy Who Works for a Living Is a Nut.
CHAPTER VI: Heroism Stinks Out Loud.
CHAPTER VII: Latabelle, I Love You. If There Was a Horse Actually Called Latabelle, I'd Bet My Last Nickel on You.

Raddled by drink, cynicism, roller skates, lost bets, and toothache, Coblenz is not the man to see a Commissioner of Sewers, however worthy, to his last home, and when Balkan insists upon trying to hold him to his promise, he waves a knife and threatens to murder the Tamburlaine of Williamsburg.

Sadly, Balkan retreats, mourning his friend's lack of nobility, and goes to his other friend in the building, Munves, the scholar, who has also promised to accompany him. But Munves is bemused by the discovery that the greatest authorities have misplaced Silwedu in Essex, stunning error. Knowing that his fame will be secure in the academic world if he can document his discovery, he loses himself in dictionaries, encyclopedias, old charts, and commits himself to the pursuit of pure, useless truth, leaving others to bury Blenholt.

Deserted in his passion by his friends, Balkan drags a protesting Ruth (she wants to see Joan Crawford that afternoon) to the funeral, leaving behind the teeming, inglorious tenement, with its children hurling grapefruit rinds filled with coffee grounds at each other, with its exasperated scolding mothers, its whining peddlers, its sorrowful legend scrawled on dumbwaiter doors:

GARBAGE COLLECTED AT SIX O'CLOCK

Have a Heart and Get the Pails Ready

The Janitor Is a Human Being Too

Although Blenholt had spoken Yiddish in synagogues and Italian at church weddings, death has revealed that he was neither Jewish nor Catholic, but in the opinion of his followers some kind of Turk, so the funeral, while attended by the representatives of religion, is a secular affair. The cortege, with its band playing appropriate airs and its open cars filled with flowers and its darkly garbed musclemen keeping the ranks of mourners in line, winds through the streets which Blenholt had lately held in fief, and Balkan and Ruth fall in with the slow parade.

Like everything else in Balkan's life, the funeral does not live up to his expectations of it. A lady in an automobile tries to drive her car across the path of the cortege and has the tires of her vehicle professionally slashed by Blenholt's bodyguards, as Balkan, man of action, tries to intervene in the cause of decorum and is cursed at and pushed around by victim and victimizers alike.

Later, in the hall rented for the occasion, the lady, on foot now, and raging, breaks into the tributes to the dead leader and once more Balkan feels he cannot remain inactive. Man of deeds, he goes up to the platform, where a confused struggle is taking place, to remonstrate in the name of peace and dignity. There he is buffeted, thrown underfoot, trampled, loses his glasses, and is pulled out nearly blind, concussed, wounded. Ruth, for whose good opinion he had thrown himself boldly into the fray, has fled in embarrassment, and he himself staggers toward home, taunted by children and berated by a passing lady who calls out that it is shameful to see a Jewish boy drunk on the street like any goy.

But in his agony, one last glimmer of hope is vouchsafed him. A man whose name his mother insists is Hot Water, has been telephoning him. Interpreting, Balkan realizes the name is Atwater, the official of the onion company he has written to with his scheme for bottling onion juice. At last, Business has recognized his talents. The last laugh is his, and his family, his friends, the inhabitants of the entire building now look at him with new respect, a man who has his foot on fortune's ladder.

Triumphantly, as the building hums with speculation on the huge sums he is bound to be paid, he goes to the rendez-vous with Mr. Atwater. But, this late in the book, there is no mercy in the author's heart. Balkan returns with a single bag of onions to show for his pains, and Mr. Atwater's assurance that onion juice, odorless, tearless, bottled, has been on the market for years.

There is nothing left for him. He announces that he is going to look for a job. Only in his father's heart is there any sympathy for him. His mother roars with laughter at the ruin of her son's hopes, and the old man, musing, recognizes "in his wife's earthy guffaws the clamorous demands of the world, its insistent calls for resignation and surrender, and he knew now that Max would never be the same again. Much had gone out of Max, aspiration, hope, life. His son would grow old and age-ing, die, but actually Max was dead already for now he would live by bread alone."

In the more than three decades since the book was writ-ten some of its comic impact has faded. Its colors seem less strong, its characters inevitably more familiar, its dialogue, which in its time was so accurate, now dated. But the dramatic gift is still there, the scenes are constructed with sure-handed skill, the tangle of many lives is confidently handled, the feel of a vanished society is transmitted, heightened but not betrayed by fantasy.

The pages are a little yellowed in this funny-sad fable of a group of Jews, but the criticism of the society that they lived in and suffered under is as valid today as it was the day it was written. And not only for Jews.

# KAY BOYLE

## ON

## WOLFGANG BORCHERT'S

# The Man Outside

### KAY BOYLE

KAY BOYLE *is a member of the Creative Writing Department at San Francisco State College. She has published thirteen novels, seven collections of short stories and novellas, four books of poetry, and two volumes of memoirs. Her most recent book is* The Long Walk at San Francisco State (*November 1970*), *which deals with the student-faculty strike at that college in 1968–1969. Miss Boyle has received two Guggenheim fellowships, and has twice been awarded the O. Henry Memorial Prize for the best short story of the year. She is a member of the National Institute of Arts and Letters, and of the National Committee of Radcliffe of the Future. She was born in Saint Paul, Minnesota, in 1903.*

~~~

### WOLFGANG BORCHERT

WOLFGANG BORCHERT *was born in Hamburg, Germany, in 1921; twenty-six years later, he was dead in a sanatorium in Basel. He had worked as a bookseller and an actor before becoming a private in the German army during the Second World War. Wounded in 1942, he spent six months in solitary confinement under sentence of death for writing letters home against the Hitler regime. His sentence was commuted, and in 1944 he was again sent to the Russian front, and again imprisoned for treason. The pieces collected in* The Man Outside *are his only published work.*

Nine years is perhaps not a remarkably long time to have lived intimately and passionately with one particular book; but to me it seems remarkable because Wolfgang Borchert's *The Man Outside* is the only book that has endured for me in exactly this way. There are days, for instance, when I have been unable to start writing without first opening Borchert's book and reading a page of it, or even no more than a paragraph, and then the miracle will happen in my mind, or heart, or wherever such things take place. At other times, I have been startled awake at night by the terrifying conviction that the book is lost, that it is missing from beside my bed, and I reach for the light in panic. To understand this, one must know that the book is out of print now, and cannot be replaced. And yet I tell myself that the fear of losing it is absurd, for even if it were to disappear, I have carried so much of it in me for so long a time that it could never be forgotten. The reasons for my dependence on this book, almost as if it were an actual person, are so deep that I have never sought to define them. I do not know if I can do so now.

To begin with, I cannot rid myself of the fantasy that I read *The Man Outside* (a collection of short stories and a one-act play which gives the book its title) long before it was actually published in English translation by New Directions in 1952. I was living in Marburg, Germany, in the spring of 1948, and Borchert's play was put on by a group of young German actors in that smug little university town, with its castle topping the hill. They had been prisoners of war together in Colorado, these young men, and on their return to Germany they had found that the only families they had left to them— either physically or spiritually—were one another. So they stayed together, and brought good (and in Borchert's case, revolutionary) theatre to the wholly chauvinistic people of the town. This spirited and cynical group also brought into being in Marburg a political cabaret. Such places of outrageous political satire were flourishing in the ruins of Hamburg, and—sharp-witted and lively as a cricket—the most famous of them all functioned without interruption, even during the Occupation, at the Théâtre de Dix Heures in Paris. But Marburg had never seen anything like it before, and certainly never wanted to again. For even then, with dueling forbidden to the university students, numbers of them met clandestinely in the university gymnasium at night and defiantly performed the ancestral ritual of slashing one another's cheeks. Wolfgang Borchert, dead at twenty-six, had, just the year before, written the last of his meager 259 pages to say, while there was still time for him to say it, that there was another Germany.

It was perhaps through my acquaintance with these young actors that long before I read the facts of his life and death in print I knew that Borchert had been born in Hamburg in 1921, and that before entering the Wehrmacht he had been a bookseller and an actor. I knew that he had died in a Swiss sanatorium in 1947, from a malaria-like fever contracted at the Russian front and in Nazi prisons. I was later to learn that Borchert wrote the play, "The Man Outside," in a few days in the autumn of 1946, and that it was produced on the air, and rebroadcast innumerable times, by the Allied-sponsored West German Radio. It was then produced in an English version on the Third Programme of the BBC—this play that Borchert subtitled "A play which no theatre will produce and no public will want to see." It was given its first stage performance at the Hamburger Kammerspiele the day after Borchert's death. Of this irony, Stephen Spender writes in his introduction to the New Directions volume: "He only had to live a day more to witness the success of his own play, and only a few months more a remarkable German recovery. But are the success and the recovery real so long as the man who was immersed to the highest possible degree in the mechanical destructive forces tells us from the grave that those forces will destroy us—unless we unite to prevent them—or unless—and this is the 'realer' challenge—we can believe in something which answers the right of the suicide to his own death in a world like ours?"

The setting of the prologue to the play is the banks of the river Elbe. The time is evening, and there is a wind, and also the sound of river water lapping against pontoons. The Undertaker (who is Death) stands on the quay and watches a man standing too close to the water for his own good. God, too, is there on the riverbank: an Old Man whom no one believes in any more. The voice that speaks the introduction to the action of the play says in part:

> A man comes to Germany. He's been away for a long time, this man. . . . Perhaps too long. And he returns quite different from what he was when he went away. Outwardly he is a near relation to those figures which stand in fields to scare birds— and sometimes in the evening, people too. Inwardly—the same. He has waited outside in the cold for a thousand days. And as entrance fee he's paid with his knee-cap. And after waiting outside in the cold for a thousand nights, he actually—finally— comes home.
>
> . . . And there he sees a quite fantastic film. He has to pinch his arm several times during the performance, for he doesn't know whether he's waking or sleeping. But then he sees to the right and left of him other people all having the same experience. So he thinks it must indeed be true. And when at the end he's standing in the street again with empty stomach and cold feet, he realizes that it was really a perfectly ordinary everyday film. . . . About a man who comes to Germany, one of the many. One of the many who comes home—and then don't come home, because there's no home there for them any more. And their home is outside the door. Their Germany is outside in the rain at night in the street.

The man who comes home is named Beckmann, an ordinary, limping German soldier, twenty-five years old, wearing the worn and faded uniform still, returning home from Siberia, where he has been a prisoner of war. His country is in ruins, his little son has been killed in a bombing, and his wife has taken a lover. So on this particular evening, with both God and Death as witnesses, he throws himself into the waters of the Elbe. But the river too rejects him, and in their brief dialogue she says to him, to the sound of the lapping waves:

> You thought no doubt I was a romantic young girl with a pale green complexion? The Ophelia type with water-lilies in her flowing hair, eh? You thought at the end you could spend eternity in my sweet-scented lilywhite arms, eh? I'm neither romantic nor sweet scented. A decent river stinks. Stinks! Of oil and fish. . . . I don't want your miserable little slice of life. . . . Your little handful of life is too damned small for me. Keep it. I don't want it. . . . Hey, lads! (she calls to the waves) Throw this baby on the sand here at Blankenese. He's just promised to have another go at it!

In his search for a new life (which takes place in the long dream of death), Beckmann meets with a Colonel; with a Girl whose husband died at Stalingrad; with a Cabaret Producer, composite figure of the producers who gave Borchert himself work as an actor and director after the war; with the rejected Old Man, who is God; and with the Other One. The latter describes himself as "the one who says Yes. The one who answers"—as the other self "who drives you on when you're tired, the slave-driver, the secret, disturbing one. . . . who marches on, lame or not." In his introduction, Spender refers to "this Otherness" as "the central point of conflict in Borchert's mind. Is it dream? Is it reality? Or is it just a name for the persistent courage which can go on creating again and again the illusion that life is worthwhile?"

Whenever I read Borchert's play anew, in whatever year, I say to myself: "This is taking place now. This is exactly what is taking place at this moment in our separate lives and in our history." To cite Beckmann's dialogue with the Colonel as the most relevant to this year, or to last year, or to the year that lies ahead, would be to slight his dialogue with the Girl, who has likewise thrown herself into the Elbe, or with the Cabaret

Producer, or with the Old Man who is God. None of these stunning and sane (sane beyond sanity, one is tempted to add) dialogues can be belittled by comparison; but it is in the anguish of his rational appeal to the Colonel, who sits eating supper with his family, that Beckmann speaks with almost unbearable relevancy to our own national and human pain.

BECKMANN: . . . I can't sleep, you know, sir, never can. That's why I'm here, why I've come to you, sir, for I know you can help me. I want to be able to sleep again at last! That's all I want. Just sleep. . . .

COLONEL: (*To his wife and children*) Just leave it to me. . . . I know the type from the troops. (*To Beckmann*) Well now, what *do* you want?

BECKMANN: (*Drunk with sleep, dreamily*) You can hear, sir? . . . If you can hear, sir, I'd like to tell you my dream. The dream I dream every night, sir. Then somebody screams— dreadfully, and I wake up. And do you know who's screaming? I am, sir, I am. . . . Every night, sir. . . . That's why I'm tired, sir, so terribly tired.

COLONEL: (*Interested*) And your dream wakes you up, you say?

BECKMANN: No, the scream. Not the dream. The scream.

COLONEL: (*Interested*) But the dream is what sets you off screaming, eh?

BECKMANN: . . . It sets me off. You should know that it's a most unusual dream. I'll just describe it to you. You're listening, sir, aren't you? There's a man playing the xylophone. He plays incredibly fast. And he sweats, this man, because he's extraordinarily fat. . . . But it's not sweat that he sweats, that's the odd thing. He sweats blood, steaming dark blood. And the blood runs down his trousers in two broad red stripes, so that from a distance he looks like a General. . . . A fat, bloodstained General! He must be a real old campaigner, this General, for he's lost both arms. Yes, he plays with long thin artificial arms that look like grenade throwers, wooden with metal rings. He must be a very strange sort of musician, this General, because the woods of his xylophone are not made of wood. No! Believe me, sir, believe me, they're made of bones! Believe me, sir, bones!

COLONEL: (*Softly*) Yes, I believe you. They're made of bones.

BECKMANN: (*Still in a trance, ghostlike*) . . . Wonderful white bones. He's got skull-bones, shoulder-blades, pelvises. And for the higher notes, arms and leg-bones. And then ribs—thousands of ribs. And finally right at the end of the xylophone, where the really high notes are, come little finger-bones, toes, teeth. . . . Now the dream really begins. Well, the General stands in front of his giant xylophone of human bones, and with his artificial arms beats out a march. "Prussia's Glory" or the "Badenweiler." But mostly he plays the "Entry of the Gladiators" and "The Old Comrades." Mostly that. You know it, sir, don't you, "The Old Comrades"? (*Hums*)

COLONEL: Yes, yes, of course. (*Hums as well*)

BECKMANN: And then they come. Then they move in, the Gladiators, the Old Comrades. Then they rise up out of their mass graves and their bloody groaning stinks to the white moon. . . . Then the nights are such that we can't breathe. Then we smother if we have no mouth to kiss and no spirits to drink. The bloody groaning stinks to the moon, sir, to the white moon, when the dead come, the lemonade-spotted dead.

COLONEL'S DAUGHTER: He's crazy, don't you hear? The moon's supposed to be white, he says! White! The moon!

COLONEL: (*Soberly*) Nonsense. Of course the moon's yellow. Always has been. Like honey bread. Like an omelette. The moon was always yellow.

BECKMANN: Oh, no, sir, oh no! These nights when the dead walk, she's white and sick. Like the belly of a pregnant girl drowned in a stream . . . No, sir, the moon is white on these nights when the dead walk and the bloody groaning stinks to the moon. . . . Then they rise up out of their mass graves with rotting bandages and bloodstained uniforms. They rise up out of the oceans, out of the steppes and the streets, they come from the forests, from the ruins and marshes, frozen black, green, mouldering. They rise up out of the steppes, one-eyed, one-armed, toothless, legless, with torn entrails, without skulls, without hands, shot through, stinking, blind. They sweep up in a fearful flood, immeasurable in numbers, immeasurable in agony! The fearful immeasurable flood of the dead overflows the banks of its graves and rolls broad, pulpy, diseased and bloody over the earth. And then the General with his stripes of blood says to me: "Corporal Beckmann, you'll take responsibility. Number off." And then I stand there before the millions of grinning skeletons, the wrecks and ruins of bone, with my responsibility, and number them off. But the fellows won't number. Their jaws jerk terribly, but they won't number. The General orders fifty knee-bends. The rotting bones rattle, lungs squeak, but they don't number. Is that not mutiny, sir? Open mutiny?

COLONEL: (*Whispers*) Yes, open mutiny.

BECKMANN: They damn well won't number. But the ghosts form up into choruses. Thundering, threatening, muffled choruses. And do you know what they roar, Colonel?

COLONEL: (*Whispers*) No.

BECKMANN: Beckmann, they roar! Corporal Beckmann! Always Corporal Beckmann. The roaring grows. And the roaring rolls up, brutal as the cry of gods, strange, cold, gigantic. . . . And the roaring grows so big, so stiflingly big, that I can't breathe. Then I scream, then I scream out in the night. Then I have to scream, scream so frightfully, so frightfully. And it always wakes me up. . . . Every night the concert on the bone xylophone, and every night the choruses, and every night the frightful screams. And then I can't go back to sleep again, because, you see, I was responsible. I had the responsibility, you see. Yes, I had the responsibility. And that's why I've come to you, sir, for I want to sleep again. . . . That's why I've come to you, because I want to sleep, want to sleep again.

COLONEL: What is it you want of me?

BECKMANN: I'm bringing it back to you.

COLONEL: What?

BECKMANN: (*Almost naïve*) The responsibility. I'm bringing you back the responsibility. Have you completely forgotten, sir? The 14th February? At Gorodok. It was 46 below zero. You came on to our post, sir, and said, "Corporal Beckmann." "Here!" I shouted. Then you said, and your breath hung as ice on your fur collar—I remember it exactly, it was a fine fur collar—then you said: "Corporal Beckmann, you will take over responsibility for these twenty men. You'll reconnoitre the wood east of Gorodok and if possible take a few prisoners. Is that clear?" "Very good, sir," I replied. And then we set off and reconnoitred all night. There was some shooting, and when we got back to our post, eleven men were missing. And it was my responsibility. That's all, sir. But now the war's over, now I want to sleep, now I'm giving you back the responsibility, sir, I don't want it any more. I'm giving it back, sir.

There are stories in this collection quite different in subject matter and in mood from the play, but in all of them is what Kafka spoke of once as "the terrifying quality of life—the heartrending quality of art." In "Thithyputh, or My Uncle's Waiter" there is beer-swilling gusto and humor: two strangers, each of whom has a speech impediment, meet and believe the other is mimicking him. In "God's Eye," a little boy sits in the kitchen and whizzes the eye of a codfish around the curves of his soup plate. "Eyes are not meant to be played with," says his mother as she puts the white fleshy pieces of the cod itself into the saucepan. "God made that eye exactly like yours." And the boy asks: "Is it supposed to be God's?" "Of course," says the mother. "The eye belongs to God." "And not to the cod?" the little boy persists. "To the cod as well. But chiefly to God," his mother answers. And then, left alone in the kitchen, the boy whispers urgent questions about life and death to the glaring, unanswering eye of God, pleading: "You, tell me. You're from God, tell me!" It ends with the bitter anger of the child's abandoning of faith, and his slamming of the kitchen door.

There are two other stories of Borchert's that I use frequently in my short-story classes: "Jesus Won't Play Any More" and "The Kitchen Clock." But what insolence it is to speak of "using" them in my classes! To "use" such stories as these in a classroom is as perilous an undertaking as cutting one man's heart out of his breast and seeking to make it function in the body of another. If the writing student has not perceived long before this that every sentence he writes must be charged with the maximum of meaning, then it is doubtful that he would learn this truth even from Borchert. Ezra Pound wrote nearly half a century ago that "great literature is simply language charged with meaning to the utmost possible degree." And he added that it is "the thing that is true and stays true that keeps fresh" for the reader.

"The Dandelion" is perhaps Borchert's best-known short story, and the truth he tells in it is not a lesser truth because it is not overtly concerned with the magnitude of war and the helplessness of God, but with a yellow dandelion growing in a prison courtyard, a "tiny, unpretending sun." Borchert was imprisoned in 1942 by the German military for speaking out too plainly in the letters he, as a soldier, wrote home. He served six months in solitary confinement. ("I've been locked in together with the Being I fear most of all: with my Self," he writes in "The Dandelion.") His sentence was commuted because of his youth, and he was returned to service and sent to the Russian front. In 1944, when he was twenty-three, he was again imprisoned on the same charge. "There were seventy-seven men in our circus ring and a pack of twelve uniformed, revolver-toting hounds barked around us," he writes in "The Dandelion." "Some might have been carrying out this barking job for twenty years and more, for in the course of the years, with so many thousand patients, their mouths had grown like muzzles. But this *rapprochement* with the animal world had in no way diminished their conceit. One could have used every single one of them, just as he was, as a statue for the inscription: 'L'État, c'est moi!' " *"Rapprochement* with the animal world" was the way Borchert described the police guards. Young dissenters today are describing the police in like terms at this moment, as I write, but they give them a more specific name.

In Borchert's "This Is Our Manifesto" and "Stories from a Primer," he speaks again for the young and spirited throughout the world who have sought, and are seeking now, to transmute their convictions into substance and act. Borchert foresaw all that was to come when he wrote: "We are the generation without limit, without restraint and without protection —thrown out of the playpen of childhood into a world made for us by those who now despise us. . . . And the winds of the world, which have made gypsies of our feet and of our hearts on roads burning hot . . . made of us a generation without farewell. . . . We are a generation without homecoming, for we have nothing to come home to, and we have no one to take care of our hearts."

Margaret Mead has described the young of the world of
1968 and 1969 as like to "the first generation born in a new
country." And she speaks of "all of us who grew up before the
war" as "immigrants in time, immigrants from an earlier world
living in an age essentially different from everything we knew
before." Borchert, as if knowing this would be ultimately confessed, calls out to her in sudden hope from the page: "Perhaps
we are a generation full of arrival on a new star, in a new
life. . . . Perhaps we are a generation full of arrival at a new
love, at a new laughter, at a new God."

The last thing Borchert wrote shortly before he died is an
exhortation to all poets, all priests, to the "mother in Nor-
mandy and the mother in the Ukraine," to the mothers in
Frisco and in London, to "girls at the counter and girls in the
office," to the men in villages and cities who are being mobi-
lized for war, and to others he calls on by name. The title of
this fierce and eloquent and tender plea is "There's Only One
Thing," and the lines of it might be borne on placards at this
instant by our dissenting children, the words of it chanted as
they demand of us, who are "immigrants in time," a new world
in which mankind can survive.

"You. Judge in your robes. If tomorrow they tell you you
are to go to court-martial, then there's only one thing to do:
Say NO!" Borchert's last summons to humanity thunders from
the page. "You. Research worker in the laboratory. If tomorrow they tell you to invent a new death for the old life, then
there's only one thing to do: Say NO!" And again: "You. Pilot
on the aerodrome. If tomorrow they tell you you are to carry
bombs and phosphorus over the cities, then there's only one
thing to do: Say NO!"

If we do not learn to say "NO," Borchert is telling us in
the final twilight of his young despair,

> then the last human creature, with mangled entrails and infected
> lungs, will wander around unanswered and lonely under the
> poisonous, glowing sun and wavering constellations, lonely
> among the immense mass graves and the cold idols of the gi-

gantic concrete-blocked devastated cities, the last human creature, withered, mad, cursing, accusing—and his terrible accusation: WHY? will die away unheard on the steppes, drift through
the splitting ruins, seep away in the rubble of churches, lap
against the great concrete shelters, fall into pools of blood, unheard, unanswered, the last animal scream of the last human
animal—

# HOLLIS SUMMERS

## ON

## WILLIAM MAXWELL'S

# They Came Like Swallows

## *HOLLIS SUMMERS*

HOLLIS SUMMERS *is a teacher at Ohio University, and has taught writing at the University of Kentucky, and at numerous writers' conferences. He has edited several anthologies and textbooks. Among his publications are several volumes of poetry,* The Walks Near Athens *(1959),* Seven Occasions *(1965),* The Peddler and Other Domestic Matters *(1967), and* Sit Opposite Each Other *(1970). He is included in the readings of* 100 Modern American Poets *distributed by Spoken Arts. His first novel,* City Limit, *appeared in 1948, followed by* Brighten the Corner *(1952),* The Weather of February *(1957), and* The Day After Sunday *(1968). Hollis Summers was born in Eminence, Kentucky, in 1916.*

~~~

## *WILLIAM MAXWELL*

WILLIAM MAXWELL, *was born in Lincoln, Illinois, in 1908, and studied at the University of Illinois and at Harvard. He ended a brief teaching career to wander, farm, and write. His first novel,* Bright Center of Heaven, *was published in 1934. His second novel,* They Came Like Swallows, *was a Book-of-the-Month Club selection in 1937. Among his other works are* The Folded Leaf *(1945),* The Heavenly Tenants *(1946),* Time Will Darken It *(1948),* The Château *(1961), and* The Old Man at the Railroad Crossing and Other Tales *(1966). Mr. Maxwell has been an editor of the* New Yorker *since 1936. He now lives in Yorktown Heights, New York.*

87

There is a story going around writers' conferences (it may not be true; it may be one of those stories people make up to tell each other at writers' conferences) about a very current writer who is experiencing a writing block with his very current novel. The book records a writer's relationship with a woman, while he is composing a novel. The writing block has nothing to do with fiction, only with life. The real-life writer cannot decide whether or not to murder his lady friend. Since his composition is a daily diary, since he believes in what he terms "the total and honest freedom of honest composition," he must kill or not kill before he can continue writing.

There is a story going around about a sculptor of no mean reputation who has recently dedicated himself to collecting used carpet pads from old stairways; personally he visits museums to toss the pads into a corner, preferably a north corner; the titles of his compositions vary. Quite recently he announced to a college reporter that the carrying of the pads was the essence of his artistic experience: the viewer must consider the carrying, not the composition.

There is a story about two English instructors of Contemporary Novel, a young and an old. The old teacher uses a syllabus and assigns eighteen novels a semester; the young teacher covers a single current book from Grove Press. The men are suing each other because of a fist fight that took place in the waiting room of the office of the Dean of Arts and Sciences, before seven witnesses.

And so I will read, and probably admire, the novel of the very current novelist when he finally decides on the handling of his real-life paramour; and so I will visit the exhibition of the tossed stairway pads, no doubt taken by the arrangement, remembering their transportation; and so I will continue to have lunch with both the old and the young English instructors, although on different days. I would not ultimately vote either for the old or the new.

Admitting the impossibility of keep-up, I still champion, these impossibly responsible days, the consideration of the recently old. I choose for revisiting, rather by chance, William Maxwell's second book, a novel I read the year of its appearance.

William Maxwell is not the very current writer; he is not the sculptor whose creative process is more important than his creation; he is not the young instructor who is dedicated to a single novel from Grove Press; and none of his books is included in the eighteen novels assigned by the old instructor.

But William Maxwell, the writer, has *meant* for me.

We have owned most of his work: *Bright Center of Heaven*, 1934; *They Came Like Swallows*, 1937; *The Folded Leaf*, 1945; *The Heavenly Tenants*, 1946; *Time Will Darken It*, 1948; *Stories* (with Jean Stafford, John Cheever, and Daniel Fuchs), 1956; *The Château*, 1961; *The Old Man at the Railroad Crossing* (stories), 1966. I could have chosen any of these books. I have gone to our untidy shelves to reread *Time Will Darken It*, whose very title I consider one of the finest of our time. The shelves hold no *Time Will Darken It;* the shelves hold no *Folded Leaf*, no *Château*. William Maxwell is the kind of novelist one thrusts upon one's friends; quite obviously he writes the novels which friends fail to return. I was disappointed that only *They Came Like Swallows* remained on our shelves.

Tender of ourselves, we cover up our pasts; revisiting any old favorite anything is a dangerous business, revealing ourselves, our common and private histories. It is often uncomfortable to find out who we were, and, in so finding, to know a little of what we have become.

But I am not disappointed in having reread *They Came Like Swallows*. Perhaps the book is not so moving as I remembered it. Were William Maxwell writing the book today he would make changes: the later books illustrate the kinds of changes he would make. The book still *means* for me. I am grateful for the rediscovery.

The title, of course, comes from Yeats:

> They came like swallows and like swallows went,
> And yet a woman's powerful character
> Could keep a swallow to its first intent;
> And half a dozen in formation there,
> That seemed to whirl upon a compass-point,
> Found certainty upon the dreaming air . . .

*They Came Like Swallows* is a dangerous book to write. The people are large, after the manner of life. The novel tells the story of the death of the mother of two young sons; one son is enormously sensitive; the other, crippled, tries not to be sensitive; the husband assumes gruffness. An insecure child, an injured child, an assertive father, an angelic mother could make the formula for sugar. A child, Bunny, contracts Spanish influenza, so does his brother, Robert; their mother dies, having borne a new baby; the father of the clan considers giving up his family; he accepts them. One can imagine the necessity of taking an insulin shot on the Contents page seeing: Book One, "Whose Angel Child."

But we are safe in William Maxwell's hands.

Here is a made book. V. S. Pritchett surely errs (in *New Statesman and Nation,* August 28, 1937) when he says, "The weakness of *They Came Like Swallows* is technical. . . . There is no unity." One wonders what Mr. Pritchett would say of the current novel about the man who may or may not kill his mistress. The novel occupies a place, Logan, Illinois, and a time, "the whole of the second Sunday in November, 1918," two days following the Armistice. The novel moves *from, through to,* with the logic of both heart and reason.

Maxwell chooses three points of focus in the three sections of his narrative; without a strictly limited point of view, the reader receives a sense of associating with the character in charge. Basically, "Whose Angel Child" belongs to Bunny, aged eight, afraid of the dark; Book Two belongs to Robert, five and a half years older; Book Three, "Upon a Compass-Point," is James Morison's, the father's. The compass-point is Ycats's point, James's, Maxwell's. Elizabeth, mother and wife, is rendered only through the eyes of her sons and her husband.

Brief passages from the three books, chosen almost at random, can illustrate the extent to which Maxwell is willing to stretch his limited point-of-view telling.

Book One:

> Outside, branches of the linden rose and fell in the wind, rose and fell. And November leaves came down. Bunny turned over upon the small unyielding body of Araminta Culpepper. Because he was eight, and somewhat past the age when boys are supposed to play with dolls, Araminta hung from the bedpost by day— an Indian papoose with an unbreakable expression on her face. But at night she shared his bed with him. A dozen times he drew her to him lovingly in sleep. And if he woke too soon, the darkness was neither frightful nor bare so long as he could put out his hand and touch her (4).

Book Two:

> The next morning Robert awoke into a bright cold room. There was snow on the window sill, and on the floor beneath. He looked out and saw that the walks were gone, the roofs buried under an inch of snow. And in the level morning light (which came neither from the sky nor the white earth but from somewhere between sky and earth) the maples stood out with meticulous clarity (155).

Book Three:

> If James Morison had come upon himself on the street, he would have thought *That poor fellow is done for.* . . . But he

walked past the mirror in the front hall without seeing it and did not know how grey his face was, and how lifeless.

It was shock to step across the threshold of the library and find everything unchanged. The chairs, the white bookcases, the rugs and curtains—even his pipe cleaners on the mantel behind the clock. He had left them there before he went away. He crossed the room and heard his own footsteps echoing. And knew that he would hear them as long as he lived (207–8).

*They Came Like Swallows* contains few tricks. The reader cares what happens next, while knowing. The plot matters because the people matter. Presenting the human beings of the narrative, Maxwell arranges for the reader to expect, while being surprised, the inevitable. Foreshadowing has rarely been accomplished better:

. . . he began to imagine what it would be like if she were not there. If his mother were not there to protect him from whatever was unpleasant—from the weather and from Robert and from his father—what would he do? Whatever would become of him in a world where there was neither warmth nor comfort nor love? (10)

*"What is Spanish influenza? . . . Is it something new? . . . Does it come from Spain? . . .*
The word epidemic was new to Bunny. In his mind he saw it unpleasantly shaped and rather like a bed pan (20, 21).

"For this time of the year," she said, "for November, it seems to be getting dark too soon."
She meant what she said, of course. And she meant also whatever she wanted to mean. Bunny was not surprised when his father stopped turning the cards and looked at her (71).

The novel is all of a piece.

And, after the manner of *made* novels, we are given subplots and minor characters: a dog, Old John; Crazy Jake, a town character; Aunt Rene and her estranged husband, Boyd Hiller; the girl cousin, Agnes; the maid, Sophie, and her Karl. And after the manner of life, the minor characters matter in their own right and in their relationship to us, the Morisons. When *They Came Like Swallows* first appeared, adjective-loving reviewers considered it *unpretentious, simple, straight-forward, natural, heartwarming, pathetic, delightful, serious, moving, individual, commonplace, complete.* It was even called, by the London *Times Literary Supplement, nice.* In an age when our compliments for novels center on *shattering, raw, searing, explosive, devastating, They Came Like Swallows* may sound like a very old-fashioned novel.

William Maxwell writes quietly. In his own real way his novels, too, are shattering, searing, devastating, after the manner of being alive. He dramatizes the difference between sentiment and sentimentality. I have come away from *They Came Like Swallows*, believing it.

But Maxwell should have the last words.

Here are two climactic scenes. The first comes from Robert's book; the parents are leaving for Decatur, where there is "a very fine specialist, who's developed a new treatment in dealing with childbirth"; the boys are to be left with the very particular Aunt Clara. The second passage belongs to the father, the last three paragraphs of the novel. To arrive at these paragraphs is worth the revisiting of *They Came Like Swallows*, realizing that the end is enormously important, while being no more important than the isolated other moments of the novel.

Book Two, Robert

For some time Robert stood before the bookcase in the library, uncertain whether or not to take his soldiers. He didn't want to go and stay at Aunt Clara's. He didn't like it there. But on the other hand, what if the house should burn down while they were gone. . . . At the last minute he decided to take both his soldiers and *The Scottish Chiefs*, which he had finished once, and read partly a second time. When he came into the hall his mother was standing before the mirror, with her hat and coat on.

"Dr. Macgregor," she said, "is outside with his car, waiting. Come bid your fond mother farewell."

In sudden distress, Robert started toward her, but Bunny was there first, tugging at her and sobbing wildly into her neck.

"Why," she exclaimed through her veil. "Crying . . . at your age. What a thing to have happen!"

And when Bunny cried the harder, "There, angel, there, please don't take on so!"

Robert hesitated for a moment.

"Good-by, Mom," he said, though there was little chance that she might hear him. "Good-by." And made his way out to the car (161–62).

## Book Three, Upon a Compass-Point

When James changed the direction of their walking, it brought them straight toward the coffin. They stepped up to it, together, and it was not as James had expected. He was not in the least afraid with Robert beside him. He stood looking down at Elizabeth's hands, which were folded irrevocably about a bunch of purple violets. He had not known that anything could be so white as they were—and so intensely quiet now with the life, with the identifying soul gone out of them.

They would not have been that way, he felt, if he had not been doing what she wanted him to do. For it was Elizabeth who had determined the shape that his life should take, from the very first moment that he saw her. And she had altered that shape daily by the sound of her voice, and by her hair, and by her eyes which were so large and dark. And by her wisdom and by her love.

"You won't forget your mother, will you, Robert?" he said. And with wonder clinging to him (for it had been a revelation: neither he nor anyone else had known that his life was going to be like this) he moved away from the coffin (266–67).

# NIVEN BUSCH

## ON

## MARCUS GOODRICH'S

# Delilah

### NIVEN BUSCH

NIVEN BUSCH *started a career in journalism at Princeton, where he worked on the boards of all three college papers.* Then he *went to the staff of* Time, *becoming a Senior Editor before he was twenty-five; simultaneously, he worked as a staff contributor to the* New Yorker. *Going to Hollywood in the late thirties, he wrote screenplays or original stories for more than thirty films, including such hits as* In Old Chicago (*nominated for an Academy Award*) *and* Duel in the Sun, *from his own novel. Of his recent fiction,* California Street (*1958*) *was a Literary Guild selection and a nationwide best seller; he had a Reader's Digest Book Club selection for* The Actor *and Dollar Book Club selection for* The San Franciscans (*1962*) *and* The Gentleman from California (*1965*). A Piece of the Action, *a new novel, is due for publication in 1971 by Simon and Schuster. He also has a play,* Private Slovik, *scheduled for off-Broadway production this year. He has contributed fiction and articles to* Life, Harper's, Saturday Review, Holiday, Esquire, *and other magazines.*

〰️

### MARCUS GOODRICH

MARCUS GOODRICH *was born in 1897, in San Antonio, Texas. He joined the Navy in 1915, resigning in 1920 as a commissioned officer and naval aviator. After attending Columbia University, he worked for three major New York newspapers as a drama critic for a while; his essay on Maugham's* Of Human Bondage *has been credited with renewing interest in that novel. He wrote*

95

*ad copy for a time, then became a scenarist for Vitaphone, MGM, United Artists, RKO, Republic, David O. Selznick, and Paramount studios. But for fifteen years he worked on* Delilah, *his only novel, which was published in 1941, became a best seller, and received the Friends of American Writers Award. That year he began work on a sequel to* Delilah, *which is now near completion. Mr. Goodrich lives in Richmond, Virginia, when he is not traveling in Europe.*

---

He was a strong, well-built man with a great air about him of being someone of importance, long before he had made his mark. That he must make his mark, that he could and would, perhaps tomorrow morning (if he had not already, in some secret way) was a foregone conclusion, an assumption he demanded of you. Those unfortunates who were not friends of his but had joined as casual listeners a group of which he was a part would jump to this assumption anyway, inevitably, so that as the group broke up they would grab you by the arm and want to know at once, "Who is he? This fellow Goodrich? What's he done?"

"Oh, it's not what he's done," you would answer. "He's done everything, according to him—served on the Mexican border as a teen-ager, chasing Pancho Villa. Then a hitch in the Navy, a long one I guess. Now he's—" and then you would insert mention of whichever of the numberless and ever-changing trades was giving Marcus bread at just that moment: cityside reporting it might be, or dramatic criticism or writing advertising copy or managing a Broadway show. He kept busy.

"But the main thing," you always added, "is, he's writing a book. Some goddamn long, preposterous book. That's what he talks about, mostly. A masterpiece! He's been on it for years. Expects to be on it for years more."

"Has anyone seen it?"

"Not a line of it."

"Uh-huh. The Great American Novel. Same old horse-shit, eh?"

"Well, I don't know. You can't tell. Not with him. Might be, but . . . hell, *you* saw him. You listened to him."

Oh, he loved to talk, all right. He would sit square on his chair, never tilting it or moving it at an angle. IIe would smoke a pipe and gesture with it occasionally, to make a point, while the gaze of his gray, mocking, stern and merry eyes, eyes like polished convex metal disks (designed, one could imagine, to become some part of a ship) roamed from one to another of the faces turned toward him, commanding attention, impatient of any boor who, under his spell, would attempt some diversionary tactic, such as a change of subject. God help the poor bastard who did that! Marcus Aurelius Goodrich would silence him merely by a beam from those eyes.

There clung about him, in the fires of his mockery, something resolute and reckless, explosive and incredibly gentle. His features were clear-cut and slightly aquiline. His voice was tempered rather for the rostrum than, where it was most often heard, the saloon or the coffee shop. On thc strccts he carricd a heavy blackthorn stick and often wore—in a period when this garment was under certain circumstances permissible at night, but never by any standards by day—an opera cape.

"The book? Ha!" he would say, the bugle pitch of his voice vibing through all other conversations, silencing them. *"The* book! Yes, it's coming. Coming along." Manufacturing a weariness that ill consorted with his evident vitality, he would convey the Herculean effort required to move the book in any direction, but above all forward—imply the colossal nature of the challenge, one that would have crushed or extinguished forever an ordinary mortal but which he, Marcus Aurelius Goodrich, could deal with, if not lightly, at least successfully. "It's *coming*—ha! But it requires—*time.* A great deal of time." From his pipe, as from the funnel of a distant battleship,

eddied a ringlet of Walnut tobacco smoke. "A *great* book isn't
written in *a day* or *a year!* A great book requires time. Mine
also involves an act of memory. Most of all, the remembrance
of things that happened long ago. Embellished by the imagination! To find a style. That's the thing. Then all else falls into
place. But time is what it takes. That's what I'm fighting for."

"And what," some intrepid soul would sometimes venture, "what is the book about, Marcus?"

"About? What's it *about?* Why, it's about a ship."

Joyfully I report—since long neglect has now made appropriate this announcement—that Marcus Goodrich wrote
the book he used to talk about. It took him fourteen years.
Farrar & Rinehart, Inc., brought out the novel in 1941, a year
when few Americans or any other people in the Western world
had inclination for reading novels, and fewer still the temerity
to write or publish them. Marcus Goodrich called his book *Delilah* and it was, indeed, about a ship. It was also, as Marcus
had so often implied, though never positively stated, a masterpiece.

She was very slim and light. She was always tense, often atrem-
ble, and never failed to give the impression of almost terrible
power wrapped in a thin and fragile blue-grey skin. The materials that went into the making of her complete being were more
curious and varied than those that went to compose her creator,
Man,—for Man, himself, formed part of her bowels, heart and
nerve centres. She ate great quantities of hunked black food, and
vented streams of grey debris. Through her coiled veins pumped
vaporous, superheated blood at terrific pressure. She inhaled
noisily and violently through four huge nostrils, sent her hot
breath pouring out through four handsome mouths and sweated
delicate, evanescent, white mist. Her function in existence was
to carry blasting destruction at high speed to floating islands of
men; and her intended destiny, at the opposite pole from that
of the male bee, was to die in this act of impregnating her enemy
with death. It was, perhaps, for this reason that she carried her
distinctly feminine bow, which was high and very sharp, with
graceful arrogance and some slight vindictiveness, after the man-

ner of a perfectly controlled martyr selected for spectacular and
aristocratic sacrifice. Her name was Delilah.

Thus, in the first paragraph of a work of 496 pages, the author
introduces his heroine. Nor do we—can we—after that, easily
turn away from her . . . or ever forget her.

The real *Delilah*—however female she later became in
Goodrich's creative vats—was the U.S.S. *Chauncey,* a destroyer on which Marcus shipped as an apprentice seaman
early in World War I. Based in the Philippines, the *Chauncey*
operated mainly in the Central and Southeastern Pacific. She
undertook, insofar as I have been able to check, no particularly memorable duties and accomplished no historically significant tasks. Neither does her fictional counterpart. Had she
done so, perhaps her literary fate would have turned out differ-
ently.

Oh, she did not pass unnoticed. No such book could,
even under the worst conditions—the pea-soup literary fog
engulfing a nation arming itself as fast as possible for war. As
for those nonmilitary, mostly nonnaval people, the critics—the
minute they realized that they were dealing with that all-
embracing, rather frightening genre which is not a genre in the
comfortable sense that such things go literarily but with a geo-
graphic, God save us, designation—The Sea—well, the critics
started looking for something else. Their bowels yearned for a
full-fledged, carefully plotted Conradian epic, a four-stacker
or a rusty freighter, it mattered not as long as that largeness
was there, The Big Plan à la the recognized staffers in this
field, from Captain Marryat to Herman Melville. In *Delilah*
the big plan was *Delilah* herself, and unless one saw with patience how everything, the lovely language, the sometimes glorious, sometimes theatrically failing episodes fitted into this,
one had nothing. The *New Yorker,* whose pitch at that time
was contralto rather than baritone, professed that the book
was "strictly masculine" (apparently a pejorative in the edito-

rial rooms on West 45th Street). *Books* went on to say that it "deals with incidents which in less able hands might miss the mark altogether," and the *Boston Transcript* admonished that "it goes hard, slowly, through many confusions, and nowhere in particular, and very hard."

I hasten to add that, in addition to the bad ones, *Delilah* got good reviews too, and some the kind an author dreams of, particularly an author who has in him the quality of genius but has been forced to follow lowly trades while he bought time— "Ha!"—to do his work. Clifton Fadiman probably said it best: "A remarkable work of art. Its defects are the defects of excess vigor and an overleaping imagination, which are perhaps preferable to the anemic virtues of caution. . . . But these are the defects of richness, and are not total. [It is] a creative work of the imagination, on a subject usually left to the writers of adventure yarns. It cannot fail to make its author's reputation."

*Delilah* charged onto the best-seller lists, where it held a place for all too short a time. But it had made readers, and these readers, like the critics who had sensed in the book the emergence of a major talent, waited for *Delilah*'s sequel—or if not another sea story, then at least a new novel of comparable stature. None came. We are left with this one work.

Rereading it after a lapse of almost thirty years, I was as much impressed as at first contact by its drive and dimension, its memorable, incisive prose, and the queer subtle spell through which Goodrich, defying the ukase that a sea story must have plot, enmeshes us in his own love for *Delilah*. Through this love he delivers us to the bony morality that knits up men at sea, binding them in a skeleton made up in part of hate, suspicion, fear, and boredom, but viable nevertheless, strong where it must be strong, bestowing enlargement. Through this love we become as familiar with *Delilah* as with the pulse, the tread, the perfume, and the proportions of a woman we have loved; we can move about her decks and use her weapons, energies, conveniences, and quarters as we would move around in our own house. Goodrich has seduced us. He has demanded and enforced our surrender, even against our conscious resistance (had we time to develop such resistance) to the codes of Navy tradition. The ship, a tiny furrow opening behind her, moves through a circular immensity of sea and sky, her furnaces blazing, her thin steel skin far too fragile for the tests she must endure, for victory or death.

She lands a monk on an island where, it is believed, he can put down an insurrection. "We have got to know what is going on in Malampaya Sound. . . ." A landing party goes ashore. Their purpose is to locate an underground river and explore a cave where there may be a stash of arms. Later *Delilah* maneuvers to escape from a squadron of Japanese cruisers rumored to be in the area. But there is no confrontation, and a wireless from Fleet Command puts the destroyer into drydock at Cavite.

The crew goes swimming and the captain, high on *Delilah*'s stern, watches helplessly while a shark attacks a young sailor, tearing off his leg. Suddenly Wright, "the slight, straw-haired Seaman who never could rid his face of pimples," dives smashingly to the hurt man's rescue. A liberty party gets leave ashore and O'Connel, the strongest man aboard, singlehand-edly destroys a Tagalog bordello, because his attentions were rejected by a "woman with a pert, pockmarked face, who had a lot of Spanish in her." Did I say nothing happens? I didn't mean to. Everything happens, but it is not *what* happens that counts. The fighting ship is what counts, the ways of her and of the men, finally knit together into a single Man, as it were—a tool of war. This and their relationships with one another and with the ship compose the true story, a tale spun out of gossamer and the most dire violence. Warrington's strange, strained friendship with Lieutenant Fitzpatrick. The resource-fulness of Ensign Snell, who leads the shore party. The cameo-hard cutouts of a dozen other characters, some major, some unimportant, but none without his own clear distillation of individuality: Barnes, the blacksmith; Chief Gunner's Mate Orlop, who serves as mail orderly; Hardwood, "a wild, formidable fighter." And above them all, in his gold braid and immaculate whites, "the captain, that remote symbol of impeccable and irresistible power who even must dine alone when the facilities of his ship provide adequate isolation . . . as indispensable a part of war on the sea as are the guns and the compass . . . the tactics on which he bases the summons to death may be as faulty as his familiar table manners [but] . . . in the end the order must be obeyed. . . . It was no crowd of cronies who responded with lethal alacrity to the command, 'Damn the torpedoes! Go ahead!' " Like it or not, it's Navy, man—not our Navy, but the Navy of precomputer, preradar, and preatom days, when to journey was to adventure, and adventure was personalized.

One leaves *Delilah* with regret—not only that *her* journey is over, but that there has been no other book since from Goodrich, and none to match from anyone else. Why? I am sure that many times in this anthology my fellow essayists will touch on the mystique and the melancholy of the author who makes himself a master, then uses his mastery only once in his lifetime. What silences him? The fatigue resulting from the effort? The fear of being unable to duplicate that first work? Lack of material for another? Or is the gag perhaps a personal problem engendered by the very success of the masterwork? In the case of Mark, I would guess the latter. David Selznick optioned or was discussing an option on *Delilah,* and Goodrich came to Hollywood. In his jack-of-all-trades career, he had been there before, but this time was different; this time he was feted by the great; this time he monologued in his ringing voice and cast his cruel, gentle gaze about him, not in pubs or all-night lunchrooms, but the salons operated by men and women running a billion-dollar industry.

Someone—it could have been I!—introduced him to

Olivia de Havilland, then coming to the peak of her career as a serious dramatic actress. They fell in love. Mark disappeared for a war stint, which he described in his stick for *Who's Who:* "commanded Naval Detachment working with Chinese guerrillas behind Japanese lines." Regardless of the interference of this apocryphal duty and its hazards, he came back to marry Olivia. They had one son, Benjamin. For a time the marriage seemed very successful, even though a person alert to such situations could detect in its outline a time-honored disaster pattern. Being husband to an actress is and always was a task more complicated than the command of the biggest warship ever set afloat. Mark wanted no crew aboard but himself. In short order he became Olivia's negotiator, her adviser, agent, business manager, and offensive (in the football sense, one insists) blocker. Once, in a bad moment, I caught sight of him in a West Los Angeles supermarket, buying the groceries. Presently Olivia went on tour and the marriage went up the spout.

If that is what stopped the second book (and when you saw Mark, he always said he had been working, though it took time, ha! it went slowly), I am sorry. Ten years ago, giving a party to celebrate some luck with a book of my own, I had undercover agents looking for him all over New York City— his native habitat when not at sea—to no avail.

Marcus Aurelius Goodrich, wherever you are, get in touch with Niven Busch. And thank you again, old friend, for *Delilah.*

# GEORGE P. ELLIOTT

## ON

## RAMÓN SENDER'S

# A Man's Place

## AND JEAN GIONO'S

# The Horseman on the Roof

### GEORGE P. ELLIOTT

GEORGE P. ELLIOTT'*s many honors and awards include two Gug-genheim fellowships and a Ford grant to write plays in connection with a theatre (1965–1966). The unusual anthology* Types of Prose Fiction *(1964) is one of two textbooks he has prepared; he teaches in the writing program at Syracuse University. A collection of his stories,* Among the Dangs, *and* Fever and Chills, *a narrative poem, appeared in 1961, and a collection of essays,* A Piece of Lettuce, *in 1964. His novels are* Parktilden Village *(1958),* David Knudsen *(1962), and* In the World *(1965). A second collection of stories appeared in 1968,* An Hour of Last Things, *and a collection of poems in 1969,* From the Berkeley Hills. *Mr. Elliott was born in 1918 in Knightstown, Indiana.*

∽꘎

### RAMÓN SENDER

RAMÓN SENDER *was born in 1902, in Aragon, Spain. His youth and much of his later life were spent in association with revolutionary causes; it is rumored that he was the model for Manuel in Malraux's* Man's Hope. *Before the Spanish civil war, he lived in Paris, Berlin, Moscow; after the war, he was an exile, until 1942, when he received a Guggenheim fellowship for study in the United States. He became an American citizen in 1946. Since 1947, Mr. Sender has been a professor of Spanish literature at the University of New Mexico. The first part of his autobiography,* Chronicle of Dawn, *appeared in 1944. He has lectured at many universities and contributed to such literary publications as the* Kenyon Review, Partisan Review, *and* Harper's. A Man's Place *(1940),* Dark Wedding *(1943),* The King and the Queen *(1948), and* The Sphere *(1949) are among his best-known works. Ramón Sender lives in Albuquerque, New Mexico.*

∽

## JEAN GIONO

JEAN GIONO *was born in Manosque in Provence in 1895. After 1930, he never left his hometown for any length of time, except for military duty. Giono's first novel,* Hill of Destiny, *appeared in 1929; other "novels of the soil" are* Harvest *(1930) and* Song of the World *(1934), which made him known in America.* Lovers Are Never Losers *(1929) won the Prix Brentano. Giono's favorable attitude toward the Vichy government put his work on a blacklist from 1944 to 1947.* The Horseman on the Roof *was published in 1951, and* The Malediction *in 1952. Giono's translation of* Moby Dick *appeared in 1953.* Sowers of Seed *(1937) is his only play. Jean Giono died in 1970.*

In 1940, Ramón Sender's *A Man's Place* was published in the United States. The publisher, Duell, Sloan, & Pearce, was respectable; Sender had a substantial reputation as a novelist, both here and abroad; the translation, by Oliver La Farge, was admirable; the book got a good many favorable reviews. And it has scarcely been heard of since. (For example, the copy in the Cornell University library was checked out ten times during the first four months, three times in 1952, and not again.) In 1954, Jean Giono's *The Horseman on the Roof* was published here. Again, reputable publisher (Knopf), respected author, excellent translation (by Jonathan Griffin), and decent reviews. And again, near silence. So far as American literary discussion has been going, it is as though these two novels had never been. I am referring not to the routine annihilators whom no book could, or at least does, deflect from their casual chant *The novel is dead,* but to those who care about fiction, read it, like to talk about it, wish it well.

I not only liked both these novels when I first read them and continue to like them on rereading; I think they are minor masterpieces, in the range with such esteemed works as Fitzgerald's *The Great Gatsby,* Gide's *Strait Is the Gate,* Mann's *Felix Krull,* or Greene's *The Labyrinthine Ways.* Whereupon out comes the jeer-gun: "Okay, wise guy, so you're right and everybody else is wrong. How come?"

I have a theory. In these books, Sender and Giono did not do homage to the great god Zeitgeist. Not only did they neglect honoring him; they did not even set out to flout him— flouting, after all, is an admission of importance. They simply behaved as though he were of no great consequence, no more than he had been before Hegel puffed him up. (Similarly, in more recent times, after Wilhelm Reich did his puff job on the orgasm, literary adepts of the new cult of Sex ignore any novelist who continues to treat orgasm as no more than he used to be, a bush god, the jolliest satyr of the bush.)

Before the Enlightenment and all that, Zeitgeist used to be known as the age ("not of an age, but for all time"), and the age was the liveliest, trickiest manifestation of the great god History. The historical religions Judaism and Christianity studied History in order to discover the will of God; historical philosophies sought in History the absolutes of man's nature. Then mighty Zeitgeist sprang forth shouting *God is dead, Everything is relative, I am where the action is,* and the nations bowed before him. His cult is known as social science (in the new pantheon, Science is so much the biggest god that his name is appropriated to all sorts of odd endeavors, Christian Science, for example), and the main occupation of social scientists is keeping tabs on Zeitgeist, for he is a god of many guises, many avatars. Uncle Tom, now a contemptuous term for a conservative American black, was a century ago a sympathetic Negro victim in a novel so radical that Z let it be thought that *Uncle Tom's Cabin* was a cause of our Civil War. His votaries have little regard for customs: at schools, our children are now taught current events or civics with the same seriousness with which formerly they were taught manners at home. What is more shameful for a true modern than falling behind, not keeping up, being out of date, out of fashion?

To artists in general Zeitgeist says, not *Make it beautiful,* but *Make it new* (think of fashionable Shakespeare productions, and Jan Kott's *Shakespeare Our Contemporary*). The large statue of an Etruscan warrior which used to be displayed in the Metropolitan Museum was generally agreed to be handsome; but then they discovered that, instead of the Etruscan spirit's having seized some anonymous sculptor to express itself through, this statue had been faked in the twentieth century for money by a jerk who was not even a proper Artist. (During the Enlightenment, divine Art acquired a new, magnifying attribute, *aesthetics;* currently, though not as powerful as Science, Art is worshiped with more fervor.) Now, they won't let us look at that statue anymore (to Zeitgeist, whether a work of art gives pleasure and is beautiful is secondary to whether it reveals him). Instead, they display big plastic hamburgers and unadorned gray boxes for us to look at, and when the city of New York a couple of years ago paid a sculptor to have a hole dug in Central Park, put in it a nonstatue of another of the transformed deities, Nothing, and then have the dirt put back in the hole, the *Times* found this amusing. Myself, I miss that warrior.

To novelists in particular, Zeitgeist says *Reveal Thou Me* and of course they do. In fact, they were doing it before he told them to. They can't help doing it, at least a little. A *novel* brings *news* of the subtlest ways people are connected, and not even sociology and psychology between them can beat fiction at that game. If a novelist is to do much, he must know custom more intimately than scholarship and invention between them can achieve, and because he must draw upon his own social experience, local in time and place, he more than any other kind of artist is limited by his age: it is inconceivable that a novel could be faked which was both as good as that Etruscan warrior and as remote from the artist's own culture. So, one of the best ways to find out what Zeitgeist is like in any given locale is to read good novels; but that does not mean that novelists necessarily adore him, write in order to reveal him or even to understand him. Maybe a novelist is telling a story of his growing up, and uses the age, as he uses his language, not just because he has to but also because he likes to—certainly not because he thinks it his holy duty to.

Z's literary avatar is "modernism" and to literary critics he says *If it's good it's modernist*. (By "it" is meant a work of literature written in the past century and a half or so, and "modernist" is the negative of "traditional," its counter, its anti.) Many do not heed him, but in New York it is hard not to. For American intellectuals, New York is the holy city of the cult, to which all go at least once to make a salaam or two and where many stay. Irving Howe, a New Yorker by birth, is one of the best critics in the country, but also a true believer— not quite a zealot and certainly not a fanatic: a true, but intelligent and therefore saddened, believer. Recently in *Literary Modernism* he gathered essays by various critics and wrote for the collection an introduction that amounts to a brief memorial to the movement now in its decline. When he and the others are speaking of such counter or anti writers as Baudelaire, Kafka, Joyce, and Eliot, they are illuminating, for there is no conflict of interests. But Z is an imperialistic god, inspiring missionary fervor in his followers. Modernist critics herd such doubtful writers as Rilke, Yeats, and Faulkner into their fold—even Frost, though he not only scanned, rhymed, and never innovated, but liked to write about goofy countryfolk who hardly knew what century they were in. But it's a strain to get them in, as you can see by the effort it cost Robert Brustein to incorporate Chekhov as a true member of his *Theatre of Revolt;* it feels pretty clear from reading his book that Brustein's main reason for including Chekhov was plain love. When the conflict of interests becomes acute, what do modernist critics do? Mostly they say as little as possible. For example, in another recent essay Howe displays great admiration for Hardy, for whose modernism he makes no claim. What do modernists do about *War and Peace?* It is, beyond serious dispute, one of the wonders of the ages, and it was published just a century ago when modernism was in the prime of youth; but Tolstoy is downright embarrassing when he blathers about History. They just don't mention it any more than they have to, preferring to talk about *The Death of Ivan Ilych,* in which Tolstoy had the minimum decency to blast the bourgeoisie. The result of such emphasis is that good modernist critics seem to obey the god's monopolistic injunction. However, if you think about it, you realize they know that the great tradition has remained alive and moderately well (though not in New York) throughout the duration of the movement. "Modernism will not come to an end," as Howe put it. "What awaits it is publicity and sensation, the kind of savage parody which may indeed be the only fate worse than death." I would join him in his mourning for the passing of literary modernism—it produced some marvels, no arguing that—except that I see publicity itself as Zeitgeist in his purest, most cannibalistic avatar.

I suspect, though I am not quite sure of this, that a novel written in obedience to Zeitgeist's command to reveal him, make it new, be modernist, revolt, will not amount to much; the best form for that enterprise, it seems to me, is journalism (think of Orwell's fiction and then of his superb journalistic essays). Norman Podhoretz is a prime devotee of Zeitgeistismus, and he has written that, though he finds fiction valuable enough, he much prefers the magazine article. Dos Passos's *U.S.A.* has faded badly, and the author long since accepted the journalistic role his devotion to Z meant him to play all along. Currently much the strongest American writer of the cult, as you can verify from the estimates of such Zeitgeisters as Kazin and Podhoretz, is Norman Mailer. Novel after novel he immolated on that altar, and book after book the god lavished with overpraise. Then, in *The Armies of the Night* (occasioned by a civilian protest march against army headquarters), Mailer has applied his fictional skills to experience and opinions of his own, with a result that is not only pleasing in the nostrils of the god but is a damned good book as well. As autobiography it is pretty fair; as reportage it is sloppy (so Dwight Macdonald, who is scrupulous and who was there, informs us); as fiction it is nowhere: it is Z-journalism pure and strong. You don't have to think very highly of the god to admire this shrine Mailer has constructed in his honor.

Sender's *A Man's Place* is set in a rural province in Spain; the narrative time is the midtwenties and the story reaches back through more than sixteen years into the first decade of this century; the action turns on a miscarriage of justice, and both oppressors and oppressed are vividly characterized; the narrator is a liberal. (Sender himself fought on the Loyalist side during the Spanish civil war; Malraux had already showed in *Man's Hope* how to sacrifice that experience to the greater glory of Z.) Now Zeitgeist sternly adjures his votaries west of the iron curtain, and maybe east of it too, that Government is bad; the State is the enemy of the individual; all inequality is unjust; the rulers and institutions of our society must be changed; dissent, reform, rebel. (Marx, that Hegelian, seems to have in Mao his extremest descendant: Mao, I conjecture, is so zealous for Zeitgeist, believes so fanatically in the spiritually enriching benefits of rebellion, that in the sixties he has been stimulating the young of China to rebel against his own regime. Surely this is a new thing under the sun?) Sender's story obviously contains ingredients useful for fulfilling Z's solemn adjurations. The second of the book's three sections centers on the trial, breaking, and long imprisonment of two innocent people; this is clearly one of the set occasions for high Zeitgeistery, as Koestler demonstrated in *Darkness at Noon* for the thirties, Orwell in *1984* for the forties, and Malamud in *The Fixer* for the sixties. Sender turned down every such opportunity, doing something quite other instead. But though (perhaps because?) he did what he did very well, this novel of his has been punished by obscurity.

To begin with, the story does not force or encourage or even permit you to identify with the victims (for some reason Z seems to be keen that readers should "identify with" characters and especially with victims). Sender is impartial: he keeps you at the same distance, emotionally and morally, from both rulers and ruled. He shows both—with sympathy, true, but also with a nearly comic detachment—as part of the same social system, yet without insisting that you see The System, The Establishment, The State, as the supervillain of which even the victimizers are victims. The crimes in the novel are all impure, even the cruel ones committed by agents of the State, and so are all the characters, even the most unfortunate and victimized. So too are the reader's emotions impure; my own got so complex that I threw up my hands, not knowing whose side to take. I took everybody's side. And this is the sin against the Holy Spirit-of-the-Age for which there is no forgiveness. What the god likes is good guys against bad guys, or, at the very least, us against them.

Giono's *The Horseman on the Roof* is set in Provence in 1838 during a cholera epidemic. (Camus had already demonstrated in *The Plague* how to sacrifice such material on Z's altar.) The protagonist, Angelo, is a brave, hot-hearted, extravagant young Italian nobleman, straight out of Stendhal, with a lot of romantic-revolutionary sentiments rattling around in his head. It is a story of wandering, and in the course

of it Giono invents plenty of adventures to show us how people
of every stripe behave; moreover, Angelo is a great theorizer,
and Giono lets us eavesdrop on his thoughts as well as on the
occasional speculative discussions he becomes involved in with
people he meets. We have every opportunity to find in the pattern of these adventures the book's message, for we are guided
not only by Angelo's theories but also by comments which
Giono makes in his own person. (An instance of his old-
fashioned, tale-telling, pre-Jamesian, authorial ease with the
reader: "For a heart like his, smitten with liberty, these inhuman solitudes had a certain charm." But for a novelist to manifest himself instead of Z is a mortal sin against the Art of
Modern Fiction, one of Z's lesser avatars.) What we find by
delving into this novel is that there isn't any message, at least
not of a variety favored by holy Z.-G. Giono instructs us on the
spirit of neither that age nor ours. The plague does not symbolize anything; it is neither a punishment from God nor a product of social injustice nor a disaster in whose glare the wickedness of Society may be exposed; it is just there in the world, a
given, like hot weather. Again, as with *A Man's Place,* the
reader is on everybody's side, even on the side of the despic-
able characters. Worse, he is with Angelo less because Angelo
has right opinions than because he is charming and full of vitality. The novel provides victims aplenty; in fact, all the characters are victims either of the plague or of fear of it. But our
delight in the fortitude with which Angelo and a few others
face the horror commingles with our contempt for the abject
baseness with which most face it, to impurify our victim-
pitying till it does not lead to indignation or other easy sentiments but to contemplation and thence to a kind of acceptance. Giono puts these words into the mouth of Angelo's dearest friend, a conspiratorial revolutionary in exile: "Republi-
cans have an unfortunate love for princes. Don't think they kill
them for any better reason. They need them and they look for
them everywhere. If they find one who's of their own skin,

they're happy at last to die for him." Imagine: a republican revolutionary openly and uncensoriously acknowledging that snobbery and envy cohabit with exalted ideals in his friends' hearts! Nor is the passage untypical of this novel. For the offenses of permitting shameless thoughts like these to enter his liberals' heads and of telling a victim-story which deplores not at all and delights a great deal, which is not relevant to any of the Problems of Our Age, Giono will not be lightly forgiven. He is even so imprudent as to toy outrageously with one of our solemner pieties, psychosomaticism; he has a doctor say to Angelo, "Cholera is not a disease, *it's a burst of pride.*" Only the intervention of a god mightier than Z, Art say, is likely to rescue this irreverent, splendid *Horseman on the Roof* from the boneyard of History.

A writer of good fiction is interested in people, the world. His moral, religious, or political opinions fade when he is actually imagining the people of his story: before he likes or dislikes them, and long before he judges their opinions, he is interested in them. It is this detached, meticulous interest which both Sender and Giono display.

But these two novels subvert Zeitgeistness even more radically than I have yet suggested. For like all novels they can be quarried, whatever the intention of their makers, for a Message for Our Time. The message that I derive from them is this: *is* before *ought.* And Zeitgeist is a duty-deity if ever there was one: you ought to disapprove, ought to keep up-to-date, ought to change the world. Oh sure, says the novelist, but let's have a look at it first. *What is there?*

Artists in general, novelists among them, tend to be viewed with suspicion by the rulers of the world, and with good reason. But revolutionaries, I think, should be wary of artists too: most revolutionaries, after all, are just rulers who aren't in power yet; the rest are nihilists hating order, and art is a kind of order. Rulers dread chaos and nihilists love it: novelists, an ambiguous breed, have use for it, as the stuff for the patterns they enjoy making. Nihilists rage: *Life has no meaning.* Maybe so, says the novelist, but telling stories means a lot to me. Rulers pronounce: *Our laws give meaning.* Oh sure, says the novelists, so do my stories. *Deplore!* Zeitgeist commands, and the novelist says, Fine, good idea, I've been needing some blue to set against those crimsons in the upper right-hand corner. The better he is, the nearer a novelist approaches the great high goods of all poetry, celebration and lament, neither of which can accommodate much deploring. *View with alarm!* I do, says the novelist, Oh I do; but then he gets so caught up in the viewing he neglects the alarm. Two characters are set on a collision course. *How dreadful!* cries Zeitgeist, efficient and dutiful and interfering the whole way, seeing in tragedy not the nobility so much as the deplorable waste. *Help them!* What do you think I've been doing? says the novelist and redoubles his efforts to help them collide handsomely. He is sorry things are in such a bad way; but he is glad that they *are,* for without them he wouldn't have anything to make stories with. A novelist is radically conservative as well as conservatively radical, and that's not just a play with words.

Out comes the jeer-gun again: "Whose side are *you* on?" Nobody's. My own. Everybody's, when I can manage it.

# ANAÏS NIN

## ON

## MARIANNE HAUSER'S

# A Lesson in Music

*ANAÏS NIN*

ANAÏS NIN *was born in Paris of Spanish-French-Danish parentage. She came to America at the age of eleven and began to write in English at sixteen. She is an American citizen. She has published a study of D. H.* Lawrence, a prose poem, House of Incest, Winter of Artifice, Under a Glass Bell, Ladders to Fire, Children of the Albatross, The Four-Chambered Heart, A Spy in the House of Love, Seduction of the Minotaur, Collages, *and in 1960 began to publish volumes of her* Diaries, One, Two, *and* Three. Volume Four *is appearing in September, 1971. Spoken Arts has recorded readings from her* Diaries.

∽

*MARIANNE HAUSER*

MARIANNE HAUSER *was born in Strasbourg in 1910. She has written occasional reviews for the* New York Times, *the old New York* Herald-Tribune, *and* Saturday Review. *Her stories have appeared in* Harper's Bazaar, Mademoiselle, *and* Perspective; *they have been reprinted in* Best American Short Stories *and in* O. Henry Prize Stories. *Her works of fiction are* Dark Dominion (*1947*), The Choir Invisible (*1958*), Prince Ishmael (*1963*), *and* A Lesson in Music (*1964*).

115

In the opening paragraph of Marianne Hauser's book of short stories one becomes aware that a fine precision instrument has chiseled this prose, enabling it to create physical and emotional portraits that have a crystalline transparency of image and meaning. The simplest of beginnings leads one into past, present, and future, and a care for detail evokes the most variegated atmospheres. The interrelation between the outer and inner worlds of men and women, between dreaming and waking action is carefully balanced. The movements of love and hatred, espousal of and recoil from experience are faithfully delineated and made perceptible. Marianne Hauser achieves sensitivity without sentimentality, irony without loss of humanity.

The first story, "Allons enfants," begins with a party in the present and ends with a re-creation of a childhood overshadowed by war. The ironic humor is immediately apparent: "Her mother blaming it all on the war—her derelict bladder, her callous grin, and the complicity between Dorette and her, and the cracked ceiling." The emotions are sharply defined, stoic, a sustaining force rather than a dissolving one. Through moods, contradictions, and the dualities of adolescence, they appear as clearly as cinematic figures.

In "The Cruel Brother," the vision is focused like a magnifying lens upon a girl hitchhiker and a driver. The details are vivid and hypnotic: "The girl . . . the endless jingle of her toy-bell voice had made him sink into a state of inertia, not unpleasant and rather like the feel of lukewarm water . . . he was showered by a fountain of words, silvery, high pitched speech that seemed to spring not merely from her mouth but from her entire body. Even the tips of her hair tingled with sound as she spoke rapidly on and on in a high, level register . . . the girl had that splintery sweetness, but her sweetness would never be still. It would ring on incessantly with words unsweet and strange."

They have a meal together, and he feels a growing compulsion to escape from her appropriation, familiarity, invasiveness, verbosity. Within the net of her youthful exuberance, all he feels is claustrophobia. At the first opportunity, when she is out of the car, he drives away, and the last object we see is her small cheap fragile vanity case left on the road. "The liquefied horizon reminding him of thirst."

The unusual quality of these stories is their range and their completeness. In each case, with a few words, the atmosphere is set, the dialogue is concise, there is no waste and no blur. "Peter Plazke, Poet," steals a wallet. As he is running away, to escape detection, he mingles with a group of writers going to a party. He is taken for one of the poets and they all seek to uncover his identity. They mistake his rough speech for a "proletarian pose" and remind him such a pose is now outdated. The misunderstanding becomes a surrealist comedy of errors. "What is there to steal?" asks one poet. "Ideas, my young friend, ideas," answers the host. The evening ends with Peter Plazke being invited to return next Thursday.

In "One Last Drop for Poor Abu" Marianne Hauser's skillfulness reaches a high point. To render the tone of Abu, she re-creates the chanting speech of the Middle East, derived from a half-chant half-storytelling art, the ballad. The humor here is absolutely free, ribald. There is a perfection to this portrait of a rogue, with his admixture of thievery and poetry, alcoholism and ecstasy, sorrow and stage performance. "How did poor Abu get from the Middle East to the Middlewest?" The combination of Middle East and "Middlewest" is deftly done. Abu, with "his right hand on the Bible and his left on the Koran and the local telephone book," swears off drink. The rooms are full of oriental objects, the only genuine one a copper tray which served the new church for collections and which he had lost in the snow. He covers his wife with beads and camel bells and spangles and peacock feathers for his imaginary harem and belly dancers. "She had clanked and glittered for him like this junkyard full of brass, only to be abused for not having read the classics." The dualities—two countries, two religions, two languages, two contrasting sets of values, aims, achievements, and their absurd relation—interplay. "There at his rolltop desk, over an income-tax form, he might bedevil his client, some farmer most likely, with that sudden other-world stare, and the monotonous chant of one word. Exemption. Deduction. Depreciation. Gross. Net. Whatever word had come up last, he would prophetically repeat into space in his lopsided office, where the walls were conventionally hung with The Last Supper and George Washington Crossing the Delaware unilluminated by any oriental brass."

Using words which sound like a prayer, but are a curse, using the quarrel like a ritual, which ends in a draw, using the utensils, copper tray, cigarette, cup, as in some exotic magic ceremony, the story ends satirically. "But it had, he thought, as he stretched out on the old divan, taken the Lord six days to create the world; the world which came to an end nightly here in this house in the corn, to be created anew by him, Flashpole, Eli. Edom. Abu."

"A Lesson in Music" is a character study. The erratic course of an emotional seismograph is meticulously recorded, with all the shadings of a Bergman film. Not a mood or gesture escapes Miss Hauser's attention, none of the subterranean pressures which might erupt into hysteria, the deviations, ambivalences, and complexities of relationships.

In "The Mouse" we go into a totally different atmosphere. It is one of obsession and hallucination. It is a horror story, a gothic tale. The man has a compulsion to cut off women's hair, and the description of his sensations is full of tension and euphoria, mingling lust and outrage.

In "The Other Side of the River," a philosophic tale, illusion and reality conflict. The woman who is content with a limited life in the present mocks her lover, a photographer, who dreams of fabulous adventures in exotic countries. He will not accept ordinary life. "He had been caught in the same old place—the wrong place, he would say, sniffing the air as for the scent of Siberian wolves. His camera had been focused on chimney pots too long. He had been hemmed in far too long a time by the East River and the Hudson River—murky functional waterways that could not compare with the Indus and Brahmaputra. Other fabled streams were to be considered, numerous smoldering virgin forests, swamps and ruins, marble hands buried at the foot of a dormant volcano."

They separate. She rediscovers him much later in a magazine. Brooks, once her lover, is now a special photographer on a trip around the world. His sharpest eye is the camera eye. "With Brooks's mechanical eye she . . . traced her lover through the thick cancerous jungles, bent over the lepers in the Chinese dust, the dead soldiers, the harvests, the dances, famines, explosions, prayers. Upstream and downstream she had sailed, on many rivers." Marianne Hauser superimposes the woman's plain, prosaic life upon her ex-lover's life of exotic adventure. "She had with the greatest of ease bathed her child in the family tub and at the same time joined the Hindu women as they dived in their trailing clothes into the Ganges, amidst the floating ashes of the dead."

Marianne Hauser's stories are both structured and fluid. They have the diversity of theme, the many-leveled vision that one remembers from her major novels. In *Dark Dominion,* she probes the relationship, dreamt and real, between a psychoanalyst and his wife, a former patient. In *The Choir Invisible,* an obscure midwestern town becomes a glittering stage of human drama. In *Prince Ishmael,* a legendary foundling, a fraud, idiot, or prince, projects a universal search for man's identity.

The stories in this collection demand the same attentiveness one would give to a rich painting, the attentiveness of meditation, because each word is meaningful. One must give the landscapes time to play their melody. The compactness of the stories is deceptive. Marianne Hauser folds, neatly and mysteriously, complete macrocosms into tiny containers. But dissolved in the mouth, they become fecund and nourishing. With attentive reading, one discovers that a double lens was used, one for intricate close-ups, another for distance, range; and thus the personal and the symbolic are wedded. Without the personal intimate core, the symbolic does not move us. With her special gift for humor, she deftly weaves the strange, the unknown, the unfamiliar, the perverse, into a fabric of human fallibilities that draws drama and farce close to us.

# JAMES B. HALL

## ON

## MARIO PUZO'S

# The Dark Arena

*JAMES B. HALL*

JAMES B. HALL *is a novelist, short-story writer, and poet. After a brief career as a merchant sailor and soldier he attended the University of Iowa (Ph.D.). Subsequently he has combined writing with teaching and university planning. He is now provost of College V, University of California, Santa Cruz. His stories are widely anthologized, and have claimed many distinctions; the most recent collection is* Us He Devours *(1964). His fourth novel is* Mayo Sergeant.

⤙๑

## MARIO PUZO

MARIO PUZO *was born in New York City in 1920. A World War II veteran, he remained in Germany as a civilian employee of the United States Army for two years, then returned to the United States to study writing and literature under the GI bill at Columbia University and the New School for Social Research. He has written three novels:* The Dark Arena *(1955),* The Fortunate Pilgrim *(1964), and* The Godfather *(1969). He has also contributed stories, articles, and book reviews to various magazines and newspapers. He now lives on Long Island.*

Only fifteen years later, the "important" fiction and non-fiction of America in the midfifties is like some gray, inflated apparition disappearing across the flat fields of memory.

Poor *Marjorie Morningstar* is now almost indistinguishable from *The Man in the Gray Flannel Suit.* They blend in memory, for Herman Wouk was only half-heartedly critical of his heroine hung up between two worlds; Sloan Wilson's ironic statements were equally compromised by sentiment and kindly understanding.

A casual recall of best sellers from the age of Ike gives us too many books which were overwritten, oversold, and—too often—overpraised. In some ways the era suggests a throwback to the nineteenth century, when ladies also wrote big, bad books: Grace Metalious's *Peyton Place* went onward and downward to a destiny on television; Mary McCarthy's *Charmed Life* now radiates some charm but not much life. And currently what dedicated, socially conscious undergraduate takes seriously Ayn Rand's *Atlas Shrugged?*

In other ways the midfifties is our Gilded Age, a time of literary false-coinage, of false report. *Andersonville* presents "real" history as an unreal novel; *Love Is Eternal* transmutes the biography of Lincoln and Mary Todd into wide-screen fiction. The "crisis" materials of *Advise and Consent* blend strangely with the largely staff-accumulated "facts" of those shaggy sociological epics *Exodus* and *Hawaii.* As for "truth," whatever happened to the alarums, the implied threats of *Masters of Deceit* and Vance Packard's *Hidden Persuaders?*

No matter, these titles became stalwarts on the *New York Times* weekly best-seller lists; furthermore, page 8 of the *NYTBR* was taken seriously. A place on the list certified—to some minds—a kind of worth, a recommendation of "quality." Even at the time, however, many writers vaguely understood one way in which our literature was being super-commercialized. If a Barnum-type editor paid a sizable advance or corporation money to an author (or for promotion), then a plucky sales force had to recoup. The common reader was expected to do his duty. Or, the public not being persuaded either by the author's personality or by the Hollywood wind machines, the paperback houses would surely buy the reprint rights and thereby save the reputations of all concerned. The process was self-perpetuating; quality became a much-abused word. No doubt at one time literary works of the imagination were— euphemistically—"presented to the public." In the midfifties, however, too many books were either ignored or were merely vended by sales techniques suited equally to depilatories or buggy whips.

Ironically, it was an age of criticism. The most energetic critics were fascinated by the puzzles of exegesis; they really did revitalize some literature of the past and very nearly saved "the Tradition." The price for their focus on the past was high: they left worthwhile literary works of their own time ill-defined and not defended. Concurrently the urbane, metropolitan critical establishment which might have been an equivalent to the critical circles of Sidney, Dryden, Johnson, or Arnold did not so function. The critical establishment in and around our literary capital was either merely partisan or not alert. For example, a number of pre-"angry" novels and precursors of the "New French Novel" and several "schools" of poetry were manifest. Yet it was the British or French critics, reading the same kind of thing in their own bailiwicks, who first described the play. The isolationist, involuted nature of one portion of the American critical establishment at the time is suggested by the sentiments and confessional tone of a later work, *Making It.* On balance the American critical effort worked not so much for a new vital literature as for itself.

These harsh things having been said, it is instructive to mention three typical works of literary quality as seen by the sophisticated reader of the mid-fifties. These prose fictions were either awarded national prizes, or were best sellers, or both. The works were by literary artists of serious intent, and each book sensitively dramatizes a distinctive stratum of life in America. The books are the *Nine Stories* by J. D. Salinger, *The Assistant* by Bernard Malamud, *The Adventures of Augie*

*March* by Saul Bellow. The strong literary virtues of these books are a matter of public record.

In addition to being well appreciated, these books have several things in common. They are portraits of urban and suburban life; they treat an appropriate squalor; there is a certain similarity of tone; and the main protagonists seek salvation in a basically disordered world.

More explicitly, the three books also share an easy optimism. Augie March is a positive-thinking, albeit insatiable character. Frank Alpine's fate is crudely upbeat, for in the final paragraphs the pain of circumcision "inspired him" and he becomes a Jew. For the most part the protagonists in the Salinger stories face a comfortable—if not okay—kind of doom.

If there is widespread sentimentality, there is also a deeper reliance on "ideas" that compromise the materials. In *Augie March,* for example, the dictates of the picaresque conventions presumably justify the structural sprawl of the final one-third of the novel; thus the "idea" of the picaresque works against structural fidelity. *The Assistant* relies in part on obvious symbol and mythic materials, most notably of Saint Francis and the birds; these evocations blur motive and help generalize and explain away the underlying social conflicts. In a similar way the *Nine Stories* substitutes small irony and the fuzz of Zen for genuine analysis or full dramatization.

Of course, none of these comments imply the three books are anything less than authentic works of literary art. Far from it: insight into the human condition and heavy emotional involvement are everywhere evident. Where commitment to a subject matter is so evident, however, exhortation, confession, and unresolved action are never quite enough. The sentiment and the evasions suggest these books are splendidly of their time. Nona Balakian discusses more fully some of the above ideas in a penetrating *Christian Science Monitor* article of May, 1970. On the same shelves and on the same best-seller lists were two nonfiction titles that embrace similar persuasions: *The Power of Positive Thinking* and *Life Is Worth Living.*

By contrast, there was another book published almost at the same time. Though by no means a perfect book, the first novel by Mario Puzo, *The Dark Arena* (1955), displays considerably less compromise in the treatment of the protagonists —Americans and Germans caught and held in the rubble of Europe destroyed.

At publication, understandably, *The Dark Arena* was not— as they say—well received although there were glowing and perceptive reviews by Maxwell Geismar in the *Saturday Review* and Frederick Morton in the New York *Herald Tribune.*

The story concerns occupation life a year or so after V-E Day in and around Bremen, in the American enclave. The city, the economy of Germany, and the lives of all survivors— American and German alike—are in shambles. Obsessively, the wind blows across the rubble; streetcars go clanging away to nowhere. A more youthful generation of German men and women is barely emergent; for the most part the Americans are louts, die-hard soldiers, Mil Gov stiffs, and rubble bureaucrats administering American policy in occupied Germany.

And what a policy: Denazification was the cornerstone, and yet almost by definition any German of substance or abilities was most certainly compromised. In addition all Displaced Persons were to be sent home: the truck convoys and freight trains left Bremerhaven headed for Poland and beyond; by nightfall most of the DPs were back again in the *Lager.* Better to be a live foreigner in Germany than a deserter or worker handed over at the border to the Russians. Of its kind the DPs' logic was nearly faultless: "We stay in *Vaterland.* For freedom. Freedom to *fight* the Russians. You *Ami* do not *think* so, but the Russian, he do come. Sometime." Then, the next week, with green branches and bouquets of flowers on the trucks, they would "depart" for home again.

The Morgenthau Plan was a confused beginning for all

later policy. Under that policy the German economy was to be only agricultural, the whole country to be one vast farm. But the day the war ended, the American army needed the German shipyard machinery and shipyard workers in Bremerhaven to refit the *Europa* to send American soldiers home. Quick.

Worst of all, our university-trained Military Government officers, the Property Control officers, the Labor Officers, the ex-government employees from Washington had little talent for governing the conquered. The most imaginative of our detachment commanders saw the occupation as a game one could not win: if the occupation were too successful, then Americans would have to feed and clothe the German populace; if the Germans were encouraged to feed themselves, there had to emerge a modern, complex, industrial state. At the top, the military government was somewhat confused; at the bottom, in the detachments, there was apathy, guilt, and fatigue. The best Mil Gov officers were at least sincere, and the worst no more than renegades, themselves perhaps of European background, bent on legally sanctioned revenge. If the war was won on gasoline and blood, the occupation was lost on whiskey.

This shadow world of compromise and confusion— partly of our own making—was a world the midfifties forgot or ignored or denied. Nevertheless, it is a world captured by *The Dark Arena* and still kept alive for our consideration. The novel is a hard look at an almost totally unregenerate world, an unpretentious book in a well-recognized, strong American vein.

For the author, no doubt, the response to his first novel was a keen disappointment. Puzo, however, continued to earn a living in and around New York as a writer; the day-to-day work was largely nonfiction articles. *The Fortunate Pilgrim* (1964) is a mature second novel which shows the rise of a magnificent Italian peasant woman and her pilgrimage from tenement to a little bungalow of her own on Long Island. The

quality of the second novel is very high: the book will continue
to claim serious readers for a long time. Certain passages concern the Italian-Sicilian role in big-city crime, and these episodes are fully explored in *The Godfather* (1969). This third
novel (in fifteen years) is less subtle and less controlled struc-
turally, but more than a year after publication, however, *The
Godfather* remained a best seller of magnitude. Needless to
say, both *The Dark Arena* and *The Fortunate Pilgrim* were
out of print before *The Godfather* appeared. Its tremendous
success happily revived them, and *The Fortunate Pilgrim* has
already sold more than two million copies in paperback.

Taken together the three novels make a broad, responsible statement about the quality of American urban life and
the traits of character required for protagonists to survive emotionally and physically in a Darwinian world. Save for an episode or two, *The Dark Arena* takes place overseas. Nevertheless, it is thematically and stylistically related to the other, later
works. In tone and in atmosphere Bremen is simply an exten-
sion of New York City.

The plot structure of *The Dark Arena* is not complex.
After service in a Military Government Detachment (Bremen),
Walter Mosca comes back to metropolitan New York. Once
home, Walter refuses to marry the girl who waited out the
war for him. This episode announces a major theme of the
book, which in the words of the epigraph is Mosca's "being
unable to love." The hero goes back to Germany as an American civilian employee of the occupation forces. His old friends
in Military Government arrange an assignment to the air base
outside Bremen. Thus Walter Mosca reenters the "dark arena"
not only of a destroyed Germany but also the area of his own
emotional "rubble."

The German chapters dramatize two main propositions.
Overtly the book shows the German-American accommoda-
tions in the first years of the occupation: the black market,
bureaucracy at work and play, the implied emergence of a new

Germany from the destroyed city. By parallel, the novel also shows Mosca's emotional "growth," his acceptance of what passes for love, and—at last—his defeat and his exodus from the hypocrisy and the betrayals of occupation life.

Mosca's acceptance of love of a domestic variety comes from his association with Hella: to see her again, he returned to the dark arena. Because of the fraternization rules, Mosca and Hella cannot marry. Nevertheless, they have a child and live well together. When they can marry officially, Walter delays too long; and because there are no "papers," an American GI dentist refuses to give Hella penicillin for an infected tooth. Hella is in a weakened condition and the infection spreads. Walter goes to Yergen—a German black-marketeer—to buy the penicillin. The black-market medicine is bad, and the seller probably suspected as much. Mosca's weak management, bureaucratic rules, and black-market betrayal combine to cause Hella's tragic, unnecessary death.

The revengeful, violent aspect of Mosca's character becomes dominant. With the cooperation of Eddie Cassin, another American, the black-market operator is lured to the American Club. While the usual shoddy dancing and drinking go on below, Mosca shoots Yergen. The party and the world outside go on as though nothing had happened. Yergen's body is abandoned on the stairs.

Mosca carries his packed suitcase and goes into the near-winter night. He feels no "sorrow, no desolation, that finally there was no one, no human being to speed him on his way." ". . . Finally he had become the enemy." He is alone on a "ruined continent he could never leave." The *Strassenbahn* clangs toward him but it "made no difference whether he caught this one or the next." The revengeful, planned nature of Yergen's death, the combination in Mosca of domesticity and the outlaw impulse, his throwing over or his abandonment of the Allied occupation's Rules-of-Play very much suggest the attitudes and the behavior of Don Corleone, the hero and the rebel-founder of a crime syndicate in *The Godfather*. Walter

Mosca's inability to love and to display emotion is a recurring pattern and also signifies the novel's major point. (Of this, more later.)

*The Dark Arena* is in the line of novels that surely must be a chief glory of American fiction: the American naturalist tradition, the literary cum scientific talents whose noble calling is to describe conditions as they are. All of Puzo's novels suggest the strength of the best regional fiction of the mid-nineteenth century and the later writers who profited from the example of Zola. Fictionally speaking, Walter Mosca could walk almost unnoticed through Frank Norris's *McTeague;* Mosca's home in New York, and the locale of the later novels is not far from the alleys where Stephen Crane's *Maggie* started down, and out; Mosca and Clyde Griffiths of *An American Tragedy* are fictional cousins. The evocation of Dreiser is justified in part, because Puzo shows with considerable fidelity —but less massively—the way institutions work and how the individual may fare in the process. Taken as a whole, Puzo's work is less public in its focus than Dreiser's work. In *The Dark Arena,* for example, there is almost nothing of the larger issues of postwar Europe and the cold war. Puzo's greatest strength is in rendering the semiprivate, inner workings of a family, and in showing what constitutes loyalty, fidelity, and right conduct in a crisis over business and money.

In general, naturalistic fiction deals with men and women of the lower social orders, and frequently the characters are victims of forces they dimly understand—if at all. These novels take place typically in the urban jungles where violence, exploitation, and brute misunderstanding are the rule. Life proceeds toward an ill-defined goal; suffering is everywhere; the clever, the strong, and the rich triumph over the weak and the sensitive. The naturalistic world is a fallen world; any resolution in human affairs is, at best, ambivalent. Clearly *The Dark Arena* is of this solid, unsentimental vein of fiction in American literature.

Not surprisingly, *The Dark Arena* displays certain

strengths associated with other novels of the naturalist school. There is a variety of lifelike characters, German and American.

Eddie Cassin emerges as a hedonistic administrator whose inadequacies drive him to the seduction of very young German girls and also to a creature whom he calls, without irony, "The Gorilla." Wolf is a former counterintelligence officer and looks very much like an American farmer; he manages to leave Bremen with his German wife and his "fortune," a successful man. Leo is a part-Jewish man who spent his childhood and youth, with his father, in a concentration camp; now he works for Jewish Relief and vacillates about whether or not to leave Germany.

Frau Meyer manages the American billets. She is trim and athletic, and was once a minor official with the *Bunddeutscher Maedel*. Systematically, she loots their quarters, and consorts with Yergen, her handyman, who, in turn, gets a new start in life by being of service to the *Ami* and to her. Frau Vlavern represents the old, German aristocratic tradition of trade, and is an efficient, necessary force in the black market. And there are also nightclub comics, flunkies, ambulance drivers, streetwalkers, and all the countless dead who hang on in the memories of everyone in the book.

In addition there are people who are for no one, not even themselves. Adlock, the dentist, casually and easily denies Hella the penicillin; Gordon Middleton is an unreconstructed American Communist, an "intellectual," who hopes the occupation will get him closer to a Russianized Europe which he feels is bound to develop. One of the few good persons in the book is Frau Saunders, who adopts Hella's baby.

Hella represents understanding and love; she even discerns Mosca's secret, his "lack of faith in her, in himself, and in all things." Hella has the spiritual resources, the right reason, the kind of motivation and understanding which shows her of finer stuff even though she was laughed at by the girls in

Berlin and was called "a farmer" because she liked to talk about children. In her death there is genuine pathos.

Yet it is Mosca who dominates the book. In some ways he remains a mystery. It is understood he was wounded in combat, and he bears a long white scar down the length of his body. While guarding prisoners, his German POW "straw boss" engineered an escape; the American GI guards find and "murder" the ringleader. Mosca bears the guilt for that killing. On the surface Mosca is the hard-bitten ex-GI: he is cynical, guarded, and tough. If he has his own standards, he still gives way to revenge and kills Yergen. Mosca needs love, and he needs another human being, but because of his temperament and his past, real love is impossible for him to accept. The understanding so slowly built up between Walter and Hella shows promise, but her tragic death leaves Mosca more isolated than ever before. Perhaps Mosca never understands one thing deep in himself: very possibly he feels things more acutely than he can admit even to himself; he is sensitive but does not know it. He expects to have conventional emotional reactions, but—of course—he never does.

To align *The Dark Arena* with the naturalistic tradition is not to deny other literary values. Details of everyday life are often selected for their symbolic suggestion: the view from Mosca's window upon his arrival in Germany when he observes a family working painfully in the dusk, their low, ruined-brick outline of four walls barely visible; the sharp, white buckteeth of Frau Meyer, who is ever a scavenger, a pack rat in her billets. The lacerated city, the rubble, the wind, and the crowds of people walking into or out of buildings are recurring details which come to signify the spiritual desert in the hearts of so many of the protagonists. The plot structure is low-keyed, and there are good touches everywhere. If Hella dies of an infected tooth, this is prefigured in the couple's first meeting upon Walter's return to Germany, for while he was gone, Hella had to have two teeth pulled. The language is straightforward and unpretentious. If the first episodes, and particularly the scenes in New York, are stiff, the novel gains momentum, and the death and burial of Hella are beautifully realized.

What then might be the larger issue, the significance of this novel for America today? As has been suggested, Mosca again and again sees himself as unfeeling, as incapable of emotional response. The point to the novel, therefore, must be related to that central trait of the American hero.

And so it is. Mosca's emotional conflict is of a classic kind. From the Greeks onward, the emotional relationship between conquered and conquerors has attracted dramatic and literary artists. Mosca's dilemma is this: if he responds emotionally to the conquered Germans, then he becomes a German; by giving, he joins the enemy. This was one of the reasons behind the Allied policy of "non-fraternization." On the other hand, if Mosca responds not at all, then he is doomed to frustration, to emotional starvation, and eventually to destruction of self. Mosca is a victim of emotional pulls which he cannot resolve. In the end, by weak management of his affairs, he helps kill the woman he has dared, illegally, to love, and he also kills Yergen, a man who suddenly and melodramatically became "the enemy." When Mosca flees the occupation scene, he is not so much running away as he is seeking a road to the kind of world where emotional conflicts can be resolved, or at least partially resolved. What Mosca seeks is not perfection; he seeks human accommodation. In a world legally divided between conqueror and conquered, humane intercourse is forever denied.

Walter Mosca's emotional state reflects one kind of criticism of American policy. His state suggests our occupation policy was aimed only at filling the needs of mere survival. In so doing the emotional life of anyone still alive who could any longer care was sacrificed.

If Mosca's career and his concomitant emotional conflict is the point to *The Dark Arena,* then there is reason to believe that when literary scholars, historians, or socioanthropologists need an austere, uncompromising vision of one part of American life at a difficult, probably dishonorable time, they may well turn to this novel.

# WARREN EYSTER

## ON

## HUMPHREY COBB'S

# Paths of Glory

---

### *WARREN EYSTER*

WARREN EYSTER, *a former editor at McDowell, Obolensky, has taught English in high school, creative writing at Longwood College in Virginia, and is now director of the writing program at Louisiana State University. He was born in Steelton, Pennsylvania in 1925. His first novel* Far From the Customary Skies *appeared in 1953, followed by* No Country for Old Men *(1955), and* The Goblins of Eros *(1957). He has three novels in progress.*

### *HUMPHREY COBB*

HUMPHREY COBB *was born in Florence, Italy, in 1899, in Casa Guidi, the house where Robert Browning once lived. In 1916, he enlisted in the Canadian army and was wounded and twice gassed in World War I. He wandered in Europe, England, and Africa after the war, then returned to the United States, where he wrote advertising copy. His literary reputation rests almost entirely on his antiwar novel* Paths of Glory *(1935), made years later into a celebrated film by Stanley Kubrick. Another novel,* None But the Brave, *ran as a serial in* Collier's Weekly *in 1938 but was never published in book form. Mr. Cobb lived for a while in Pasadena, California; he died at Port Washington, Long Island, in 1944.*

The copy I hold here in my hand of Humphrey Cobb's *Paths of Glory* has been ingloriously yellowing in a college library for thirty-five years. Published in June, 1935, and acquired by the library shortly thereafter, this book has not been taken outside its walls until now. Perhaps—even probably—I am the only person ever to have read it. Therefore, to classify this utterly neglected novel as a *re*discovery is to misrepresent the evidence. Books filled with blank pages might have attracted more attention. The dusty and mice-smelling lower stacks with thousands of manuscripts whose pages resemble rusty apple cores—that infernal region which even scholars visit as rarely as their schedule for promotions will permit—would have provided a more courteous epitaph than the prominent shelving position in the main reading room which Cobb's novel has occupied for almost half a century, while its once bright red and blue cover wasted into colors suggestive of dried blood and faded loyalty.

Did *Paths of Glory* deserve this fate?

In a century when war and war novels have been equally common, when every American sailor or soldier or marine with literary ambitions has penned tales of blood and guts, fungus and dry rot, battle-cry horrors and prison-camp atrocities, and when every retired admiral and armchair general and former ambassador has posted memoirs of wartime London, wartime Washington, and wartime Honolulu, what makes this story of the last days of World War I worth rediscovering?

Humphrey Cobb was not a great artist. Matched against the giants Yeats and Pound and Eliot, Conrad and Joyce and Faulkner, Fitzgerald and Lawrence and Wolfe, he was a talented amateur, a journalist with a message too untimely for newsprint and too unpalatable for family magazines.

Even among war writers, Cobb did not rank foremost.

*War and Peace* dwarfs his little novel. Tolstoy spanned

half a century and half a continent; Cobb's military action was confined to seventy-two hours and a few hundred yards of muddy trench. Tolstoy spread before his readers' eyes a historical panorama as wide as Napoleon's ambition and Russia's destiny; Cobb's vision was as narrow (or concentrated) as the dugout in which his pfc's huddled, and as insignificant as the fortified hill called "the Pimple" for which they senselessly and unwillingly died.

Cobb did not possess Stephen Crane's remarkable eye for both accurate and supraphotographic detail. Nature, indifferent to man's existence, was transformed by Crane into a magnificent and overwhelming setting wherein men acted out their brief and futile biographies, cringing beneath a cannonade on a bloody Southern battlefield, or facing, in a small open boat, slate-gray Atlantic waves outrageously high, or finding a lonely death beneath the cold blue winter skies of Nebraska, or acknowledging the passing of an era upon the sun-blazed sands of Texas. The universe of Stephen Crane held readers spellbound as it dramatized materialistic macrocosm versus spiritual microcosm—a world of vast space and awesome powers experienced and recorded and opposed by fragile creatures whose perishability mocked their sensibility and underscored the absurdity of their resistance. This vision of the world Cobb shared, but could never adequately express.

Nor did he possess Hemingway's skill for surrounding the dismal and drab conditions of modern warfare with natural beauty and symbolic significance, so that despite the feelings of inconsequence and impotence associated with all individual acts and decisions on battlefields where soldiers witnessed the impersonal ugliness with which modern weaponry performed mass executions; despite the horrible and senseless international carnage, the incredible waste of human lives, ordered by the military and justified by political slogans; despite the substitution of vicious denunciations and of firing squads and carabinieri for the once noble tradition of Periclean praise and for the patriotic devotion of earlier times and earlier wars; and despite the daily battlefield proof that Samson and Achilles were of no more value in modern warfare than the most primitive pygmy or dwarf, Hemingway's heroes remained essentially chivalric, inwardly yearning to enact legendary romances or to be seated at the Arthurian Round Table. Humphrey Cobb's soldiers simply wanted to get the hell out of the trenches and go home!

For the bizarre, he could not match Ambrose Bierce.

For personal involvement, he could not equal Wilfred Owen's descriptions, that read like prophecies of his own death (which occurred one week before the Armistice, perhaps in a battle as futile as the one Cobb described). "Gas! GAS! Quick boys!"

Cobb lacked Auden's erudition or rapport with the classics that would have permitted him to compare the "marble well-governed cities of ancient Greece" with the modern world in which life had become

> A million eyes, a million boots in line,
> Without expression, waiting for a sign.

Nor had he e. e. cummings's satirical powers and language skills to sing of Olaf and assert the conscientious objector "more brave than me: more blond than you."

Humphrey Cobb was certainly not the only artist to testify against warfare as an internationally sanctioned method of committing impersonal murders on a massive scale; nor first to relate individual instances of cold-blooded killing and other inhumane behavior. John Dos Passos, Robert Graves, Siegfried Sassoon, Erich Maria Remarque, Arnold Zweig, and Franz Werfel, to name only a few, all contributed evidence, and some of them with greater literary skill and more documentary authenticity than Cobb did.

But *no* writer has ever opposed the power structure that exists within modern armies more relentlessly than Cobb. No writer has shown the gap between officers and enlisted men, between front-line troops and the high command, to be so tragic and absurd. Indeed, Cobb hated war to a degree that makes Remarque's *All Quiet on the Western Front* seem merely sentimental, and current anti-Vietnam talk a mere kindergarten protest. Hatred for war and for the corrupt chain of command that permitted bad officers to issue bad orders and then escape the consequences of their own folly through a court-martial system designed to substitute scapegoats for justice—this hatred issues from almost every sentence Cobb wrote. It became his main artistic fault, and, paradoxically, his novel's most lasting value.

That is why *Paths of Glory* deserves to be rediscovered.

Shortly after the novel was published, P. R. Redman called it "a masterpiece of anti-war propaganda that should be broadcast for the good of the world."

That is why *Paths of Glory* needs to be read.

Humphrey Cobb's novel is more topical for the American today than it was at the time of its original publication. No current explanations of the morale problems of United States troops in South Vietnam, and no current investigations of reported atrocities at My Lai, Song My, and Son Thang offer such graphic evidence of the real causes for inhuman behavior and moral perversion as *Paths of Glory*. However sincere the efforts to reveal the facts behind alleged murders of civilians, to determine responsibility for the issuance of such orders, and to establish the motives for inhumane and shameful behavior, reminiscent of the worst Nazi atrocities, the truth will never be known. Cobb's novel warned us thirty-five years ago that military and political considerations prevent accurate tracing of the hierarchy by which general instructions from a commanding officer become specific orders to the individual sergeant or corporal or pfc. Cobb warned us then that military law never seeks justice, but merely selects a scapegoat; a court-martial is merely the formal ritual or ceremony of condemnation.

No wonder the reviewer for the *Christian Science Monitor* stated back in 1935 that the novel attacked "not the slaughter and stink of the 'field of honor' so much as the rotten, ruthless system of militarism that robs men of their most primitive rights." No wonder he urged that it "should be read in every schoolroom of every land."

Of course there are important distinctions between conditions on the western front for war-exhausted French troops in 1918 and the battle conditions American GIs confront in Vietnam. The very nature of warfare in which the enemy does not consistently wear uniforms, in which snipers may be bearded papa-sans or baby-faced schoolboys, and in which young girls and pregnant mothers plant mines and booby traps with the same tender care that once was reserved for rice shoots, mocks efforts to distinguish between foe and friend, military personnel and civilians. This nasty aspect of warfare Cobb did not include in his novel, since the Boche were sporting enough to remain clearly and even proudly identified (except when an artillery shell blew them into small pieces). But there weren't many ugly bits of reality that escaped Cobb's attention, including the trench named after a war-castrated man, and the fact that metal buttons on uniforms turned bullets into dumdums.

The plot of *Paths of Glory* is remarkably simple. The emotional impetus behind the novel came from a dispatch to the *New York Times* on July 2, 1934, which appeared under the headline "French Acquit 5 Shot for Mutiny in 1915; Widows of Two Win Awards of 7 Cents Each," and from *Le fusillé,* by Blanche Maupas, a widow who obtained exoneration of her husband's memory and was awarded damages of one franc. Small wonder, with such inspiration, that the novel from cover to cover relentlessly exposes and dissects military wickedness and corruption, and "the shocking events that lead with the objective inevitability of a Greek tragedy to the ghastly end."

A French regiment, the 181st, under the command of

Colonel Dax, had been withdrawn from the trenches for a much-needed and well-deserved rest. It was on its way to the rear when a sudden new command countermanded the rest-and-recreation orders. A headquarters communiqué had mistakenly announced the capture of a hitherto impregnable sector of the German line, a heavily fortified position known as "the Pimple." Since the army commander wished to avoid the embarrassment of correcting or retracting an official communiqué, and since the decision to launch a probable general offensive depended upon control of that high ground, General Assolant, divisional commander of the sector, was asked to take the hill within forty-eight hours. He issued orders for immediate recall to duty of the 181st. A foreshadowing of disaster occurred when the regiment lost thirty-two men returning to the trenches. Severely undermanned because of losses in a previous battle, and with untrained and raw recruits serving as replacements, the men were gloomy and pessimistic. But the general had a reputation for being gung-ho and he was ambitious, so he calculated the odds: "Five percent killed by their own barrage, ten percent lost crossing no man's land, and twenty percent more getting through the wire . . ." The regimental adjutant, a more practical man with long experience in estimating probable casualties, cut the requisition for food rations in half.

Dawn came. Zero hour came and the men went over the top. L. H. Titterton wrote in his review of *Paths of Glory,* "From the moment when Mr. Cobb begins to describe the failure of the attack, he lifts this novel up into the very first rank of war novels."

Whistles sounded along the jumping-off line.
Charpentier climbed onto the smoking parapet, shouting and waving to his men to follow. He stood there, waving and shouting, an heroic-looking figure, fit for any recruiting poster. He did not feel heroic, though. All he felt was the blister on his heel and the intoxication of the vibration all around him.

Men started to scramble over the parapet, slipping, clawing, panting. Charpentier turned to lead the way. The next instant his decapitated body fell into his own trench.

Four other bodies followed right after his, knocking over some of the men who were trying to get out. Three times the men of Number 2 Company attempted to advance, and each time the parapet was swept clean by the deadly machine-gun fire. It couldn't be done, that was all. The men, with one accord, decided to wait.

Number 1 Company got as far as its own wire . . .

Minutes later the remnants of the regiment crawled back into their trenches. General Assolant, infuriated by what he considered a mass display of cowardice, ordered the artillery to shell the French trenches and force the men forward. But the artillery officer wisely refused unless the order was put into writing and signed.

Within half an hour it was all over. The ill-conceived plan, attempted under impossible conditions and at the most futile hour of the war (November, 1918), came to an end.

All that remained was the need to select a scapegoat. At first General Assolant was determined that an entire section from each company must be shot. He insisted that the survivors were guilty of mutiny. Colonel Dax made a vain effort to defend the 181st regiment, declaring, "On my honour, gentlemen, they weren't cowards. Far from it. They were heroes . . ." And when he saw that General de Guérville, chief of staff of the Fifteenth Army, was preparing a compromise in which forty men, ten from each company, would be executed as "examples," Dax replied, "If it's an example you want, sir, one man will do as well as a hundred. But I wouldn't know how to choose him. I'd have to offer myself. After all, I'm the responsible officer."

"Come, come, colonel," said de Guérville, "I think you're overwrought. It isn't a question of officers."

Eventually it was decided that four men, one from each company, would be court-martialed and then shot. The selec-

tion of the soldier to be offered as a sacrifice for the honor of
the French army (and to assure continued discipline) was
made the responsibility of each company commander. Because
one officer, Captain Renouart, refused to carry out these orders, stating, "There is no member of my company against
whom charges of cowardice in the face of the enemy can either
be made or be found tenable," and because his name happened
to be the same as that of a high politician to whom it was
feared he might be related, only three men stood trial.

Langlois, sensitive, intelligent, was selected by lottery on
the second drawing, when the first draw resulted in a dispute
over whether the number pulled out of the hat was 69 or 96.
His letter to his wife, shortly before his execution, is the most
tender and poignant expression of personal feeling in the entire novel:

> Please, please, get a lawyer and have my case investigated.
> Your father will help you. Get all the influence you can, borrow
> money if necessary, carry it to the highest court, to the
> President himself. See that my murderers pay the penalty of
> murder. I have no forgiveness in my heart for them, whoever
> they are . . .
> How I love you, my only one. The pocket-book you gave
> me is in my hand. I touch it. It is something you have touched.
> It will be sent to you. I kiss it all over, a sad attempt to com-
> municate some kisses to you. Poor, worn, greasy little piece of
> leather. What a surge of love pours from me upon this forlorn
> object, the only tragic, personal link I have with you . . .

Didier, a brave soldier who had, unfortunately, seen his
company commander kill one of his own men with a grenade,
died while strapped to a stretcher in a mock crucifixion pos-
ture, too drugged with morphine to know what was happening
to him, after having promised his wife that he would face the
firing squad like a brave soldier. Delirium had robbed him of
the pride and dignity which were his greatest assets.

Ferol, the ex-convict, never had enough respect for life to

fear death. When the priest asked him, "Don't you believe in God and Jesus Christ?" he replied, "I may have once. I don't remember." At the hour of his death, he stood roped to his post, muttering. "The last drink of cognac was now in full possession of his brain and he therefore saw twelve men in front of him who were partially effacing twelve others, duplicates of themselves. Time meant nothing to Ferol. Nothing meant anything to him . . ."

Despite much fine writing, Cobb never did quite master the art of the novel. He relied too heavily on dialogue, and often upon that artificial-sounding kind of dialogue playwrights call, in their more apologetic moods, "necessary exposition." Having noticed certain structural similarities between portions of Faulkner's *A Fable* and Cobb's novel, I once asked Faulkner whether he had read *Paths of Glory*. He answered rather testily that Humphrey Cobb was a hack journalist, hardly worth serious discussion. (I have learned since that Faulkner did acknowledge indebtedness to Humphrey Cobb in an interview published in the *Paris Review*.) But although the reply was less gracious than I had expected, it was, from Faulkner's viewpoint, perfectly accurate. For to a novelist who regarded art as a precarious balance of time and event, of mood and personality, of ironic juxtaposition and psychological complexity, Cobb's blunt, unvarnished (and sometimes poorly varnished) tale must have seemed something of an eyesore beside his own masterworks.

Yet *Paths of Glory,* despite its numerous defects, received good reviews and was a Book-of-the-Month Club selection. Given every chance to succeed, it had a quiet public reception and then gradually faded. Written with a simplicity of language and style that should have made it a favorite with the general public, it became instead a novelist's novel. Not in the sense that Ford's *The Good Soldier* or *Parade's End* became examples of expertise in craftsmanship and construction. *Paths of Glory* became a germinal novel for, I think, a quite different reason. It contained powerful materials which many writers instinctively sensed could be employed in different and more artistic ways. Hence Faulkner's *A Fable*. And Herman Wouk's *The Caine Mutiny*. And the futile assault upon the mountain in Norman Mailer's *The Naked and the Dead*.

But whether the similarities in these more recent novels were due simply to coincidence, or perhaps to some archetype of warfare rooted deep within man's collective unconscious, one special quality of Cobb's novel has never been duplicated —the intensity of its moral condemnation of military power. For if Crane saw the world as indifferent to man, and Hardy saw Chance or Fate as certain to roll snake eyes just when a man most needed to make his point, Cobb saw the chief enemy of man as man. And the most glaring examples of man's inhumanity existed within the military, where a hierarchical system was imposed upon men through a chain of authority and official regulations.

Cobb reminds me most of Hemingway, especially in his attitude toward religion. But there is much deeper despair in Cobb's novel. Hemingway's soldiers dramatized their boredom and pretended a bravado which seemed to them befitting to their situation; in their hearts, no matter how grave the danger, they believed themselves capable of saving their own lives, of miraculously escaping death. But the battlefields of Italy and Spain mocked such optimism. Only nature, up in Michigan, or sometimes in the green hills of Africa, would support such innocence; and even nature, though it confirmed man's concepts of the free and the wild and the beautiful, denied his spirituality and made his pretensions to immortality an absurd exercise of vanity. Grudgingly Hemingway acknowledged man's frailty and his uncertain existence in a world where a scratch without iodine sometimes meant death. He came to believe that good form and dignity and precision and, for the aged, a clean well-lighted place were the sole weapons man could oppose to the persistent intent of the universe to force death upon him.

Cobb's soldiers never had possessed such innocence. The men of the 181st regiment stared endlessly at mud and shell craters, not noble nature; at death via raw gas and shrapnel and bayonets, without memory of a chivalric age; at cold-blooded slaughter, mathematically executed for mathematically predicted results which were reported through the sterile language of the daily communiqué. For noblesse oblige in Cobb's world no longer existed within the conduct of men, but only within the propaganda of official reports. The soldiers of the 181st had abandoned all hope of exercising any control over their lives. No survival was possible for men who remained in the front-line trenches. Death was a lottery with a daytime and a nighttime quota of six to the hour, with a higher risk rate, of course, during the sunrise bombardments.

Poor Humphrey Cobb! He agreed with much that Hemingway related about war, but he was too damn serious about the horror of the trenches to run about splashing attractive pigments on his pages—too sick with disgust to dip his fingers in the warm blood of the dying, to taste the cheese and sour wine in the soldier's mouth, to capture the symbolic significance of the slogging muddy boots of a retreating army, or to feel upon the back of his neck the premonition of death in the cold rain. To Cobb, mud was mud, and rain was rain, and dying was dying.

And that is why I have remembered him all these years. He was a soldier first, and then a writer. He was an antiwar propagandist first, and then a novelist. He was a concerned human being first, and then an artist.

Privately, Hemingway's pessimism went much deeper than the shallow eat-drink-and-screw philosophy by which he protected his heroes from serious moral confrontations. Publicly, Cobb's commitment to arousing public indignation against the arrogance of the military screams from every page. Elizabeth Bowen wrote: *"Paths of Glory* has been compared to *All Quiet on the Western Front*. It entirely lacks, however, the Teutonic mawkishness and is not gratuitously revolting—physically at least. Its horrors are on a different plane, and more frightening because they have a more general relation to life. Mr. Cobb makes war not so much a specific malady . . . as a mobilization of every human faculty to suffer and to deteriorate."

Cobb must have been confident that he got his message across. He never published another novel.

Or did he discover that the reading public accords books the same bored, predetermined, and unheeding pretense of attention that a military court-martial offers to its victims?

Did he discover that even a Book-of-the-Month Club couldn't break through public apathy or prevent the then-infant Pentagon from becoming the power center of America?

Poor Humphrey Cobb!

And poor fools who believe in rediscoveries!

# HARVEY SWADOS

## ON

## BORIS PILNYAK'S

# The Volga Falls to the Caspian Sea

*HARVEY SWADOS*

HARVEY SWADOS, *novelist and essayist, was born in Buffalo, New York, in 1920. The recipient of many grants and awards, he has taught for many years at Sarah Lawrence College and more recently at the University of Massachusetts; he has also been a teacher at San Francisco State College, the Writers Workshop at the University of Iowa, and Columbia University, and served as a judge in the 1970 National Book Award competition. He is the author of ten books.* His collected essays, A Radical's America, *appeared in 1962; he has also edited two anthologies,* Years of Conscience: The Muckrakers *(1962) and* The American Writer and the Great Depression *(1966).* He has written three volumes of short stories. *His novels are* Out Went the Candle *(1955),* False Coin *(1960),* The Will *(1963),* a National Book Award nominee, and, most recently, Standing Fast *(1970).*

*∽✸*

*BORIS PILNYAK*

BORIS PILNYAK *was born Boris Andreyvitch Vogau near Moscow in 1894. His literary name was taken from a never-published novel of the same name. A precocious talent, Pilnyak wrote for prominent Russian journals as early as 1915. In 1921, his first novel,* The Naked Year, *the earliest attempt to depict the Revolution, produced a sensation and sold half a million copies. The* Volga Falls to the Caspian Sea *appeared in 1930; an early version of that novel,* Mahogany, *published in Berlin in 1927, was denounced as antirevolutionary and banned in Russia. In 1931*

147

# 148 REDISCOVERIES

> he toured the United States; his bitter impressions are recorded
> in O.K. (1933). He also traveled widely in Europe, England,
> and the Orient. Pilnyak's criticisms of the regime led many to
> believe that he was liquidated in 1938.

---

> . . . I cannot write otherwise than I do write. I am unable
> to, and I will not, even though I should want to violate myself;
> there is a literary law which makes it impossible to violate a lit-
> erary talent—even with your own brain . . .
>
> Boris Pilnyak<br>28 September 1923

Forty years ago Boris Pilnyak was recognized throughout Europe as "one of the giants of the modern novel," in the words of the dust jacket on his now-forgotten *The Volga Falls to the Caspian Sea*. At this point in time the phrase seems more a publisher's blurb than a just appraisal. I quote it that we may measure the distance traveled by Pilnyak between 1931, when Farrar & Rinehart published this work in Charles Malamuth's translation ("His books sell in the millions, the present literary generation considers him its master"), and 1938, when he was apparently shot in Moscow's Butyrskaya prison as a Japanese spy. And 1970, when he remains—unlike his posthumously rehabilitated contemporary, Isaac Babel—practically an unperson, an unwriter in the land where he was once a literary star.

We do now have available in translation several volumes of Pilnyak's short stories. But his early avant-garde *The Bare Year* (published in this country in 1921 as *The Naked Year*) is long since out of print; and for the ordinary reader *The Volga Falls to the Caspian Sea* is almost as difficult to come by here, and as undiscussed, as in the Soviet Union. For this reason I am emboldened to write of an author whom I am unable to read in his original language: If Pilnyak is much spoken of in literary and political histories of his time, it is almost always in terms of his early experimentalism; his stylistic dependence on Andrey Bely and Alexei Remizov (he dedicated "The Third Metropolis" "to A. M. Remizov, 'The Master,' in Whose Workshop I was an Apprentice"); his leadership—along with the bold and brilliant Eugene Zamyatin—of the All Russian Union of Writers in the struggle against the vulgar Russian Association of Proletarian Writers; his humiliation during the Stalinist era; and his ultimate disappearance at the height of the great purges. Much is made of the circumstances surrounding the composition of *The Volga Falls to the Caspian Sea,* which are seen as either pathetic or degrading, but I am unaware of any serious commentary on the book itself.

Unquestionably, *The Volga Falls to the Caspian Sea* can be studied as a kind of casebook of literary equivocation, if not downright crawling, put together not so much from inner conviction as from personal weakness and ambition. Its real merits however are all the more remarkable when one takes into account the conditions attendant upon its appearance.

Pilnyak had gotten into hot water several years earlier with the publication of his story "Tale of the Unextinguished Moon," subtitled "The Murder of the Army Commander." Despite Pilnyak's denials, it had been all too clearly inspired by the death in November, 1925, of Frunze, Trotsky's successor as Commissar for War; and it suggested that Stalin was responsible, if indirectly, for that death.

In 1929 he published in Berlin (for copyright reasons) a short novel called *Mahogany,* and was promptly assailed for having arranged with a White Guard publisher to print abroad a book considered unsuitable for Soviet readers—a charge with which a new generation of Russian writers has become all too painfully familiar. The charge was as baseless then as now, for as Pilnyak observed in a letter to the journal that had attacked him, "the books of my comrades in Soviet literature are published there: Andreev, Vera Imber, V. Kaverin, Nikitin,

Romanov, Tolstoy, Fedin and others, and I had found not one single name of an émigré author." The editor responded by calling this a "formal evasion," and Pilnyak found himself charged with being "an agent of the class enemy" and a criminal. His true crime had consisted not in publishing abroad, but in leaning toward Trotskyism, criticizing various aspects of Soviet life, and propounding a heretical critique of Marxism (about which more in a moment).

Responding to parallel attacks, Pilnyak's colleague Zamyatin withdrew with dignity first from the All Russian Union of Writers and then from the Soviet Union itself ("I have been sentenced without trial," he wrote to Stalin in requesting an exit visa, "to what amounts, for a writer, to capital punishment—silence"). Pilnyak however undertook to square himself and buckled down to the task of producing a politically acceptable novel. The result, incorporating substantial segments of *Mahogany* into a grandiose narrative of socialist construction, was *The Volga Falls to the Caspian Sea*. According to the historian Robert Conquest, the repellent Nikolai Yezhov, Stalin's creature, and later head of the secret police (until his own downfall and disappearance), "personally oversaw the production, listing fifty-odd passages for amendment."

This effort, together with a number of other abasements, bought Pilnyak a certain temporary relaxation of the campaign against him; at least he was enabled to travel to the United States. There he was lionized by writers like Theodore Dreiser and Sinclair Lewis at a New York literary banquet, driven across the country by Joseph Freeman for more lionizing by Hollywood producers like Irving Thalberg, and enabled to acquire an American automobile. He returned to the Soviet Union with the car, and the material for a put-down of his American experience, which he entitled *O.K.;* but in the end of course nothing helped, and degradation was followed by extinction.

One cannot help feeling that the largely adverse verdict of historians and critics on *The Volga Falls to the Caspian Sea* has been inspired to a considerable degree by the unheroic conduct of its author and to a lesser degree by aspects of his method and style that in fact antedated his harassment by party hacks and thought police. Pilnyak was in the habit (not unique among modern writers) of reworking stories, of pillaging earlier productions; if he can be castigated for converting *Mahogany* into *The Volga Falls to the Caspian Sea* and for inserting crude paeans to the Party and assaults on Trotsky, he can also be saluted—at least by those of us who have not been subjected to such pressures—for insisting on retaining much of its thematic material. It was an insistence that may very well have contributed to his final downfall.

Two sets of brothers are principal characters in *Mahogany:* they remain such in *The Volga Falls to the Caspian Sea.* The brothers Bezdyetov are mahogany furniture restorers of Moscow who go to the backwater town of Kolomna and stay with Yakov Skudrin, an old peasant representative, whose brother Ivan, "a half-mad idealist expelled from the Communist Party," lives nearby in an underground dugout. The Bezdyetovs "were devoted to the art of antiquity and anonymity. . . . This art continued to be the business of nameless individuals, of cellars in towns, of wretched serfs' quarters in the huts of the manors, of bitter vodka and of the cruelty of loneliness. . . . When serfdom, which nurtured this art, was abolished, furniture factories replaced the masters who were serfs. But the nephews of the masters—through vodka—remained alive. These masters construct nothing new. They merely restore the antiques; but they have preserved the habits and the traditions of their uncles."

If the symbolism of these figures is fully obvious, that of the old Communists like Ivan Skudrin is scarcely less so. In a time of exhaustion and venality, Ivan is an extraordinary reminder of the revolutionary vitality that had swept everything before it—and that is now an encumbrance to Stalinist consolidation.

"In the year twenty-two," Ivan explains, "I was kicked

out of the party for drunkenness. . . . However, I am a Communist. . . . Our first revolution, the Bolshevik, the October one, was a social revolution; then came the second revolution, the cultural one. What we want is a revolution of honor, of conscience, that all may become honest; otherwise, we shall perish."

When he troubles to, Pilnyak can be as physically pungent as the earlier masters of the Russian novel. He describes Ivan's old brother, Yakov, thus: "For the last forty years or so, Yakov Karpovich suffered from hernia, and when walking he supported this hernia with his right hand put through the seam rent of his trousers; his green hands were swollen with dropsy; he would put a lot of salt on the bread from a common salt-cellar, crunch it, and then carefully put the remainder of the salt back into the salt box."

Despite the fact that Yakov's heretical theory, propounded in *Mahogany,* must have been one of the reasons for the storm raised by that book's publication in Berlin, Pilnyak persisted in including it in *The Volga Falls to the Caspian Sea.* It is worth quoting as an example not only of Pilnyak's persistence in clinging to his "errors," but of what may also be regarded as his prescience.

"The theory of Marx about the proletariat," says Yakov, "is rank nonsense and will soon be forgotten, because the proletariat itself is destined to disappear. . . . Revolution is to no purpose, it is a mistake made by history, a little mistake at our expense. Two or three more generations will pass, and the proletariat will disappear—first in the United States, in England, and in Germany. Marx expounded his theory at a time when labor was based on muscles, having decided that labor will be forever based on muscles. And yet it turns out now that mechanized labor is replacing muscles; soon engineers alone will remain to guide the machines, and the proletariat will be transformed into engineers. The machine is run by five men, and in the office there are forty; the office employees will become proletarians. . . ."

The engineers of whom Yakov speaks are the principal figures of *The Volga Falls to the Caspian Sea.* If they are carelessly introduced and cursorily characterized, if their life experiences are narrated in a disjointed and fragmentary fashion, if their chronology is maddeningly confused, this can be only partially attributed to their having been created, so to speak, *sur commande;* for this had been Pilnyak's mode of writing, in emulation of Bely's *St. Petersburg,* from the time of his earliest successes. If we trouble to disentangle the intertwined lives, it is because even the black and white traitors and patriots have incandescent moments in which they emerge, almost despite themselves, as creations of a writer of quality.

Old Professor Poletika, a Bolshevik Marxist, "a scientist with a European reputation, a great theoretician and a great practical man, a builder," is the hydraulic engineer supervising the design of a new channel, for which a monolith must be constructed near Kolomna to buttress and throw back the waters of the Oka and the Moscow rivers. "Professor Poletika, senile and professorially odd, never drove in automobiles and always went out in a frock coat." On the very next page, however, we are told that twenty-five years earlier he had been "a beardless engineer who had just graduated from the institute," which would indicate that he is now a senile old man of forty-eight or forty-nine. And when this old man who never drives in automobiles arrives at Kolomna, "a Russian Nami [explained in a footnote as a new brand of Soviet automobile] took . . . Poletika to the monolith." Such slapdash carelessness seems always to have been present in Pilnyak's fiction, alongside a painstaking mosaic of interlocked themes and life stories.

Let us return to the oddly intricate relationship among the engineers. Poletika, who had loved "only once in his whole life," had been married for eleven years to Olga, a movie theatre pianist, when she deserted him with their children in 1915 for Edgar Laszlo, tutor of their son (killed on the western front later in the war). Laszlo subsequently becomes an engineer and finds himself working on the construction of Poletika's monolith. He was "forever bound" to Olga, but "was not physically faithful to his wife, like many men of that epoch, and just as many women were not faithful to their husbands. In freight cars, in sleepers, on a visit to various towns, on casual nights—for the everyday life of all was broken in those days and each one had at his back a zero at stake in the desperate game—were scattered women who did not impose any obligations, who gave joy with their femininity, which seemed to be eternal, which destroyed the zero that was ever-present. The conflagration of the revolution did not leave mental capacity for anything greater, and the women were lost at dawns and on new roads."

Laszlo has been involved for some three years in an affair with Maria, wife of a dedicated and heroic engineer, "risen from the workers," Fyodor Sadykov. "Maria Fyodorovna Sadykova loved Edgar Ivanovich, and she remained his mistress when he arrived at the construction. Maria came with everything that was beautiful in her—to give herself up to him. She loved, her love treading the paths of classical music, without justifying herself, without thinking of justification."

When Sadykov learns of his wife's long-term affair, he calls her and Edgar Laszlo into his office: "We are building a new society and a new morality. It seems to me, Edgar, that there is no reason why we should quarrel. But you understand that I cannot allow any disrespect to my wife. Since you love each other, I propose that you should marry and dispense with unnecessary lies."

Shamed, Edgar returns to his wife Olga with the news. "Fyodor acted cruelly and honestly in accordance with communist morality. You can judge as you like. I cannot fail to accept his challenge. I cannot abandon a woman who has honestly given herself to me and whom previously I took in a way that was not quite honest."

Olga, who has had a daughter by Edgar as well as a grown daughter, Lyubov, by Professor Poletika, replies: "Tomorrow my daughters and I will leave you to save your honor, if this honor of yours demands that you should abandon your daughter and your old wife."

And her older daughter, Lyubov, cries out bitterly, "I am also a Communist. . . . Your honor, Edgar Ivanovich, is the honor of a coward and a thief who is canonizing his theft."

In such wretched circumstances Edgar marries Maria, who soon becomes aware of the painful truth: "You don't trust me; I am a stranger to you. You needed me as a mistress, but I am not fit to be your wife. I have not read either Marx or Goethe; I cannot advise you; I am unnecessary to you. I wish I could trust you, yet I cannot and do not trust you, just as you do not trust me."

Edgar's plea—"We must love each other, do you hear? We must! We love each other, we are chained to each other"— does not persuade her; she hangs herself.

The death of Maria becomes "the symbol of Woman's destiny" to the female laborers of Kolomna, who had been living in squalid barracks for several years and had been gossiping over the affair between Edgar and Maria: ". . . in every women's barrack, assuming seventy-one women in each, there were seventy-one sorrows. . . . Women, made equal to men in civic rights, were not rendered equal in everyday life and were certainly not made equal by biology, once children are left to the care of the mothers. In the barracks were collected single women, old women over forty; from thirty to forty, widows with children; from twenty-two to thirty, old maids; up to twenty-two, young girls whose future destiny was to remain in these barracks. All these women's destinies were determined by the absence of men; and it was but natural that in such barracks sex questions were treated with intense interest, woman's fate being bitter and doomed to unhappiness."

When the women learn of Maria's death they take the occasion, in a scene reminiscent of Zola's *Germinal*, to demonstrate against rape, molestation, and favoritism. Edgar, who has followed Maria's coffin to her grave, is surrounded by "a hundred faces, copper and stone faces, that looked past him, as if he were a black." Suddenly he is set upon by his serving maid, Darya. " 'Push him into the hole and send him to hell!' shouted Darya, and again struck him on the chest. . . . The women shouted, thunderously, terribly, and crowded toward the grave. The faces of the women ceased to be like copper or stone; they became human. The trees surrounded the grave in silence. The grave diggers hurriedly filled the grave, looking at the crowd with fear and anxiety. The dead woman was forgotten. Darya mastered her tears. 'Comrades!' shouted Darya, stopped short and waved her red kerchief. 'Comrade women! We are the organized proletarian women. Maybe the court will aquit him, but we, women, must live and build up our own life: we condemn him. It is for us to live, for us to judge!' "

Pilnyak's nervous, disjointed report of the deprivations and personal agonies of technicians and working men and women, laboring together in dismal conditions on grandiose projects, oscillates erratically between the terrible and the ridiculous. If what I have quoted thus far seems to point more in the latter direction, I hasten to add that even when Pilnyak, a Russian nationalist and a basically unpolitical novelist, is composing a scene obviously skewed to follow political directives, certain of his true beliefs are apt to burst through much as do curiously affecting moments in the commercial scenarios of hired writers who are better than hacks.

Fyodor Sadykov, the worker turned engineer, is a clockwork figure that could have been wound up for any of a dozen dishonest books about high-minded proletarians. Nevertheless at key points in his marriage to Maria he comes to life (it is perhaps revealing that only in their sexual connection do most of Pilnyak's people acquire a texture of reality). Maria, we are told, "was of a type that possessed the greatest feminine force —namely, weakness." The daughter of an engineer, her par-

ents had been killed during the civil war, and after hiding in
their cellar for a week she had come to the revolutionist Fyodor, her eyes vacuous. "Kill me too, if you like! I have nothing
to live for," she says helplessly.

"She became the wife of Fyodor Sadykov. Fyodor took
her because of death, from pools of blood at the front, just as
newly born kittens unwanted by anyone are taken from cess-
pools by the scruff of their necks. Fyodor Ivanovich was what
is called a coarse, unrefined man; he had his life's work
mapped out for him by the revolution."

Far more significant in Pilnyak than such spontaneous
reflections are the recurring appearances of the carefully
rhythmical leitmotif, one of the stylistic devices he had bor-
rowed from Bely. When he is ruminating on the fitful nature of
the relations between the sexes as a necessary consequence of
the revolution, he observes: "The palm of a woman's hand
placed on a man's eyes may sometimes conceal the whole
world, not merely by the physical law of vision; it may so conceal the world that the palm becomes larger than the world
itself; while the naked knee of a woman can possess the heart
even as do thoughts of death under fire in battle, for not only
are death and love zeros, but they are also equal to each
other."

After Edgar has had to give up his wife Olga in order to
marry his mistress, Maria, Pilnyak reverts to the metaphor, in a
new context: "Every man knows of the happiness of possessing
a woman and every man knows of the still greater happiness of
possessing a human soul—a wife, her head, her hair, her voice,
her words. . . . The palm of a woman's hand can shut out the
whole world not merely by the physical laws of sight; it can
shut out the whole world to such an extent that the palm of the
hand becomes greater than the world. And at such hours Edgar
Ivanovich was most intensely aware of the fact that Maria was
of no use to him, not necessary to him."

In his last, climactic scene with Maria before her suicide,

Edgar thinks: "The wife Olga, with her face growing old, her hair turning gray, her warmth, her caresses, could force a human being to open his heart, and something beautiful dominated that which had given life to red-haired Leessa. The knees of a woman may be more majestic than Mont Blanc. The knees of Maria were stripped naked; they were the knees of a weak townswoman, almost a girl, and nothing more . . ."

Until now I have not so much as mentioned, in a novel that commences with a listing of twenty-one Principal Characters and eighteen Minor Characters, the villain of the piece, who in his monstrousness stands astraddle of its entire concept. Yet another construction engineer, Evgeny Poltorak, is first seen by the unworldly visionary, Professor Poletika, in the restaurant of the Great Moscow Hotel. And in the very first descriptive words we become aware of yet another of Pilnyak's symbolic themes, Russian duality, his people's destiny to face both the East and the West.

"Poltorak was dressed like a foreigner, but his cheekbones were defiantly Slavic. His blue coat was made not only for the eyes of strangers, but for the lordly comfort of its possessor. His parted hair shone with brilliantine. His index finger was decorated with a shining diamond in an old setting. It was precisely this ring that arrested the attention of Professor Poletika, who, only after examining it carefully, glanced at the perfectly courteous face of the engineer. Poltorak's eyes looked energetic, clever and precise, 'and yet they are the kind no decent man should have,' thought the professor. 'He is right in concealing them behind the diamonds.' "

Pilnyak cannot let it go. He must point out that "Poltorak always evoked in Poletika a feeling of dirty stickiness."

Poltorak, the novelist informs us, "lived behind the trenches of history." The image might well apply not only to privileged engineers, but a fortiori to those Soviet writers who could manage, like Pilnyak himself, to produce work acceptable to their rulers. The itemization of Poltorak's worldliness in the materially deprived Russia of the twenties reads like an inventory of the luxuries with which "honored artists of the republic" have been a suborned: Moscow cabarets, suppers, foxtrots, meetings at early dawn in the actors' circle, Saturdays at the Casino, Sundays at the turf, evenings at home with children who are taught English, maids in white apron and cap, carpets, bronzes, paintings, a "severe" telephone, wine, fruit, caviar, sturgeon laid out for guests on porcelain—and the recurring mahogany which serves to remind us of the scavenging Bezdyetov brothers, searching out the handicrafts of the old regime.

"Poltorak was ill," we are informed bluntly. Curiously, Pilnyak attributes the villain's "illness" not to his bourgeois origin, but to something brutally simple: "He was ill because of women, having unchained his instincts."

The catalogue of Poltorak's amatory adventures is punctuated with a leitmotif: "Poltorak knew well how the heads of women bend at the behest of lips, and how their eyes quiver under a kiss—how enfeebling words are uttered—how to lay his head on the lap of a woman, face down, baring her knees, when, beyond drunken shouts and whispers, conscience falls to pieces."

So he moves from his aging wife Sophia, "a tired and worthy woman," to his mistress Nadezhda to his wife's sister Vera, dying of tuberculosis in the Crimea; and to Lyubov Poletika, Olga Laszlo's daughter by her first marriage to Professor Poletika. Only Lyubov, the young Communist archaeologist studying "the obscure history of those stone-women that are dug out of the ancient tumuli of the steppes," succeeds in resisting him because of her adherence to the principles of Communist morality.

"Poltorak wanted to believe that the girl was giving her time to those antiquities because of erotic mysticism," Pilnyak informs us and promptly destroys the insidiousness of this evil reverie with the hasty assurance: "nevertheless it was not true

so far as Lyubov was concerned. Lyubov was digging into the
ages in order to give them to the future."

If, atop this painful obviousness, we observe that Poltorak has successively betrayed Sophia (Wisdom), Vera
(Faith), Nadezhda (Hope), and Lyubov (Love, or Charity),
we may leap to the conclusion that Poltorak is simply comical,
and in a way that Pilnyak hardly intended—particularly when
we see the engineer's predictable but irrational hatred of the
patient proletarians at a production conference ("He began to
understand in anger that he was dependent upon these
people"), his predictable but unmotivated acceptance of "English pounds sterling" from one Sherwood in a plot to blow up
the dam, his predictable but absurd involvement finally with
the half-mad idealist Ivan Skudrin in this plot, and his predictable murder by Ivan's old brother Yakov.

But we should be wrong. Pilnyak succeeds in investing
Poltorak with a horrid Mephistophelian aura that touches
everyone about him with its phosphorescent corruption. Particularly in the cases of Nadezhda and Vera, the erotic overtones, with their mingling of sex and sickness, are irresistibly
reminiscent of similar decadent involvements in the novels of
Thomas Mann—women dying of tuberculosis, or of cancer,
whose sexual passion is heightened by the fetid breath of approaching death.

Poltorak leads Nadezhda to a hotel assignation in Kolomna through "corridors that smelled of mice and creosote, of
disinfectant," to a room in which she announces, "With you I
want to be the cynical European, the tourist—the kind who
may do anything. You too may do anything now . . ."

"Poltorak closed the shutters. The armpits of women
smell of sealing-wax. And the room with its bastionlike walls
that were sinking into the darkness stolen from the dawn, this
room of a provincial hotel through which Russian provincials
had passed, the morning, the kisses—all became the office of
passion, very terrible, like all such offices of provincial rooms

with hotel beds. European morality had forbidden third parties to reveal the secrets of these offices."

After Poltorak has met his fate, Nadezhda gets drunk at a party given by the Bezdyetov brothers, the furniture restorers, and tries "to play the part of an eighteenth-century marquise in alcohol." She rants on about the love affair of Sergei Yesenin and Isadora Duncan, and finally, drunken and naked, surrounded by mahogany, announces, "I don't know who's the father of my child, and it's utterly immaterial to me. I'm pregnant, and I shall not submit to an abortion. I'm not afraid of life. We're modern people. Nations perish, but I shall have a son of my own, born of the epoch . . ."

The next morning, Nadezhda goes to the doctor's office: "The doctor, washing his hands after examining the case, said to Nadezhda that she actually was pregnant, but that, moreover, she was ill with syphilis."

The seduction of his wife's sister Vera, however, is beyond doubt the most lurid of Poltorak's sins. His wife had pawned her watch and brooch to pay for his ticket to the Crimea, in order that he might go south and bring Vera home to die. At Yalta, he meets the dying woman. "Aside from physical changes, she displayed also psychic changes, which suddenly excited Poltorak and pleased him."

On the night train from Sebastopol to Moscow he plays the attentive brother-in-law to the feverish Vera. "He unlaced her shoes, pulled off her stockings. And he felt the restless attack of his ailment, the one which he had contracted no one knows when."

"Like a skilled orator," he makes love to her. "Before the zero of death, everything is nonsense. Carnal love will remain until the zero comes; all the other truths are wrong, except this one."

Vera survives long enough to die in the arms of her sister, who sends her husband a telegram: VERA JUST DIED BOTH OF US SAY BE ACCURSED YOU SCOUNDREL.

All of this is unashamedly operatic, but it is grand opera, as were many of the nineteenth-century Russian novels before Pilnyak, as was Pasternak's *Doctor Zhivago* after him. And Pilnyak does not hesitate to move from the pathetic particulars of Vera's life—"there was a girl Verochka, there was an adolescent gymnasya student Vera, there was a student at the Moscow Philharmonic, Vera Salishcheva, there was a middling actress of provincial theatres Vera Poleyaya,"—to her apotheosis in flames: "In the chamber of the crematory at a temperature of two thousand degrees Réaumur, in two minutes the coffin and human clothing burn up into nothing, and there remains only the naked corpse—and the naked human being begins to move; the dead man's legs bend under him, his hands crawl to his neck, his head is sucked into the shoulders. Should a living human being with broken nerves stand at this little window through which may be seen how two thousand degrees of Réaumur destroy a man, then the hair of this living human being would turn gray and the last human convulsions will seem to him to violate death. The dead man assumes shameless poses, and a quarter of an hour later only a handful of ashes remains of the man. . . ."

When Pilnyak returns to this leitmotif in describing the cremation of Maria after her suicide, he converts the erotic element of the writing cadaver into another configuration: "A naked body remains and the naked man begins to move. These last human convulsions may appear supernatural, violating the laws of death, but they are subject to a strange law. The feet of the dead man are bent under him, his arms stretch toward his neck and then are crossed on his chest, the head is drawn into the shoulders; the man, before he passes into non-existence, assumes that pose which he had in his mother's womb, when he arose out of the same non-existence."

At the very end of their lives, Poltorak engages Edgar Laszlo in a lengthy conversation that is all but a monologue. It is difficult to imagine that Poltorak's fury-filled assault on life

in the Soviet Union does not reflect in some degree those perceptions of the author which got him into such terrible trouble
that he too, like his engineers Poltorak and Laszlo, wound up
with a bullet in his head.

"Have you ever noticed," reflects the doomed engineer,
"how our—yours, not mine and none the less ours—how our
government régime is choking from roguery, flunkeyism, treason, moral dissolution. The government weapons are armies of
controlling organizations. The people's commissariat of the
workers' and peasants' inspection is a moral institution, just as
those placards in the streets, on the stairways, in street-cars, in
inns, in institutions: 'Beware of pickpockets.' 'Don't spit.'
'Don't smoke.' 'Pull the chain in the water-closet.' 'Don't lie.'
'Don't rape.' In my house on the stairway there's an inscription
under the electric lamp: 'Thief, do not take the trouble of
stealing the lamp; it is soldered.' And in Moscow they put up
posters teaching people to act as stool-pigeons. 'Citizen! Your
duty is to watch the taxpayer.' You see how the whole country
is turned into a moral placard; the placards of morality have
come out into the streets because there's nothing left of it in
their so-called souls. In Russia, people are guilty by the mere
fact that they are alive!"

If Boris Pilnyak deliberately set out to write a bad book
in an effort to ingratiate himself and purchase at least a temporary personal security, it must be acknowledged that he was
partially successful—and with a certain vulgar panache,
hymning socialist construction with engineering data on problems of hydraulics, earth moving, and geology worthy of a
Steinbeck. I would suggest however that *The Volga Falls to
the Caspian Sea* can also be measured by the extent to which
Pilnyak failed in this task. His failure—the voice of the artist
cheating his paymasters, bursting through the braggadocio and
the burlesque of Bolshevik realism—does him honor that
should be recognized by us, if it cannot as yet be in his native
land.

Even here, the final words should belong to Pilnyak himself, and to the tortured novel in which they glow:

"The shelves of years are like the shelves of books. The shelves of human years are like books, for every book is surely a human convulsion of human genius, of human thought breaking the law of death, striding across death, even like the convulsions in a crematory. Assuredly every man must—sometimes at night, when alone in his study among the shelves of books—every man must be horrified in the face of these books; must feel that every book is a counterfeit of real human life, every book is a convulsion of thought cheating death. . . ."

# JESSE HILL FORD

## ON

## KNUT HAMSUN'S

# Growth of the Soil

*JESSE HILL FORD*

JESSE HILL FORD *was first published in the* Atlantic, *winning the 1959 Atlantic "First" prize for "The Surest Thing in Show Business." Other stories followed, and three have appeared in O. Henry Prize Stories collections. He is included in the 1970 Doubleday volume containing the best short stories of the past fifty years. A collection of his stories,* Fishes, Birds and Sons of Men (*1967*), *followed his second novel,* The Liberation of Lord Byron Jones, *a 1965 Book-of-the-Month Club selection. A movie version of this novel, released in 1969, was directed by William Wyler. His first novel,* The Mountains of Gilead (*1961*), *won an Atlantic grant. His third,* The Feast of St. Barnabas (*1969*), *is his most recent. He is at work on* Elias, *a saga-novel, scheduled by Atlantic–Little, Brown for 1972. This year he completes a two-year stint as writer-in-residence at Memphis State University. He lives with his wife and four children on a farm near Humboldt, Tennessee.*

✧

*KNUT HAMSUN*

KNUT HAMSUN *was born in Lom, Norway, in 1859. He emigrated to the United States in search of a livelihood, and roamed about Wisconsin and Minnesota for a time, returning to Norway in 1884; during a second stay in America in the Middle West, he lectured on literature in Minneapolis and was a horse-car conductor in Chicago. His first novel,* Hunger (*1890*), *published a year after his return to Norway, was a success; he settled in a*

165

*fishing village near Grimstad and devoted himself to writing.
Growth of the Soil (1917) is generally considered his best novel;
in 1920, it won for him the Nobel Prize for literature. Pan
(1894) is another of Hamsun's well-known, widely translated
novels. Knut Hamsun was sympathetic to the Germans during
both world wars; in reaction to this, thousands of his embittered
countrymen returned to him by mail their well-read copies of his
numerous novels. He died in 1952 in Norway.*

---

Knut Hamsun was in his eighties when Norway was occupied by Adolf Hitler's armies. Hamsun's beloved native
land was destined to suffer a full five years of misery and depri-
vation under the invading conqueror's heel. One result of that
occupation would be the entry of *Quisling* into many languages as a synonym for "traitor." Another would be the children of that occupation, and their children after them, who
would continue, as they were taught under the Nazis, to eat the
entire orange, peel and all, the entire apple, core and all, and
never to leave one scrap of food on one's plate.

Hamsun (tragically for Norwegians who knew him as
their greatest novelist) welcomed the goosestepping Germans.
Did he imagine that they were true supermen come to set Norway back a few years in time, to the robust era in which, as a
youth in Nordland, that region of the iron darkness of winter,
the young Hamsun partook of a world in which every man was
his own policeman?

It would be hard to know what passed through Hamsun's
mind those tragic last years, but we can guess, by reading his
works, filled as they are with such fierce independence of spirit,
that the old man mistook conquering bullies for heroes. However that may be, his name was banished from many Norwegian tongues, his books were swept from a great many shelves,
and the reputation of the man himself went into an eclipse that
had only begun to lift when, as a Fulbright scholar, I went to

Norway in 1961 to read the Icelandic sagas and study Norwegian literature.

I devoured Hamsun's works—peel, core, and seeds. From *Sult* (*Hunger*) straight on through to the last essay, the last poem, the last word of Knut Hamsun's that I could find. Along the way I struck with *Markens Gröde* (*Growth of the Soil*, 1920) and the novel has stuck with me ever since as certainly one of the very finest stories ever written—in any language.

In 1968, Alfred A. Knopf, which has kept *Growth of the Soil* in print, came out with a new edition of *Hunger*. Only recently, *Hunger* was filmed as a motion picture in Europe. A Hamsun revival is on, and it is eminently well deserved. We have time to thank for the fact that the man has been forgiven; we have Hamsun himself to thank for a glowing warmth that reaches over years, that spans oceans and the barriers of language to afford perhaps the richest experience that literature has to offer.

Isak, the protagonist of *Growth of the Soil,* is a great barge of a man. We are never told his past life. Perhaps, Hamsun muses, "the little scars on face and hands" were wounds of war, or the marks of toil. Isak is "a strong coarse fellow, with a red iron beard."

Isak enters the great wilderness landscape of the north country as a protean hero. Where did he come from? We are not told. The last look we have of him—an affirmation—is not on his deathbed, but rather, sowing grain. Where is he going? "Isak? why, he is going on, and on!" Hamsun seems to say.

It is the affirmative quality of Hamsun's writing that endears him to us in this, our own era of negation. *Markens Gröde* is so powerful that it casts a strong shadow of belief in the goodness of life. Through Hamsun's eyes, man's effort on earth seems monumentally worthwhile. His credo—man laboring in cooperation with a kindly earth, a true mother nature, as opposed to the simpering conceits of the Lake Poets or those parsimonious intellectual flights of the Transcendentalists— has a freshness that will not leave the mind. Nor will it let the heart go.

While *Markens Gröde,* like Pearl S. Buck's *The Good Earth,* traces the progress of a family from poverty up the twisting and generally tortuous trail to relative prosperity, Hamsun's novel differs radically from *The Good Earth* in nearly every other respect. *The Good Earth* closes on a note of cynicism—an old man, unable to stand on his own feet, hangs supported by his two sons. The old man fears that the land he has labored his life away to acquire will be sold and the proceeds squandered. While assuring him that the land will not be sold, the sons are smiling over the old man's bent shoulders, having already entered into the conspiracy to sell.

What a contrast to Hamsun's ending:

> The evening sunlight falls on the corn that flashes out in an arc from his hand, and falls like a dropping of gold to the ground. Here comes Sivert to the harrowing; after that the roller, and then the harrow again. Forest and field look on. All is majesty and power—a sequence and purpose of things.
> *Kling . . . eling . . .* say the cow bells far up on the hillside, coming nearer and nearer; the cattle are coming home for the night. Fifteen head of them, and five-and-forty sheep and goats besides; threescore in all. There go the women out with their milk-pails, carried on yokes from the shoulder: Leopoldine, Jensine, and little Rebecca. All three barefooted. The Margravine, Inger herself, is not with them; she is indoors preparing the meal. Tall and stately, as she moves about her house, a Vestal tending the fire of a kitchen stove. Inger has made her stormy voyage, 'tis true, has lived in a city a while, but now she is home; the world is wide, swarming with tiny specks—Inger has been one of them. All but nothing in all humanity, only one speck.
> Then comes evening.

It has become fashionable to talk about the Third World. I prefer to think of the Third World not as a single sector of our world or national population, but as a condition in which we all find ourselves: I see the Third World, in short, as a designation of our position in history. We are *living* in the Third World.

Just as the First World was ended by World War I; and as the Second World was brought to an end by World War II; so, I believe, this Third World will end (and perhaps along with it the physical earth itself insofar as it shall have the power to sustain human life) with the coming of a Third World War—World War III. Thus the Third World may be our last world. And if it is not suddenly ended by World War III, then it is almost sure to die of poisoning: a poisoned atmosphere, a poisoned sea, an earth poisoned by atomic and other industrial wastes.

How difficult it is to see the state of man now as it could be seen by a robust genius like Hamsun: man in harmony with nature. Mankind is out of harmony with nature. As never before, the forces—all man-made—that can destroy life on earth loom like dusty clouds on the horizon of earth's immediate future. One reads beyond the serenity of *Markens Gröde*, back into a world that once was, into a world that should be, into a world well worth striving to preserve. Yet what if life should pass from this earth as a result of man's mechanisms? What if the neo-industrialists should lead all life down the dark cinder path to doom? What if World War III explodes?

We can say, I believe, that man is and that man was and that man will have been *worthwhile* if he shall have written with the calm assurance and affirmation of Knut Hamsun about those things which are moving, real, and generous. And if man shall have written with the humor and the incisiveness that Hamsun displayed, then life shall have been worthwhile.

Taken in the light of what has been written in fine books by fine writers like Hamsun, men have always been about as they are now, far from perfect. They have been capable of great evil, but they have been capable of great good—great dreams, great visions, great works of the imagination.

It is just as important now to write well, as ever it has

been. Hamsun shows us by example in *Markens Gröde,* how important it is, even in the face of the firing squad, to conceive and to carry to fruition ambitious works of the mind. Even if all of reality turns out to have been a freak of imagination; though the gods be dead, though the heavens themselves explode, it shall have been worth it, to have experienced Hamsun's works. Indeed, the greatest good that we may know and the greatest we may experience, may, as it happens, turn out to be contained entire within the boundaries of the kingdom of the imagination.

This is no meager world, imagination. It has lived and has abounded since the first human consciousness. It would be foolish of us now insistently to contend that men, in nature, are more important than animals; that men are more necessary to life than birds, shrubs, meadows, herds. Our conduct may point to a sickly attitude on the part of man himself—that he is above nature, that he conquers it, that he turns the world upon its axis to his, man's own purposes.

The truth is quite opposite. All of us, like Inger, have been specks, tiny specks. Not merely the world, but the universe swarms with them. What do they mean? If they have meaning, Hamsun better than any other man I have read, elucidates the essence and the purpose of life and of mankind in the world.

# GEORGE GARRETT

## ON

## MARY LEE SETTLE'S

# Beulah Land Trilogy

### GEORGE GARRETT

GEORGE GARRETT *is poetry editor of* Transatlantic Review. *He teaches at Hollins College in Virginia; he was writer-in-residence at Princeton in 1964–1965; and he was the first novelist to write a play in the Ford Foundation's program to involve poets and fiction writers in the theatre. He has written television and movie scripts.* The Reverend Ghost: Poems *(1957) is one of four volumes of his poems that have been published. He edited an anthology of stories on a common subject,* The Girl in the Black Raincoat *(1966). His works of fiction are* King of the Mountain *(1958),* The Finished Man *(1960),* Which Ones Are the Enemy? *(1961), and* Do, Lord, Remember Me *(1965). His poems* For a Bitter Season *were published in 1967. Mr. Garrett was born in Orlando, Florida, in 1929.*

◝◞

### MARY LEE SETTLE

MARY LEE SETTLE *was born in Charleston, West Virginia. Her first piece, a poem, was published when she was nine. In addition to the trilogy* O Beulah Land *(1956),* Know Nothing *(1960), and* Fight Night on a Sweet Saturday *(1964), Miss Settle has had two other novels published,* The Love Eaters *(1953) and* The Kiss of Kin *(1956). She has also written a movie script, and her stories and articles have appeared in* Harper's Bazaar, *the* Paris Review, Harper's, *and* Contact. *After several years' residence in England, Miss Settle now lives in Rhinebeck, New York.*

171

A natural generation ago, the form of the trilogy was still possible for the American writer. At least it was possible still for the American writer of that generation to consider building a triform structure, three separate novels not necessarily sequel or in sequence to each other, but close enough kin to be in large and sum more than any of the separate parts. Offhand one thinks at once of Stribling and Faulkner, of Henry Miller. And, if one includes the British, Cary's two trilogies or the four-part grand designs of Durrell and Ford Madox Ford. It could be said (no doubt it *has* been) that the modern trilogy is a shadowy image, its present function gone and forgotten, of the nineteenth-century habit of the three-volume novel. A size, then, and a division into units which no longer have practical aim or purpose. And there is some truth in that.

There is another truth involved, though, in the varied fashions of writing, publishing, and reading—the simple truth that very, very few of our contemporary writers, now mature and presumably at the peak of their gifts and powers, have been able or willing to engage themselves in the slow construction, the long-term investment of time, energy, and spirit, of large-scale designs. The curious circumstances and chaotic economics of modern American publishing are a factor. But, the world we live in being more seamless and whole than we care to admit, it is inevitable that writers should share in the general view, the short-term sprinter's view of things which limits the arts in much the same way as it limits plumbers, politicians, merchants, and all the multitudinous chiefs. Fascinated by change in all its mysterious forms and celebrating change as if mutability were newly discovered, we shy away from overt commitment to anything for long.

No wonder that the very idea of a trilogy seems at best naïve, at worst arrogant and enforced with the strength of invincible ignorance.

There are some important exceptions. One thinks of Shelby Foote, who turned from a promising and productive career as a young novelist to devote more than fifteen years to his great history, *The Civil War,* the third and final volume of which is almost complete now; turned, with what now seems extraordinary courage and faith, to a work which would require, he knew, a minimum expense of fifteen years. Turned to work in steady patience and long silence between the publication of the separate volumes.

And one *should* think of Mary Lee Settle's *Beulah Land* trilogy, conceived and designed as such and, however long in the making, published between 1956 and 1964. Conceived and designed by a reasonably successful, highly intelligent, and certainly sophisticated young writer who had two bright novels, *The Love Eaters* and *The Kiss of Kin,* behind her and a different and more conventional future ahead if she had chosen it. Conceived, designed, and most important, *executed* —despite the added difficulty that her publisher (Viking at that time) deliberately chose to ignore the fact these works were part of a trilogy, bringing out instead each book, including the last, as an entirely separate and distinct work. Ballantine Books managed to remedy that situation somewhat with its paperback editions, including a brief foreword by Granville Hicks on the general structure of the trilogy. (Hicks is one of the very few reviewers or critics who treated the work in terms of its intention.)

Since the last volume of the trilogy, *Fight Night on a Sweet Saturday,* Mary Lee Settle has published an exceptionally fine autobiographical book, *All the Brave Promises,* dealing with her time and duties as an American girl in the British WAAF during World War II. Due apparently to mismanagement, above and beyond the deplorable average, by her latest publisher, this book was so lost in the seasonal shuffle that it was scarcely noticed by any of the reviewers and consequently reached very few readers indeed. Perhaps *All the Brave Prom-*

*ises* will have its second chance, depending on the relative success of her next novel, or her next. . . .

The odds against second chances for our writers have grown formidable in recent years. But whatever becomes of Mary Lee Settle's work, early or still to come, the trilogy is *there,* challenging even the most deep-rooted, rhino-hided abilities to ignore it, not so much daring as justly demanding attention. And with any attention at all, it must come, sooner or later, to receive the simple recognition of genuine achievement.

Superficially the trilogy is straightforward in design, chronological. *O Beulah Land* deals with pioneers and settlers in 1774. *Know Nothing* treats the descendants of these people in the middle years of the nineteenth century. *Fight Night on a Sweet Saturday* is here and now, could have been last weekend or might be the next. The three stories are linked together by bonds of family kinship. Moreover the trilogy is held together by the communion and character of place—in this case the West Virginia of Mary Lee Settle's home and ancestry. Though style and manner vary appropriately with time and subject, a gradual diminishment and tightening of point of view, for example, from a large, omniscient overview in *O Beulah Land* to the single third-person view of *Know Nothing* to the quite precise restrictions (and freedom) of a first-person narration in *Fight Night,* the general method is clear, clean and spare, polished to transparency and, thus, calling attention not to itself or the *making,* carefully nonexperimental. Superficially, then, the books might appear, allowing for the rarity of the trilogy form, conventional, and the storytelling "classic." Yet, for all that, none of these novels is "easy reading." In an important sense Mary Lee Settle is working against the grain of her material throughout. Devising a counterpoint against the line of the conventions. In the novel as much as the sonnet or any literary form, conventions and precedents are always there. They can be followed openly or in a dazzle of disguises;

they can be seemingly ignored (though ignorance of them is no salvation); they can be challenged, twisted, and changed. Or, and this is rare and difficult, they can be *assimilated*, becoming in a new context not less than but something more than they have seemed. This is what Mary Lee Settle has done with the conventions of the historical novel and with the form of the trilogy.

Her characters are complex and fully dimensional. Encountered, they react in unconventional ways. They can be known only as we "know" each other, acknowledging the limitations of our knowledge and the mysteries of self that continually seem to ambush all easy certainty. The place is oddly just off-center: Southern, but not completely so, naturally rich and desperately poor, a land and a weather of betwixt and between. And history itself, events and reactions, is slightly out of focus, something unfinished from any viewpoint, a series of beginnings with no end in sight. *O Beulah Land* ends with the rage of the Indian Wars still unresolved, the Revolution coming. America has not happened yet. *Know Nothing* ends with the Civil War just beginning, inevitable to us because it was, but to those intricately involved, the characters, more circumstantial than inevitable; still possibly to be avoided. In *Fight Night* the violent death of Johnny McKarkle, itself a kind of confirmation of the premonitions in the mind of the narrator, his sister Hannah, happens and many questions are resolved; yet more are raised in the mind of the reader. And the isolated acts of violence of the story seem to hover upon the edge, a ragged, indefinite horizon, of some more enormous and terrible violence yet to come. Already since 1964 this feeling has been confirmed in "actual" history by real events.

History, then, or rather *this* history of the land and the people of West Virginia, covering a span from the time when the rich and virgin land was fiercely inhospitable, to a time when the land seems denuded and defeated by the careless and brutal descendants of the originals, history would appear to be deceptive beyond all knowing, an almost aimless and irregular sequence of spasms, its only pattern being in ruthless randomness. That certainly is one of the thematic burdens of each of the separate novels. Although the evidence is there, and easy to see in retrospect, it is not easily accessible to any of the characters, no matter how sensitive or perceptive. They cannot imagine (and therefore cannot believe) the random horror at the heart of things, preferring instead to grasp for, then to cling to some notion of a grander pattern in time than time allows them to perceive. It is, it seems, their greatest and most lamentable weakness, their (our) tragedy.

Not surprising that the paradoxes and ambiguities of *knowledge* should be one of her most urgent subjects. Mary Lee Settle, both as critic and artist, has been a dedicated admirer of the work of Conrad. Not incidentally she has done work for British film companies on scripts from Conrad stories. Yet precisely in the sense that Conrad's finest work defies the kind of analysis which becomes more translation than interpretation, that just at the moment of purest simplicity, the final unveiling reveals not naked truth but a veiled figure, so in this trilogy the sense of the whole contradicts, strongly opposes the thrust of the separate stories.

In terms of knowledge, it is we, the readers, who can know cumulatively more than any or all of the characters. We know truths beyond their means. We can see, for example, that the narrator, Hannah, of *Fight Night,* as moral and right-minded as she seems to be, as courageously perceptive, is no more so than Hannah, a thief and a whore from London, who fled into the wilderness after the Indian massacre at Fort Duquesne, completely lost and alone, to stumble upon the cabin of Jeremiah Catlett and so was the first of the long line who would, in our time, come to suffer from the delusions of ancestor worship (never knowing *that* Hannah or her chronicle) and crippling pretensions to aristocracy. The "last" Hannah of *Fight Night,* almost the mirror image of the original

Hannah, flees also from her inheritance, repudiating past and present (insofar as she can know either), and her final view of the land from the window of a banking airplane is oddly like Hannah's first view of it in the Prologue of the first volume. The two Hannahs reflect upon each other, unwillingly. For the modern Hannah has something of the whore in her heart just as her long-dead ancestor had—more clearly because of the skillful dramatization of the first-person narrator in *Fight Night*—grace and courage and an impeccable moral stance. Each is incomplete without the other. They reach across centuries to touch, to join hands in the same dance to the same music, though neither can know this or hear more than faint fragments of the tune they must dance to.

Which, so simplified and abstract in the critical telling of it, dramatically illustrates a *cyclic* view of history, emphasizes a sense of pattern and mysterious order which refutes the effect of the separate stories. And, curiously, this sense *reverses* one's reaction to the limitations of knowledge and imagination of the characters. For, while it does not deny those limitations, it confirms that their apparent folly in believing, against the evidence, in the pattern (which once might have been called Providence) is in truth the beginning of wisdom.

Thus the pattern they seek to find, and fail to, is there. And their failure to find it, their *inability,* becomes as much a blessing as a curse. Thus the care with which Mary Lee Settle manages (without a checklist rigidity) to include examples of most of the conventional complaints against "the American dream" and what happened to it is valid enough; for at the last, we must concede that we, too, are caught in the web of our own times and concerns and no more able to see our own pattern than they, her characters living and dead.

The reader's perception of this larger pattern leads not to the comforts of assumed superiority, but instead to a learned humility. In effect, the reader is invited to join the dance too.

Which, one instance among many, demonstrates the validity and strength of the *form* she chose to revive. Rightly so, for revival is her theme though the events retailed are often terrible to behold.

Which also, briefly and inadequately, suggests the subtlety of her work, in design and execution made to look, by grace of art and craft, easy. . . .

And all this, these words of mine, adding up to a brief and inadequate appreciation, a mere passing salute, to something rare and fine.

All that stands between the reader and the deep pleasures of recognition is the fuzzy circumstance of *reputation*. Reputation, the last refuge of the *secret* whore, the creation of our modern version of the medicine show, the elixir that cures everything and nothing at all. Perhaps the ironies of likeness in the two Hannahs who open and close the *Beulah Land* trilogy can teach us something about *that,* too.

Meanwhile the trilogy is there, in or out of print, but alive, patiently waiting for the readers who will, sooner or later, come to discover it. And in that discovery they will also find the artist who made it, one of the few and finest of our times.

Perhaps it will please that imagined and imaginary reader to discover that the artist did not need him to make her brave promises come to be. Just as it pleases me to realize that nothing I can say here or elsewhere will add to her lonely triumph. That is hers and hers alone. We are most graciously invited to share only the ripeness. Which is, precisely, all.

# JUDSON JEROME

## ON

## MARIANO AZUELA'S

# Los de Abajo (The Underdogs)

## JUDSON JEROME

JUDSON JEROME *was born in Tulsa, Oklahoma, in 1927. Chair-*
*man for several years of the literature department at Antioch*
*College in Yellow Springs, he is Director of the Writer's Institute*
*at the Washington-Baltimore Campus of Antioch. His thinking*
*about education is reflected in* Culture out of Anarchy: The Re-
construction of American Higher Learning *(1970). The author*
*of several volumes of poetry and of an excellent textbook,* Poetry: Premeditated Art *(1968), Judson Jerome has been poetry*
*editor of the* Antioch Review *and of the* New Campus Writing
*series; he has written the "Poetry: How and Why" column for*
Writer's Digest *for eleven years. His first novel,* The Fell of
Dark, *appeared in 1967.*

〜✎

## MARIANO AZUELA

MARIANO AZUELA *was born in Lagos de Moreno, Jalisco, Mex-*
*ico, in 1873. After studying medicine in Guadalajara, he re-*
*turned to Lagos in 1909; two years later, his first novel,* Andres
Perez, maderista, *appeared. As a liberal, he supported Francisco*
*I. Madero's uprising, and in 1911 he was made director of ed-*
*ucation of the state of Jalisco. He served as a doctor with Pancho*
*Villa. He emigrated to El Paso, Texas, where he wrote* The
Underdogs *(1915), first published in an obscure Spanish-lan-*
*guage newspaper. In 1949, he was awarded the National Prize*
*for literature and another prize the following year for his drama-*
*tization of* The Underdogs. *He is considered the first of the nov-*

179

*elists of the Mexican Revolution. Among his other novels are*
*The Flies (1918), Mala yerba (1909), and The Bosses (1917).*
*Up to the time Azuela died in 1952, he was engaged in writing*
*and practicing medicine among the poor in Mexico City.*

---

It might be today—anywhere in a volatile world in which the oppressed have access to arms:

If a man has a rifle in his hands and a beltful of cartridges, surely he should use them. That means fighting. Against whom? For whom? That is scarcely a matter of importance.

The endless wavering column of dust moved up the trail, a swirling ant heap of broad straw sombreros, dirty khaki, faded blankets, and black horses. . . .

Driving across desert stretches of Mexico, one sees people crouched at the doorways of adobe huts, their clothing and the houses themselves blending into the sun-beaten hills. It is like passing a prairie dog town, knowing the shy rodents will dive for the interior of the earth if approached—except that the level of life appears to be below the bestial. It is almost chemical, like the lives of insects: food, water, and heat generate patterns of action and reaction, flow and decay. On this minimal fringe, desert life has not changed for centuries. It is stubborn, crusted, thorny, the color of dust. In that stillness, movement comes in flicks, like those of a lizard's tongue.

Imagine, now, that life somehow aroused. Isolated men come together in bands—Indians from the mountains, peons from the plains, laborers from their huts in parched villages—gathering, armed with knives and obsolete rifles, scythes and clubs. Mothers and children disappear into hiding. Men (and occasional women) drink tequila around campfires. They scurry silently in the black morning. Ambush, pillaging, racketing shots in the blaze of day, the clatter of hooves, celebration in captured haciendas: "War Paint rushed in shouting jubilantly, attempting to drag a splendid black horse into the dining room. 'My booty! My booty!' she cried, patting the superb animal on the neck. It resisted every effort she made until a strong jerk of the rope and a sudden lash brought it in prancing smartly. The soldiers, half drunk, stared at the beast with ill-disguised envy."

The time is about 1910. We are following one of the armies roving the country creating indiscriminate disorder: under Madero, Carranza, Obregón, Zapata, Pancho Villa. . . . Who can tell which? Who cares? Are they Yippies? Hell's Angels? SDS? IRA? Striking migrant workers? The troops of General George Washington? Rabble storming the Winter Palace? The Blacks of Newark? Someone has kicked the ant hill and the oppressed of the earth are in arms, spilling in rampage.

> "I killed a storekeeper at Parral because he gave me some change and there were two Huerta bills in it," said a man with a star on his hat and precious stones on his black, calloused hands.
> "Down in Chihuahua I killed a man because I always saw him sitting at the table whenever I went to eat. I hated the looks of him so I just killed him! What the hell could I do!"
> "Hmm! I killed . . ."
> The theme is inexhaustible.
> By dawn, when the restaurant was wild with joy and the floor dotted with spittle, young painted girls from the suburbs had mingled freely among the dark northern women. Demetrio pulled out his jeweled gold watch, asking Anastasio Montañez to tell him the time.
> Anastasio glanced at the watch, then, poking his head out of a small window, gazed at the starry sky.
> "The Pleiades are pretty low in the west. I guess it won't be long now before daybreak. . . ."

Azuela's novel, lean and hard as one of his peasant revolutionaries, first appeared serialized in an El Paso paper in 1915. As a medical student and journalist, he had accompanied one of the armies under Pancho Villa and had become disillusioned as he saw suffering exploited by the ambitious and saw violence become an end in itself. Compared to other great novels of revolution (such as *Man's Fate, Les Misérables, For Whom the Bell Tolls, The Grapes of Wrath, A Tale of Two Cities*), *Los de Abajo* (literally "Those of Below") is distinguished by its unsentimental record of brutality, viciousness, and squalor. It is comparable to Orwell's *Homage to Catalonia* in that its intent is somewhat counterrevolutionary: it is an exposé of the sordid aftermath of unleashed revolutionary energy.

In 1949 when I first read the novel (Azuela died in 1952), it radicalized me in an uncanny way; I have not recovered. There are times when disruption of the social order is simply necessary—and no less so because the revolution is ugly and devoid of any but the most hypocritical idealism. Reading this novel one might reflect that a society must be destroyed which creates such beasts as these revolutionaries— and that they are the ones most fit to destroy it. A logical outcome of oppression is that the oppressed become ignorant, savage, and dangerous to the regime. In their unflinching accounts of the corruption and cruelty generated by a revolution, Azuela and Orwell convey an implicit compassion for people whose lives have been so distorted, so deprived of possibility of goodness. Moreover, though the rabble may be composed of bandits, thrill-seekers, sadists, and louts, these are all relatively innocent compared to the politically ambitious intellectuals and professionals who use the revolution as a means to gain power and to create new tyrannies as bad as those overthrown.

In style the novel is astonishingly crisp and understated. Were it not for its early date, one might guess it was influenced by Hemingway. The irony is tight-lipped, repressed, and is likely to be missed in the novel's swift movement. For example, the first words are: " 'That's no animal, I tell you! Listen to the dog barking! It *must* be a human being.' The woman stared into the darkness of the sierra." Only with the accumulated experience of the novel does one catch the full significance that beasts are no threat, but the approach of a human being strikes terror in the home.

It is, in fact, soldiers—the Feds—approaching the isolated mountain hut of Demetrio Macías. Demetrio hides, but he returns to the hut when the soldiers are abusing his wife. The Feds leave, but Demetrio rightly suspects they intend to return. He, his wife and child are climbing the dark mountains when they look back into the canyon to see their house blaze up in the night.

Demetrio assembles threescore social derelicts into a troop that attacks garrisons, collects arms, and lives by what it can commandeer. When Demetrio is wounded, they move in on a group of houses: "These proved to be a few wretched straw huts, dispersed all over the river slopes, between rows of young sprouting corn and beans. . . . Groups of squalid Indians sat in the dark pits of the huts, men with bony chests, disheveled, matted hair and ruddy cheeks; behind them, eyes shone up from floors of fresh reeds." The people gladly share what they have with the rebel band; they are united in spirit by their grievances against the Federal troops which had visited and ravaged them before.

A deserter from the Federal army, a young medical student and journalist (like Azuela) joins the band. He ponders:

> Can the accounts given by the Government newspapers and by myself be really true and are these so-called revolutionists simply bandits grouped together, using the revolution as a wonderful pretext to glut their thirst for gold and blood? Is it all a lie, then? Were their sympathizers talking a lot of exalted nonsense? . . . Well, it looked as though the revolutionists or bandits, call them what you will, were going to depose the Government. Tomorrow would therefore belong wholly to them. A man must consequently be on their side, only on their side.
>
>     "No," he said to himself almost aloud, "I don't think I've made a mistake this time."

Self-consciously, this young man, Luis Cervantes, creates
a role for himself as the camp intellectual and rhetorician in
residence. Demetrio tells Luis about how he became a rebel:
he insulted a local landowner in a barroom row, and the landowner reported him to the government as a subversive. Luis
says:

". . . It is not true that you took up arms simply because of
Señor Mónico. You are under arms to protest against the evils
of all the *caciques* who are overrunning the whole nation. We are
the elements of a social movement which will not rest until it
has enlarged the destinies of our motherland. We are the tools
Destiny makes use of to reclaim the sacred rights of the people.
We are not fighting to dethrone a miserable murderer, we are
fighting against tyranny itself. What moves us is what men call
ideals; our action is what men call fighting for a principle. A
principle! That's why Villa and Natera and Carranza are fighting; that's why we, every man of us, are fighting."

"Yes . . . yes . . . exactly what I've been thinking myself," said Venancio in a climax of enthusiasm.

"Hey, there, Pancracio," Macías called, "pull down two
more beers."

Fired by the encouragement of Cervantes, Macías takes
his band to join the siege of Zacatecas. He is commissioned as
a colonel in the revolutionary army—and soon becomes a general. This coppery Aztec of few words has great courage and
cunning. Once he was relieved of the oppression of the Feds in
his local area he would have been content to go back to his
family, rebuild his hut, and peacefully continue his marginal
existence. He hardly understands the politics or the ideals of
the revolution. When faced with factionalism that requires him
to choose between two or three of the rebel leaders, he follows
the general who promoted him because he cannot grasp the
issues of the dispute. He likes the excitement of battle, the
glory, the rank—but he does not seem personally acquisitive
or hungry for power. What carries him onward? A dis-
enchanted intellectual describes the inertial force of the revolution: " 'You ask me why I am still a rebel? Well, the revolu-

tion is like a hurricane: if you're in it, you're not a man . . .
you're a leaf, a dead leaf, blown by the wind.' "

Though pillage is certainly a strong motive among many
of the bandit-soldiers, it seems more a thrill of the moment
than a means of gaining wealth. A society is crumbling; the
forces operating seem beyond human will, like laws of physics
or chemistry. The reasons for the behavior of the rebels are
simultaneously obvious and mysterious. They have been oppressed—and are throwing off oppression. But the oppression
in their lives has been so pervasive, so complete, that their
efforts to throw it off are like thrashing—aimless, wild, furi-
ous, and ecstatic.

A typewriter is an excellent symbol for the Establishment
—for the language of control, the machinery of office, the opu-
lence of power:

> "Who'll buy this thing?" one of them asked. He had carried
> his spoils long: he was tired. The sheen of the nickel on the type-
> writer, a new machine, attracted every glance. Five times that
> morning the Oliver had changed hands. The first sale netted the
> owner ten pesos; presently it had sold for eight; each time it
> changed hands, it was two pesos cheaper. To be sure, it was a
> heavy burden; nobody could carry it for more than a half-hour.
> "I'll give you twenty-five centavos for it!" Quail said.
> "Yours!" cried the owner, handing it over quickly, as
> though he feared Quail might change his mind. Thus for the
> sum of twenty-five centavos, Quail was afforded the pleasure of
> taking it in his hands and throwing it with all his might against
> the wall.
> It struck with a crash. This gave the signal to all who carried
> any cumbersome objects to get rid of them by smashing them
> against the rocks. Objects of all sorts, crystal, china, faïence,
> porcelain, flew through the air. Heavy, plated mirrors, brass
> candlesticks, fragile, delicate statues, Chinese vases, any object
> not readily convertible into cash fell by the wayside in frag-
> ments.

It is property itself which is oppressive—and the revolution will not change that. The momentary joy of liberation one

feels hurling a typewriter onto the rocks is dysfunctional. Others will keep typewriters and learn to use them. They will accumulate property and power. And the masses will remain oppressed—by these Feds or those who replace them.

Thus the revolution is permanent. The ants may return to their hill and remain quiescent until some overt abuse brings them out again, but the motivation to rebel smolders or flames forth continually. Such energy can be organized and directed by the Mafia, by Brown Shirts, by Black Panthers, by Garibaldi or Mussolini. It is terrifying, dangerous—and heartbreakingly innocent; voracious and selfless; passionate and numb. Man seems to have a need of hierarchy, of status, of control of others. Inevitably the victims are the masses, *los de abajo,* those below, and inevitably they will seethe and occasionally erupt.

Azuela reports such phenomena with grim objectivity, as though he were giving us the scenario of a frightening documentary film. The novel has little in the way of plot: it is a chain of events. It has little in the way of characterization: its people are like the epical figures in murals of Orozco and Rivera—bold outlines, earthy tones, simple postures—crude people, tense and vivid with contained drama: "She wore a silk dress and heavy gold earrings. Proudly her pale blue gown deepened her olive skin and the coppery spots on her face and arms. Riding astride, she had pulled her skirts up to her knees; her stockings showed, filthy and full of runs. She wore a gun at her side, a cartridge belt hung over the pommel of her saddle." What emerges from the novel is a sense of inevitability, of primitive truth. It says these things occurred; they will occur again; they will occur this way.

W. B. Yeats wrote of the Irish revolt of 1919: "A terrible beauty is born." When oppressed men are moved to militancy —no matter how senseless and destructive it may be—they acquire a strange splendor and new dimensions; their capacity for membership in one another is evoked and they are bound to one another with glowing webbing. Student rioters at Harvard described a sense of passionate community; they recognized that they accomplished nothing, that they had nothing specific to accomplish: "But while we were in there, boy, *we were together; we were beautiful.*"

Destruction itself has an eerie beauty—the geyser of flame, the cascade of rubble, the collapse of proud, arching structures, the folding of façades. We must pray silently, "Deliver us from order. Deliver us from the System. Release us from these corridors, these citadels, these machines." Our nerves race to sinister music. Eyes sharpen. Our breath comes fast and light.

Standing on the crest of the hill, they could easily sight one side of the Bufa peak. Its highest crag spread out like the feathered head of a proud Aztec king. The three-hundred-foot slope was literally covered with dead, their hair matted, their clothes clotted with grime and blood. A host of ragged women, vultures of prey, ranged over the tepid bodies of the dead, stripping one man bare, despoiling another, robbing from a third his dearest possession.

Amid clouds of white rifle smoke and the dense black vapors of flaming buildings, houses with wide doors and windows bolted shone in the sunlight. The streets seemed to be piled on one another, or wound picturesquely about fantastic corners, or set to scale the hills nearby. Above the graceful cluster of houses, rose the lithe columns of a warehouse and the towers and cupola of the church.

"How beautiful the revolution! Even in its most barbarous aspect it is beautiful," Solís said with deep feeling. Then a vague melancholy seized him, and speaking low:

"A pity what remains to do won't be as beautiful! We must wait a while, until there are no men left to fight on either side, until no sound of shot rings through the air save from the mob as carrion-like it falls upon the booty; we must wait until the psychology of our race, condensed into two words, shines clear and luminous as a drop of water: Robbery! Murder! What a colossal failure we would make of it, friend, if we, who offer our enthusiasm and lives to crush a wretched tyrant, became the builders of a monstrous edifice holding one hundred or two hundred thousand monsters of exactly the same sort. People without ideals! A tyrant folk! Vain bloodshed!"

On land fertilized by carnage, new and oppressive institutions arise rapidly, invulnerably. The dictatorship of the proletariat ("A tyrant folk!") squats on the heart as does any other domination. The burden of the present is intolerable, as is the burden of the new regime to replace it. In the interim is revolution, "revolution," as Abbie Hoffman puts it, "for the hell of it." Perhaps liberation is possible only in the period of flux; a vision of liberated man is a vision of permanent revolution, a kind of Dionysiac orgy unto death.

As the novel ends, Demetrio's army is ambushed on the site where it had ambushed the Feds long before.

> The sierra is clad in gala colors. Over its inaccessible peaks the opalescent fog settles like a snowy veil on the forehead of a bride.
> At the foot of a hollow, sumptuous and huge as the portico of an old cathedral, Demetrio Macías, his eyes leveled in an eternal glance, continues to point the barrel of his gun.

Like Robert Jordan manning his last machine gun, he has no hope for himself but some hope for the continuation of the life spirit. Like Tom Joad disappearing in the night, promising to "be there" whenever men are clubbed by cops or gather in the name of freedom, Demetrio is futile in himself, significant as spirit.

In the struggle itself he achieved dignity, self-actualization, freedom; these accrue as man resists institutions, but the institutions are stronger than he is and, moreover, he cannot survive without them. The revolution is man's resistance to his own inventions, his "mind-forg'd manacles," his abstractions, his own need of order. Perhaps there is no such thing as victory; the revolution is simply the continued spirit of resistance correcting the tendency of our social forms to become rigid and oppress whoever happens to be on the bottom.

Azuela was embittered by his realization that the human condition is replete with such paradoxes. He obviously has great contempt for the character of Luis Cervantes—and obviously that character represents the role he himself played in the army of Pancho Villa. It is indeed perplexing to recognize and accept one's complicity in the human race as this novel portrays it, but I find my own reaction (whether Azuela intended this or not) to be one of compassion and awe. Having heard the worst, as it were, I am left sympathizing with man in his necessary revolution.

# JACK MATTHEWS

## ON

## NORMAN DOUGLAS'S

## South Wind

*JACK MATTHEWS*

JACK MATTHEWS *was born in Columbus, Ohio, in 1925, and is Distinguished Writer in Residence at Wichita State University for the academic year 1970–1971, on leave from Ohio University in Athens, where he teaches regularly. A volume of his poems,* An Almanac for Twilight, *appeared in 1966, and a collection of his short stories,* Bitter Knowledge, *in 1964; approximately ninety of his stories have been published in various literary magazines. He has also written a number of essays.* Hanger Stout, Awake! (*1967*), Beyond the Bridge (*1970*), *and* The Charisma Campaigns (*1972*) *are the first three of a quartet of novels, being published by Harcourt Brace Jovanovich. Harcourt has also scheduled another novel of his, independent of the tetralogy,* The Tale of Asa Bean, *for April, 1971.*

❧

*NORMAN DOUGLAS*

NORMAN DOUGLAS *was born in Scotland, in 1868, of a very old Scottish family. Dissatisfied with the English public schools, he studied modern languages and the sciences in Germany. After serving with the British Foreign Office in England and in Russia, Douglas settled on the island of Capri, resolved to become a writer. His* Unprofessional Tales *appeared in 1901 and "promptly sold eight copies."* South Wind, *his best-known work, appeared in 1917. His other novels,* They Went (*1920*) *and* In the Beginning (*1927*), *were not nearly so successful. In 1933,*

190

*Douglas's autobiography,* Looking Back, *appeared. He died in Capri in 1952.*

---

For years I have read liberally in that strange, seemingly incestuous type of literature called "Books About Books," in which collectors give expression to their enthusiasms, their travails, and their convictions. This kind of book was very popular from about the turn of the century to the 1930s, coinciding with the careers of such great collectors as A. Edward Newton and A. S. W. Rosenbach. It is interesting to read about the opinions of such men—particularly their opinions of their contemporary writers, as reflected in auction prices at the time.

Their judgment has proved sadly human in many instances. High prices spent years ago for first editions of Rudyard Kipling, and ALSs (autographed letters, signed) of Christopher Morley are sufficient to make any active collector pause. These bookmen, for all their expertise and all their love for literature, had it within them to be monumentally wrong.

But they could be right, too. And I can think of no better instance of their rightness—and a corresponding "wrongness" on the part of contemporary literary judgments (at least in the United States)—than the almost universal admiration of collectors during this period for the novels of Norman Douglas. He was, everybody—collectors, scholars, and general readers—agreed, a great writer. And his novel *South Wind* deserved to become a classic.

One day a few months back I came across the 1939 Heritage Club edition of *South Wind* in an old junk store, where I go periodically to try to snoop out bargains. This was a large (page size, 7 by 10 inches), handsome book, illustrated by Carlotta Petrina. Inside was the Heritage Club monthly announcement, quoting Professor George Saintsbury in the first paragraph, as follows: "I have read more novels than a man of seven hundred and fifty ought to have done. I have come across just two novelists who have given me something that I can recommend to a friend. The author of *South Wind* is the second in point of time, not rank."

This splendid praise, it was said, appeared in a letter the seventy-five-year-old Saintsbury had written to Douglas, six years after the publication of the novel. It was very impressive, I thought; but of course one acquires a certain immunity to dust jacket rhetoric (and that was how I viewed the quotation at the time). One would have to wait and see, which in this context gives emphasis to the former word.

But the seed was planted, and eventually I did take time to sit down and read those marvelous opening lines (the Heritage Club was right in pointing this out for admiration, as well): "The bishop was feeling rather seasick. Confoundedly seasick, in fact. This annoyed him. For he disapproved of sickness in every shape or form." When I finished, 383 pages later, I closed the book with that marvelously lucid conviction that one experiences only rarely of having participated in a book where art, humor, intelligence, and humaneness are all of a piece. *South Wind* must surely be acknowledged a classic if those qualities I have just listed continue to be (or will someday once more be) admired by human beings.

How could the majority of otherwise civilized men have forgotten this book? Since this question itself has to do with those very qualities that I have claimed for the book, it is appropriate that one of Douglas's characters should throw light upon the question, and that it should be the nauseated bishop of that first sentence. American democracy, the bishop says, "has substituted progress for civilization." He goes on to admit that an intelligent appreciation of beauty is compatible with progress, but to create things of beauty, he says, a man "requires intelligence and something else as well: time. Democracy, in abolishing slavery, has eliminated that element of time —an element which is indispensable to civilization."

It is good to be able to report that the bishop is not always so anti-egalitarian and pontifical, but his aristocratic views give us a place to start in describing the book: it is old-fashioned (the characters are full of strange humors, indeed, and not all southern by any means); it is sly; it is not suspense-fully plotted (which is to say it tends toward the discursive); it is not "progressive" (whatever that might mean); it is not "relevant" in terms of almost any activist's use of that word; it is civilized; and it does contain some of the most delightful characters and some of the brightest and most entrancing con-versation in our language.

The locale of the book is the Mediterranean island of Nepenthe, which everyone thought on the book's publication was obviously Capri. The South Wind of the title is that infa-mous wind, the sirocco, which allegedly influences men to strange notions and sometimes stranger actions as surely as the moon is reputed to influence them to lunacy.

On Nepenthe are a group of Englishmen: Mr. Keith, an aging sybarite who believes that English culture is largely the result of constipation; young Mr. Denis, who is suffering from an identity crisis, before that psycholiterary disease, much diagnosed by undergraduates, was named; Mr. Eames, a doc-trinaire antiquarian devoting his life to the study of the works of an early Nepenthean writer; Miss Wilberforce, an aristo-cratic tosspot with a bibulous compulsion to take off her clothes after dark, no matter where she is; the Duchess, who is about to become a convert to Roman Catholicism; and Mr. Freddy Parker, a scoundrel, coward, and nincompoop of clas-sical accomplishment.

In addition to the English colony, there are Madame Steynlin and her paramour, who is a member of "the Little White Cows," an exiled Russian religious sect; Bazhakuloff, the ancient and near-vegetable leader of the sect, Count Calo-veglia, whose wise conversation and classic sympathies reveal the fact that he has made of his sensibility an art (a lost art, one is compelled to say); Don Francesco, a shrewd and toler-

ant priest; Cornelius van Koppen, a wealthy American manufacturer of contraceptives; and Don Giustino, a Machiavellian
attorney from the mainland, who might have stepped out of
the pages of *The Ring and the Book* or the commedia dell'arte.

These are most—not all—of the dramatis personae.
Their stage, as I have said, is the half-mad island of Nepenthe,
and the background music is the South Wind itself, eroding
away the vestiges of normality in those who inhabit the island.

I have mentioned that the novel "is not suspensefully
plotted," but this is far different, of course, from saying that
nothing happens. A great deal "happens." There is, for example, a murder that turns out to be simply a more-or-less sa-
lubrious excision of an undesirable human specimen. The
murder leads to a superbly comic courtroom scene—simply
the best I have ever read—in which Don Giustino reveals himself in all his glory: "Don Giustino made a point of never defending innocent people. They were idiots who entangled
themselves in the meshes of the law; they fully deserved their
fate. . . . 'I never defend people I can't respect,' he used to
say."

He begins by defending motherhood generally (it follows
that motherhood is always "guilty"), and then the innocent
(beyond his knowledge) Nepenthean charged with the crime.
The Accused had a mother, Don Giustino reasonably argues;
therefore he bears some connection with motherhood, which
everyone knows is holy.

However, upon being tipped off that the poor wretch was
an orphan, Don Giustino adroitly changes his tack and begins
to lament the fact that the Accused was deprived of a mother.
He argues so passionately and forcefully that the mayor who is
hearing the case faints dead away from emotion.

There is vastly more to amuse and edify us. There is, for
example, the sudden shower of ashes from the island's volcano
that turns the sky black in the middle of the day. The resulting
confusion needs a Rossini score. Some turn to drink and others

go on a religious procession toward the volcano, praying to Saint Dodekanus—the island saint. The infamous upper-class dipsomaniac, Miss Wilberforce, is caught outside, unfortunately deep in her cups, and her familiar but mysterious instinct is triggered: she thinks it is night, and commences to undress.

So it goes. The comedy is endlessly delightful—various and distinctive, vast and subtle. It is also protean: often rich with the ironic joy of Fielding, now and then whimsical and recondite, as in the catalogue of the various fountains upon the island—a marvelous mixture of superstition and medical lore. Here is a sample:

> The Fountain of Saint Feto had, by virtue of its smell alone, applied to her nose as she lay in her coffin, raised from the dead a certain Anna da Pasto.
> The Fountain popularly called "La Pisciarella" was peculiarly adapted to those ailments which are incidental to childhood and youth—to wit: chlorosis, St. Vitus' Dance, constipation, ringworm, otoötitis and other perimingeal disturbances, urticaria, moon-sickness, scrofula and incontinence of urine.
> Lastly, the Fountain of Saint Elias, sulphurous and saponaceous, was renowned for its calming influence upon all who suffered from abuse of lechery or alcohol, or from ingrowing toenails.

The above is worthy of Sterne, but there is here and there a Dickensian quality, too, with its emphasis on large-featured sensibilities, as in the scene of that rascal Freddy Parker's crisis as "Commissioner" of the local social (English) club.

Above and beyond the delightful scenes, however, is the abiding sense of (if I may be forgiven the phrase) "authorial authority." Incisiveness of mind, lucidity, magnanimity—these are the realities created. The ironic light in which the characters move and act is constantly fascinating, but in the last resolve, it is the characters themselves who show forth most of the rich possibilities of mind (one of whose functions is, of course, error). The characters are all, in this old-fashioned novel, engaged in the excitement of discovering the implications and resources of the life around and within them. The wind that blows upon the island is not only the south wind of madness and eccentric humors, but the breath of mind, and of life, both *animus* and *anima*.

"I have not been bored since I was twenty," the bishop says, and this is true of the characters generally. The aging Mr. Keith has such a passion for learning that he says he would like to "take geology by the throat." But Mr. Keith's intelligence is part of his eccentricity, for he can be a perverse and whimsical casuist (the author himself refers to "Mr. Keith's sententious irrelevancies"). The lack of existential despair, the absence of brainless *Angst,* the unquestioning love of sun, talk, and human plenitude give to this book a spirit of intelligent innocence of heart that is blended so subtly with sophistication of mind, that *this* becomes its truest genius. It is a pagan and civilized book, not a modern and savage one.

"What a man postulates is truer than what exists," says Cornelius van Koppen, the wealthy American manufacturer of contraceptives. Many things are not true until a lot of people believe them, causing the beliefs to operate statistically in a culture. Like many great novels, *South Wind* comes to us as a sort of hypothesis: this isn't the way people live, and it isn't necessarily the way people have *ever* lived; but it shows the way people might live, for these are recognizable human beings, in the last analysis, on a recognizable island. More importantly, this is the way people might be regarded—with intelligence, compassion, and—always—humor.

# JANE MAYHALL

## ON

## GERTRUDE STEIN'S

# Things As They Are

*JANE MAYHALL*

JANE MAYHALL *has written several volumes of poetry; her poems and stories have appeared in numerous magazines, including* Partisan Review, Harper's Bazaar, Botteghe Oscure, Sewanee Review, *and in the anthology* Cross Section. *She has taught writing at the New School and at many summer workshops.* Givers and Takers (*1968*) *is her most recent volume of verse. Her first novel,* Cousin to Human, *appeared in 1960. Work in progress includes a new novel and some plays. The author was born in Louisville, Kentucky, in 1921.*

*GERTRUDE STEIN*

GERTRUDE STEIN *was born in Allegheny, Pennsylvania, in 1874, and was raised in Vienna, Paris, Oakland, and San Francisco. A favorite pupil of William James's, she spent four years at Radcliffe, specializing in psychology. She also studied medicine at Johns Hopkins, but she did not earn a degree from that institution. In 1903 she went to live in Paris, returning to the United States for a lecture tour and to see a performance of her opera* Four Saints in Three Acts (*1934*). *Among her more than thirty books, perhaps the best known are* Three Lives (*1909*), Tender Buttons (*1914*), The Making of Americans (*1925*), *and* The Autobiography of Alice B. Toklas (*1933*). Selected Writings *appeared in 1946.* Things As They Are *was first published posthumously in 1950. Yale University Press has reprinted much of her early work. Miss Stein died in 1946 in France.*

*Things As They Are* is a new and shocking book, written in
1903. It is shocking because it does not presume to be
shocking. It is new, because the departure from the old seems
neither premeditated nor manufactured. Considering the general assumptions of what literature is about, and what stale
ideas—whether by ten-ton syllables or the four-letter word
syndicates—are brought to bear on every work of art, there is
more than a hint in this book of a kind of spontaneous generation. If the impulse of its young author, Gertrude Stein at the
age of twenty-nine, was to strike for new ground, the mystery
is (then and now) whether she knew how far she had gone.
Because what she produced in this, her first novel, was neither
experiment nor exercise, but a highly developed species, already bursting with life and demands.

But what did she do with the odd achievement? She put it
away. And Stein never again directly pursued the subject,
which was a lesbian love story, or the method, which was total
intellectual candor. The manuscript was finished in Paris,
while she was living with her brother Leo. The title she gave
the book seems mad, or of a tremendous recalcitrance aimed
at throwing off any reader who might mistake the tale for mere
frankness: *Quod erat demonstrandum.* But of course, there
was the Stein humor, and she was good at the cheerful deception. Was it, too, a part of her wit, that she claimed (in *The
Autobiography of Alice B. Toklas*) to have "forgotten" the
book? Presumably it lay unnoticed until she happened upon
the pages thirty years later and showed them to Louis Brom-
field. The year was 1933. But the novel itself was not published until 1950, and then in a limited edition and posthumously. At this time, the Banyan Press brought it out,
beautifully printed and with a different title, *Things As They
Are.*

Edmund Wilson wrote a review, speaking of the book's

candor and lack of the scandalous. The "sobriety" and "abstractness of language" recalled to him Benjamin Constant. Donald Sutherland, in his study of the Gertrude Stein *oeuvre,* refers to *Things As They Are* as a preliminary exercise for Stein's novelette *Melanctha,* but he feels that the latter had the advantage of using "uneducated speech." (One assumes Mr. Sutherland means that not using her own vocabulary was, for Stein, a liberating process.) Elizabeth Sprigge, in the comprehensive *Gertrude Stein: Her Life and Work,* quotes freely from *Things As They Are,* more to present a self-portrait of Stein than to give the book individual praise. Despite the pleasures that critics express about Stein's first novel, obviously it is regarded as something left behind, or a meander by the wayside. And inversely, they are right. How can a landmark be pointed to where the road was never taken? Where the author herself seems to have blocked up the way, or consciously moved in another direction?

Yet, on a serious rereading, one is struck by the irony. Here may be, after all, Stein's most daring book. If only in terms of subject, it is outspoken, coherent, ultramodern. To a large measure, it outdistances what is now considered bold. That is, the third sex (as it were) is not isolated to nerve endings, but is presented as a moral reality. There are, in this book, no voyeurs or peeping toms. All such puritanisms have, in fact, been expunged. From the first pages, we are drawn into an unselfconsciousness, much like our own; albeit, banked by masses of shifting thought and identities. The relations of three persons in a love triangle have a spontaneity and freshness. Adele, Helen, and Sophie are young college women, traveling on a boat to Europe. It is shortly clear that they are, no doubt, white—and their romantic preferences are lesbian. I state it in this peculiar way because what is extraordinary, I think, in Stein's approach is (though no one would have thought of saying this in 1903) that they could as well be heterosexual or black, so convincingly are they depicted *in depth,* and with

such rigor and articulation are the conflicts expounded. It may
not be possible that people be viewed as essences. But Stein,
with her essayistic fervor and sharp analyses, comes very close
to that effect. The chief character, Adele, who is undoubtedly
the voice of the author, gives only minimal allowance to background allusions. For instance, we never know how the
women got into their predicament, of needing each other instead of men. What we are faced with is the situational immediate, three persons, ultimately a *ménage à trois,* reacting each
to each. Pornography is not required to know what is going on.
Incidents fuse, loving fingers brushing lips, ardor, impatience,
"a kiss that seemed to scale the very walls of chastity." The
facts are, if anything, plain. How the affair *is* seen is through
the intelligence of Adele. Her ideas, in their range, are stun-
ningly anarchic. Without the excuse or support of conventional attitudes, the plight of the round-robin lovers becomes
at once both more savage and more civilized. There are no set
moral standards to repair to. What they enact will depend
upon choice, or a capricious honesty.

   Such freedom has its terrors, as we are existentially
taught, and when it serves as material for fiction, a writer can
easily land at dead end. By the same token, the writer may fall
prey to the lures of philosophy, losing touch with the very
spark that whirled the mind into orbit. Occasionally, one feels
that Stein apprehends this danger. (I will indicate, at the conclusion, how she may have succumbed in other ways in her
better-known work.) Philosophy was her life style; she was
metaphysically trained, having studied the works of William
James, Whitehead, Bergson. But, in *Things As They Are,* she
is saved by a streak of sensuality. On the boat, "They remained
. . . quietly in the warm sunshine looking at the bluest of
blue oceans, with the wind moulding itself on their faces in
great soft warm chunks." The characters are alive and their
feelings are tactile. Adele, with her "simple instinct for comfort," sunning on the deck, is physically, almost poignantly
aware, "nestling close to the bare boards as if accustomed to

make the hard earth soft by loving it." Descriptively, she is realized by a few brief strokes; when in Rome, she "looked as brown and white and clean as if [she] had just sprung out of the sea." Even Sophie, the villainous member of the threesome, has a strong physical cast, her "American womanhood" that suggests "the body of a coquette"—which body "often encloses the soul of a prude and the angular form of a spinster [that] is possessed by a nature of the tropics." Sophie's face is rank and present: "It was pale yellow brown in complexion and thin in the temples and forehead; heavy about the mouth, not with the weight of flesh but with the drag of unidealized passion, continually sated and continually craving."

Another way Stein eluded the trap of metaphysics was by her natural sense of comedy. She loved to stand values on their heads. Ideas taken for granted are pulled apart and arranged in a different sequence. In the book's first paragraph, she is kidding and truthful. "A little knowledge," she says, "is not a dangerous thing, on the contrary it gives the most cheerful sense of completeness and content." Adele moves in and out of emotional complexities, buffeted, but not destroyed. At the height of suffering, when she feels Helen (whom she adores) is rejecting her, she is caught between a "laugh and a groan." Further, she is rather amused at her own ability to look at patterns. In her reactions, there is always a kind of witty stamina. The problems of love give trouble, but there is some entertainment in observing how the psychology works. Helen is beguiling, difficult, flirting with Adele, and then declaring loyalty to Sophie. Adele thinks, "Like Kate Croy—" (a nod to Henry James) "—who would tell me 'I shall sacrifice nothing and nobody' and that's just her situation, she wants and will try for anything, and hang it all, I am so fond of her and do so much believe in her that I am willing to help as far within me lies. Besides I certainly get very much interested in the mere working of the machinery. Bah! it would be hopelessly unpleasant if it didn't have so many compensations."

Pathos, or a joke? There is detachment, as in a charade.

But alternately, the roots of character are exposed, and go very deep. When Adele exclaims, in apposition to the foolish manner of women (even her friends), and their habits of hypocritical pleasantries, "I always did thank God I wasn't born a woman!" there is a funny taste of bitter-sweetness. Humor has strength when painful undercurrents contribute. The unstated theme of renunciation, peculiar to the lesbian sense of being "different" from others, makes itself felt—but lightly. The initial thoughts of Adele are almost like a parody of the romantic young woman on a lonely sea voyage, viewing the other ship's passengers and feeling out of sympathy: "It was very easy to think of the rest of the passengers as mere wooden objects: they were all sure to be of some abjectly familiar type that one knew so well that there would be no need of recognizing their existence . . ." The sour, and delicious, grape, of feeling like an outcast. A few pages later, the same sensitivity applies itself to a more specific stratum. Sophie and Helen have argued as to whether Adele is middle-class or not. When the matter is brought to Adele, she replies by simply turning the old concept inside out. And, by doing so, she reveals her own independent conscience. "You have," she says, "a foolish notion that to be middle-class is to be vulgar, that is, to cherish the ideals of respectability and decency is to be commonplace and that to be the mother of children is to be low. You tell me that I am not middle-class and that I can believe in none of these things because I am not vulgar, commonplace and low, but it is just there where you make your mistake. You don't realize the important fact that virtue and vice have it in common that they are vulgar when not passionately given."

Adele feels that whatever masks one wears (of virtue or of vice) it is passion that spins the plot. But it *is* vulgar to be false. Therefore, within ourselves, the natural laws operate. I stress this, because condensed on the first pages is the book's theme. Where there is *no* morality, there has to be *all* morality, the self-created laws, evolving with unique innocence and force, and fitted to each new problem that may arise. The story whisks along these lines. Here is a brief résumé: Adele, the stranger and neophyte, meets two women who are having an affair. She does not comprehend the ingredients of their friendship, but basks in the sexual atmosphere, and gradually falls in love with the good-looking Helen, "the American version of the English handsome girl." It is Helen who courts her; but later back in America, Adele learns through Sophie the nature of Helen's and Sophie's relation. Adele is horrified on two counts. One is in Sophie's manner of telling, which is both an unwanted confession and, underhandedly, a breaking of Sophie's confidence with Helen. The other horror is in Adele's sudden comprehension of the treacheries possible in love, and of the deep waters that may lie ahead. In spite of Sophie's intention, which, the reader may assume, is emotional blackmail, Adele is more strongly attracted to the undecided Helen—if only to try to help her, or sift out complexities.

The episode is intensely ugly, and—feminine. It is to Stein's artistic credit that she so clearly reveals, in the character of Sophie, the backwaters of catty women. If ever one had a picture of the proclivities of the weak, and saw to what furtiveness and tyranny they are driven, it is in the insidious person of Sophie. Part of the fine persuasion is in the laboratory exactitude, which reminds one of Gertrude Stein's former medical training as a student at Johns Hopkins. Her eye was quick at discerning pathologies. In the Sophie scene, motivations, like connective tissue, are appallingly revealed. But mixed with the scientific temper is a strong humanity. Adele does not become rigid on the subject. She is the participating observer, vulnerable even to the responses of the villain. After the confession Adele says: "Poor Sophie, I could almost find it in my heart to be sorry for her. I must have looked dreadful." The subjectivity-objectivity (remarked upon by Elizabeth Sprigge as a quality of Stein's) comes out rather hangdog and egoistic. But the victim's concern, as to how she may appear to the victimizer, is typically Adele, and quasi-funny.

As the story moves to a climax—or, more correctly, to a

series of climaxes, in little firecracker bangs of language and realization—we are never far from comedy. Such comedy, I admit, is of a special order, expressing a determination not to get mired in a lugubrious self-pity. In the isolation of these women, there could be something quite sullen, brooding. But it is precisely from the morass that Stein extracts her humor. Gently, she mocks the inertia of Adele, the changeableness of Helen, the proprietorship of Sophie. Life is devious, but facts are actual. Despite the baseness of Sophie's character, the possessive schemer who is unworthy of Helen's love, Adele still realizes that it is she—the interloper—who is on the wrong side of the triangle; she is like an animal treading on the territory of another.

The central issue is that Helen herself is resistant, and appears under some bondage to Sophie. Should Adele attempt a rescue, by guessing Sophie's claims? Or, is it even any of her business? Against a background of Europe and America, specifically Florence, Rome, Siena, Boston, New York, Stein adroitly deals out these questions. We are not denied, either, the candy-box trimmings, stolen kisses in passageways, secret letters discovered. Meanwhile, the psychological texture becomes more intricate; this intricacy includes Adele's playing up to Sophie, with an almost perverse infatuation, because she (Sophie) represents the obstacle to love. The reader may be reminded, in the full allowance given to the most minute awareness, of a sort of bare-ribs Proust—with the language, of course, holding to a Spartan economy. On the face of it, there is no sharp crisis, denouement or ending. As in life, the forces of disintegration are, partially, as expected.

And so, from unfolding clues, Adele learns to decipher Helen and discover the basis of her ambivalent attitudes. Part of the devil's brew is pity. Helen feels a great pity for Sophie, and "in the extreme cases if she [Helen] had to give up some one it would be Adele and not Sophie, as Sophie would be unable to endure it, and Adele herself were strong enough to support such a trial." But also, mixed with the compassion is the actuality that Helen depends on Sophie for money. The truth is deadly, universal (not confined to lesbian relations, one might observe), and part of the condition that Stein effects to show is how cleverly human beings deceive themselves and each other—in the guise of honest probings. But, by not finally admitting "things as they are"—the quote is from a last letter Adele writes to Helen—they not only break each other's hearts, but do evil against "reality." ("Reality" is the word Stein has employed throughout, discreetly enough, to indicate, one gathers, the happiness of a sex relation.)

The book ends with this deadlock, and Helen's inability to face the truth. As remarked, the finale does not resound. Adele has lost her love, but the fact is too well comprehended to adapt to a lachrymose idiom. Technically, it wouldn't fit, neither in the pace of the sentences, nor in the style of character. Stein's method of winding up the plot is, here, penultimately modern. Emotions wear out, and conflict has to stop. But, there is a kind of hard-core exhilaration we have come to associate with twentieth-century tough-mindedness, familiar on the many levels of current literary usage.

The style seems pivotal. Not only is there a lack of nineteenth-century embellishment, but the dialogue is amazingly contemporary, audacious. Particularly is this true of the Adele-Helen exchange; their remarks are abrupt, spouting tensions, overly intimate. Listen to Adele's emphatic "you are certainly right about most of your talk, it does bore me . . ." enlarging into "you always make me feel at no period did you ever have the thoughts that you converse with. Surely one has to hit you awfully hard [in the context, Stein means "stimulate" or "impress"] to shake your realer things to the surface . . ." Here is the nervous, stinging rudeness one accepts of modernity. In fact, I was reminded (curiously, or not) of Beckett's two tramps in *Waiting for Godot,* and their prison world of neurotic mutual dependence. Or, in the descriptive

passages, one gets strange *postponements* of feeling, the kind
that the reader experiences in the (much later) prose of Hemingway. Emotions at one remove, and essentially what we
think of now as an American genre. A good example of this is
in the New York harbor scene, when Adele has been in the
mood of a "despairing endurance." But, "just escaped from
this oppression, Adele stood in the saloon of an ocean steamer
looking at the white snow line of New York harbor. A little
girl of a family who had also fled from England after a six
months' trial, stood next to her. They stayed side by side, their
faces close to the glass. A government ship passed flying the
flag. The little girl looked deeply at it and then with slow intensity said quite to herself 'There is the American flag and it
looks good.' Adele echoed it, there was all America and it
looked good; the clean sky and the white snow and the straight
plain ungainly buildings all in a cold and brilliant air without
spot or stain."

In the patient listing of items, there is an almost simpleton
tranquillity—which Hemingway, as disciple (if he was) perhaps
repeated, for an effect of limpid thought—as in *The Sun Also
Rises*—with all the rough, unwinnowed feelings waiting just
beyond. In the case of Stein and Hemingway, and their famous
friendship, it may not be possible to know where styles were
interacting. Nor can we do more than speculate on when, or if,
he ever read her first novel. *Three Lives* is a presumed influence on Hemingway and Sherwood Anderson. But, along with
its extraordinary innovations, this was where Stein became
more deliberate, taking on the stance of willful slow-minded-
ness, and in her style making use of what Edmund Wilson
termed the "ominous banalities." Such "banalities" certainly
bore fruit, transmitting through the various channels. And
whatever the ambience was, it was considerably attractive to
the American aesthetic, from Hemingway, to Bogart gangster
movies, to good pulp tales and daily journalese—others before
this, I am sure, will have noted the lines of descent. And, with

impunity, they may observe that impetus as being carried several steps further, to its current deterioration and to today's literary produce of uncommitted feelings. The results are active not only in the best-selling sadistic plum cakes, but contribute to that endless grocery list of pop absurdities. All were once, no doubt, founded on authentic literary principles of simplicity and detachment. But harking back to Stein: in the matter of *Things As They Are,* to these disciplines (simplicity and detachment) had been added a cogent, human, downright honesty.

As I've said, Stein herself did not follow that first direction. Not that it can be said she stopped telling "the truth." But she evidently ceased to let it be important. Reason, emotions were accordingly put aside. They were replaced by the brilliant word games, and tantalizing dissociative patterns that the general public came to regard as the work of Gertrude Stein. One cannot propose, in so short a space, to assess a whole career. It would be tempting, though, to elaborate on how even in *Three Lives* (her second book, yet containing some warmth of event) the charming persiflage had already begun, how despite the genial evocations of, supposedly, naïve persons, the reader may have been deprived—in the portrayal of Negro and German women—of what is truly complicated, protean. This view, I realize, is open to argument. But one cannot help noting (excepting the chatty vigors of *The Autobiography of Alice B. Toklas*) how the complex inner consciousness of the author-speaker Adele was, in the later books, repressed, slowed down, fragmented. From that speedy epigrammatic mind of *Things As They Are,* concentrated on dilemmas of interest—love, sex, and their fatal interlockings—we are offered mainly the mood and gloss of their models. It is one thing to "reproduce the movements of consciousness," as William Troy described the task Stein set herself, and another to express *what you are conscious of.* The difference (I would like to risk saying) is, perhaps, between the safety of building puzzles, and going on the really dangerous pursuit of a live enigma.

For the freedom to choose a direction, Gertrude Stein was possessed of infinite skills. But here, I think, is the impressive irony. For the greater part of her life, she sought to create a radical art. But this she had already accomplished at the beginning. *Quod erat demonstrandum* was a truly remarkable overturn. Its abstractions were concrete, its re-formation inherent. So sophisticated *and* adventurous was the author, that in every candid statement lay a critique testing life, even if it unsettled her own rules that she took for granted. The thinking was atomistic. But so much so, that even lawlessness, or nonconformity did not profess to glamor. In the sexual deviation there was delicacy and health.

Beneath the lucid diction, the mind does double takes. If, occasionally, the reflex feels hermetic, the reason is, mayhap, that the cast of characters could be expanded. What Stein might have done with a larger, intelligible canvas! Her brilliance was many-faceted; she apparently had a grasp of history and social studies. One senses, anyway, a potential for the vast communication. Elizabeth Sprigge called *Things As They Are* eminently readable. Certainly, that is part of the impact. But, clear meaning, straight feeling, or some deep literacy of abandon, that was the road Gertrude Stein never took. Whether she should have or not, what can we say? But the book should be read anew.\* Where else will we ever know such clarities, amidst disorder?

---

\* As the proofs for this book were being corrected, the firm of Liveright, New York, announced that *Things As They Are* is to be included as "Q. E. D." in *Fernhurst, Q.E.D., and Other Early Writings* by Gertrude Stein, scheduled for publication this summer. For this new edition the text of the novel has been set from Miss Stein's manuscript, now in the Collection of American Literature at Yale University; the name of one of the three principal characters has thus reverted to Mabel (from Sophie) Neathe, and a few phrases altered or deleted for various reasons in the first publication in 1950 have been printed as Miss Stein originally wrote them.

# GEORGE LANNING

## ON

## ELIZABETH'S

# The Pastor's Wife

*GEORGE LANNING*

GEORGE LANNING, *former editor of the* Kenyon Review, *was born in Lakewood, Ohio. He has lectured widely at writers' conferences and is the coauthor, with Robie Macauley, of a book on creative writing,* Technique in Fiction *(1964), coeditor, with Robie Macauley, of* A Gallery of Modern Fiction: Stories from The Kenyon Review *(1966), and coeditor, with Ellington White, of* The Short Story Today *(1970). His short stories have appeared in* Sewanee Review *and other literary quarterlies. His first novel,* This Happy Rural Seat *(1953), was followed by* The Pedestal *(1966) and* Green Corn Moon *(1969).*

c~⌐o

## "ELIZABETH"

"ELIZABETH" *(Mary Annette Beauchamp, Countess von Arnim and later Countess Russell) was born in 1866 in Sydney, Australia. She was a cousin of Katherine Mansfield. She met her first husband, Count Henning von Arnim, in Florence while on a grand tour with her father. In 1916, she married Lord Francis Russell (Bertrand's brother); he died in 1931. Elizabeth and Her German Garden (1898) was one of her most famous books; it was followed by other Elizabeth works, signed "Elizabeth." Her nonfiction and fiction works sold very well. Among her novels are* The Pastor's Wife *(1914),* Vera *(1921),* The Enchanted April *(1923); and her last novel,* Mr. Skeffington *(1940), which was a Book-of-the-Month Club selection, and later was made into a memorable Bette Davis movie. Her auto-*

*biography,* All the Dogs of My Life, *was published in 1936. To escape the ravages of the Second World War, the countess moved to the United States; she died in Charleston, South Carolina, in 1941.*

---

In the latter part of the 1940s, I spent an evening in Cambridge, Massachusetts, with Pamela Frankau and her husband—a tall, pale man, somewhat her junior, I think—named Dill. They occupied half the second floor of a decaying house in a dismal street not far from Harvard Square. They seemed oblivious to any sense of being slum-dwellers, and possibly I exaggerate their circumstances out of my persistent feeling that Cambridge is one of the most unlovely of American cities. I was surprised that someone I already thought of as a famous novelist (Pamela Frankau was in later years to become far better known, though never so famous as she seemed to me then) should live in such a place. She told me that I was not only the first American she'd met who had read her books but the first who even knew she was an author.

I had just been lent *The Merry Wives of Westminster,* the latest in a series of reminiscences that Mrs. Belloc Lowndes was then publishing. A part of it dealt with Gilbert Frankau, Pamela Dill's novelist father; her grandmother, who had written successfully under the pseudonym "Frank Danby"; and the great Frankau house in Belgravia—right on the square, if memory serves me. Coincidentally, I had recently managed to buy a copy of *Christine,* that notorious best seller of World War I which, though it was signed "Alice Cholmondeley," was widely considered to be the work of "Elizabeth"—Countess Russell in private life and before that the Gräfin von Arnim-Schlagenthin of the vast Schloss at Nassenheide and later and more briefly tenant of the Gutshaus on the estate at Schlagenthin, both in Pomerania. *The Merry Wives of Westminster* contained an unflattering but fascinating portrait of Elizabeth and in addition much material on the Frankaus.

With Mrs. Belloc Lowndes's comments about Elizabeth Russell fresh in my mind, I asked Pamela Frankau whether she and the Countess had met. They had, although once only, and only briefly. But the image was sharp, if unexpected in the context of what I then knew about Elizabeth. The encounter had taken place on a street in one of those hilly villages along the Italian Riviera. "We were walking up and she was coming down one blistering, sunny afternoon," Pamela Frankau said. "I'd never have recognized her, though I must have seen pictures, but my friend had been introduced to her somewhere. She was a little old lady covered over in dusty black, and she had a face like a crumpled football."

That was all, but for contrast it was enough. How could one reconcile this unprepossessing, solitary woman with the famous London hostess, the austere beauty, the femme fatale whose liaisons were almost as notorious as her ill-fated second marriage? This was the woman who had employed E. M. Forster and Hugh Walpole as tutors to her children, who had created at Nassenheide a German garden which became so world famous that Forster privately circulated a pamphlet denying that any garden existed. This was the celebrated novelist who became a best seller with her first book about that garden and by and large remained one through *Mr. Skeffington* (1940), her triumphant last. Though she had begun sweetly (or seemingly so), writing about flowers and books and her husband, the Man of Wrath, and the April, May, and June babies, she had gone on to startle her readers with such novels as *The Caravaners* (1910), a high comedy that was nevertheless a chilling forecast of Germany's intention to conquer England, and *Vera,* a *roman à clef* at least on the psychological level, about her disastrous marriage to Francis Russell. And possibly her intimates blinked a bit when she published *Love.* There was also the unsigned *In the Mountains,* a rather oblique description of her slow recovery from her second marriage.

I am trying to suggest that this elderly person in dusty

black, encountered in an Italian village, didn't accord at all
with the common impression of a glamorous woman who
moved comfortably through international social and literary
circles, was mistress of H. G. Wells, sister-in-law to Bertrand
Russell, cousin of Katherine Mansfield (they were both born
Beauchamps),* and friend of statesmen, writers, scholars, and
the aristocracy of several countries.

It wasn't until years later, when I read Leslie de Charm's
biography, that the two disparate images came tentatively together. But that is a partisan work, at least where the life is
concerned (one suspects the pseudonymous author is a daughter of Elizabeth's), and blurred otherwise by a zealous ama-
teurism that simply does not always know where to omit or
condense and where to expand. It is the best reference to date,
however, and almost all we have except for scattered comment
in Frank Swinnerton's volumes of literary essays, Rupert Hart-
Davis's biography of Hugh Walpole, some letters of Katherine
Mansfield's, a few lines in Bertrand Russell's autobiography,
Mrs. Belloc Lowndes's comment, and Elizabeth's own, severely
restricted autobiography, *All the Dogs of My Life* (1936). She
is a minor writer, but it continues to surprise me that references to her should be few when she knew well so many articulate and often indiscreet people. On the whole, Swinnerton
serves her best. In *Figures in the Foreground* he writes: "She
was extremely kind. Her judgments of men and women, however, being unsentimental, were often destructive. . . . The
lucid ridicule of dullness and brutality that quickens nearly all

---

* Elizabeth's real given names were Mary Annette, although her family
called her May. Why she chose the pseudonym that in later years became
so firmly affixed to her is a mystery. Frank Swinnerton, to whom I appealed on this matter, suggests that the choice may have been due either
to her admiration for a famous nineteenth-century novel, *The Wide,
Wide World* by the pseudonymous Elizabeth Wetherell, or to the fact
that Elizabeth was the given name of an eminent Arnim forebear. In any
case, it would have been unthinkable for the wife of a highborn German
to have signed her own name to her books.

her books was what produced for every hearer an awful delight in her more intimate conversations. I have never known any woman with the same *comic* detachment of mind." He goes on (with some unintentional horticultural imagery): "Perhaps because of this characteristic, she had loyal admirers rather than a great literary reputation. It was as long ago as the eighteen-nineties that she first set a fashion of 'garden' books and drew to her side, whenever she was in England, so many of the cultivated people of her day."

By way of summary comment Swinnerton says:

> Now a literary life of nearly fifty years is long enough to allow any reputation to wax and wane. Whether there is any other example of a writer who scored such tremendous successes of delight with her first and last books as Lady Russell did with *Elizabeth and Her German Garden* and *Mr. Skeffington* I cannot say. In her case the progress was from demure comedy to rueful hilarity. It was from the young wife pitilessly regarding the idiosyncrasies of a Man of Wrath to the ageing flirt who discovers that, one by one, she has lost her adorers, and that while charm may be perpetual, allure inevitably dies. . . .
>
> Her style did not change. She unobtrusively depicted herself as she was or had been, surrounded by husbands or friends seen with what Jane Austen called "open pleasantry". Her talent lay in fun, satirical portraiture, and farcical comedy, qualities which are scorned by those obsessed by what a correspondent describes to me as "the modern dilemma". Her fame has therefore sunk. If it ever recovers, as I hope it will do, she may find a place below the highest but in a discreet jostle with Fanny Burney, Emily Eden, and Rhoda Broughton.

Comedy in fiction has been supplanted in our time by scatological joking, a form of alienation and life-denial that seems to suit our present temper better than a literature of affirmation, which is what comedy traditionally has been. But Elizabeth has more than her attitude toward human life working against her now. As Swinnerton notes, her style didn't change—except, perhaps, to become slightly more baroque as

she grew older. We now admire a demotic style, or what passes
as such. Perhaps we think of it as writing with no style at all
(although some examples seem to me as consciously mannered
and artificial as anything Lyly ever came up with). It is possible to read Elizabeth for her punctuation alone, a statement
that would probably enrage any contemporary writer to whom
it was applied. I have never read a study of the evolution of
English punctuation, but my impression is that in early fictions
—at least from the pens of serious writers—it follows the
rhythms of speech. Where, to our eyes, irrational or irrelevant
punctuation occurs, I have assumed that we were to think of
the speaker as pausing, perhaps in mid-gust, to catch his breath
or rephrase his thought, or to emphasize what would come
next. I will say arbitrarily, and with the freedom that total ignorance confers, that this engaging disorder reaches its peak
and its splendid apotheosis in Jane Austen. After her, as the
century moves along, punctuation becomes more orderly,
though no author of my reading has ever subscribed consistently to common rules. Elizabeth lived until 1941, but she
grew up in what might be called the period of High Punctuation, when, for instance, conjunctions were preceded and often
followed by commas, when interpolations required both a
comma and a one-em dash, and prepositional phrases and in-
troductory adverbs and even short appositives were usually set
off by themselves. Here, from the opening of *Mr. Skeffington,* is
a characteristic example of Elizabeth's style and her copious
punctuation:

> Fanny, who had married a Mr. Skeffington, and long ago,
> for reasons she considered compelling, divorced him, after not
> having given him a thought for years began, to her surprise, to
> think of him a great deal. If she shut her eyes, she could see him
> behind the fish-dish at breakfast; and presently, even if she didn't
> shut her eyes, she could see him behind almost anything.
>     What particularly disturbed her was that there was no fish.
> Only during Mr. Skeffington's not very long reign as a husband
> had there been any at breakfast, he having been a man tenacious

of tradition, and liking to see what he had seen in his youth still continuing on his table. With his disappearance, the fish-dish, of solid silver, kept hot by electricity, disappeared too,—not that he took it with him, for he was much too miserable to think of dishes, but because Fanny's breakfast, from the date of his departure to the time she had got to now, was half a grapefruit.

Contemporary readers either like this style and habit—believing that it possesses a clarity and is capable of a subtlety that the demotic headlong tumble cannot achieve—or else they are entirely put off. Obviously, I like the way Elizabeth writes. But it is a kind of writing that can become unbearably arch if control isn't maintained, and most of Elizabeth's books are flawed by passages that make even the most ardent reader flinch. Worse still, like many satirists she possesses (in her books if not, as Swinnerton suggests, in her life) a vein of gush, often sentimental in its origins, which sometimes spoils what might be her best effects. This is most evident in her early works until we come to one of the last, *The Jasmine Farm*, the only novel of hers that requires an act of will to get through.

Nevertheless, the quality of most of her work is generally good. I'm especially fond of *The Adventures of Elizabeth in Rügen, Fräulein Schmidt and Mr. Anstruther, The Enchanted April, Father,* and *Mr. Skeffington.* I've selected *The Pastor's Wife* rather than any of these others because in several ways it is uncharacteristic of her fiction. It is, to begin with, a detailed study of lower-class Prussian society in the years preceding the First World War. All Elizabeth's books, even the nonfiction ones, might roughly be termed comedies of bad manners, bad temper, or neglect, and the particular society is sketched in sparingly, no more being given than is necessary for an understanding of the action. Another reason for my choice is that *The Pastor's Wife* is the most naturalistic of Elizabeth's novels —a quality that will not, of course, recommend it to today's more sophisticated readers. But to me it is interesting to see how a comedic writer can work successfully within the form without sacrificing her special gifts. *The Pastor's Wife* is sad, funny, rueful; the reader is less a spectator than a participant in the action because he is given such a thorough experience of the pastor's household and community.

Until recently, I hadn't looked at *The Pastor's Wife* in more than twenty years. It remained in my memory among a number of other affections whose lineaments, like those of childhood friends, had grown vague. I took the book up again at a particularly bad moment in my life: my father had just died unexpectedly only a matter of months after my mother's unexpected death. It was impossible for me to concentrate on anything; I had sunk into that apathy and physical fatigue that grief and shock bring on, and I had as little desire to reread *The Pastor's Wife* as I had to write about it.

These private difficulties may account for my feeling that the book begins slowly, and that there are passages that represent Elizabeth at her most ordinary. The narrative starts when Ingeborg, the heroine, comes up to London to have a tooth pulled and on impulse, instead of going straight home again, takes a conducted tour to Switzerland. (This unlikely name for an English girl is due to the fact that her maternal grandmother was a Swede.) It is on this tour that she meets her German husband. Within fifty pages she is betrothed, and by page 119 she has faced the wrath of her family and been married. That suggests a novel that is moving along at a respectable rate, but my impression persists that the story doesn't really begin to quicken—in both senses of the word—until the scene shifts to East Prussia and to the village of Kökensee, where Ingeborg will spend the rest of her life except for one other impulsive excursion. (Though I should add, in fairness, that there are some splendid scenes in Redchester, her home, when she returns to break the news of her engagement to her father, the most eminent of Anglican bishops, and her mother, who long ago "had found the sofa as other people find salvation.")

Elizabeth—at least in her work—often took a dim view

of Germans, but this never seems to have affected her response to the German countryside, especially to those areas near or bordering the Baltic. That flat land of murmuring pine forests and lakes and vast fields of rye evoked a lyricism that is almost unique in her writing (I say "almost" because on occasion she also wrote lovingly of Italy and Switzerland). It is against the immensity and under the sunlight of this lonely landscape that Ingeborg and Robert Dremmel, her pastor husband, finally emerge as individuals, and that their problems become more than those to be found in any amusing, skillful romance about unlikely partners. Ingeborg, dominated all her life by her father, ignored by her mother, eclipsed in the family by the rare beauty of her sister, has until now lived submissively. When, for instance, she faces her parents with the news of her engagement, it is with "the real courage found only in the entirely terrified." In Kökensee, she believes that an altogether new and different life will open before her: "spacious untouched canvases on which she was presently going to paint the picture of her life."

On the tour to Switzerland, it is the immense amount that Ingeborg and Herr Dremmel find to say to one another that first draws them together. The delight turns out largely to be Ingeborg's, though. Herr Dremmel's real passion is that of the experimental farmer. Once the couple marries, the pastor resumes his taciturnity. Ingeborg "seemed to sit in his mind on the top of a slope up which he occasionally clambored and caressed her. Eagerly on these visits she would buttonhole him with talk and ask him questions so that he might linger, but even as she buttonholed his gaze would become abstracted and off he slid." (I suspect the sexual imagery is unintended.)

Ingeborg takes long walks, exploring forest paths, or with picnic provisions paddles a punt down the lake adjoining Kökensee, tying the punt where the forests begin. "The forests were quite out of the beat of tourists or foreigners, and the indigenous ladies were too properly occupied by indoor duties to wander, even if they liked forests, away from their home anchorage."

The parish is well satisfied with its pastor: he has trained his parishioners to be "unobtrusive in return for his own unobtrusiveness." Herr Dremmel spends almost all his time in his experimental fields or in his laboratory. He has no need to prepare a weekly sermon, having years before worked up twenty-six of them which he regularly repeats. The most popular is the Advent sermon on "Isaiah lxv., part of the 4th verse, *Swine's flesh:* This sermon filled the church. In spite of the poor opinion of pigs in both the Old and New Testaments . . . in his parishioners' lives they provided the nearest, indeed the only, approach to the finer emotions, to gratitude, love, wonder. . . . Herr Dremmel on pigs was full of intimacy and local warmth."

During the six months which her idyll lasts, Ingeborg's life is marred by only three people: her disapproving mother-in-law, her daily servant (known as Müller's Ilse), and Herr Dremmel's patron, the Baron Glambeck. Baron Glambeck knows that nothing can be done in the face of the parish's opposition to a change in pastors and has ceased to attend divine services at the church. "Until Herr Dremmel brought Ingeborg to make his wedding call he [the Baron] had had no word with [Herr Dremmel] for three years." Müller's Ilse has "surprisingly" thick legs but persists in wearing short skirts and no stockings. When Ingeborg gently protests, "Ilse raised her voice and said that she had no money to get a husband with but at least . . . she had these two fine legs."

Ingeborg's rapturous happiness does not last long. By Christmas Eve she learns she is pregnant—and none too soon according to local views. Becoming pregnant is the first popular thing she's done since her arrival. "She could not if she had planned it out with all her care and wits have achieved anything more dramatically ingratiating [this is because she collapses during the Christmas Eve service, and has to be carried from the church]. The day was the most appropriate day in the whole year." But the pregnancy is a particularly difficult one, and when the child (a boy) is born, Ingeborg at first can feel no interest in it—or in anything else. Later, she is brought to some form of affection, but the child is too grave.

Five more children are born in the next six years, although only the first and second (a daughter) survive, and the glorious canvas that Ingeborg has planned to make of life grows steadily more somber. The daughter of an eminent churchman, the friend of the rich and influential, she finds that in East Prussia a pastor's wife has no more social status than a peasant. Quite literally, she has no one to talk to (not even Robert), no one to invite to her house or to visit. Even parish calls are frowned on.

During these years, a single event, touching in its briefness and casualness, brightens Ingeborg's life. The famous British portrait painter Edward Ingram comes as a house guest to the Glambecks, and one day Ingeborg encounters him in the road when he is returning from a day of sketching. He is intrigued with her because, though an Englishwoman of obvious breeding, she is a pastor's wife living in a village nearly on the border of Russia. But he is even more intrigued —or provoked—when he learns that she has no idea of his international reputation as an artist. Perhaps largely from pique, he admonishes her to enlarge her plainly limited outlook. " 'Read, read, read—everything you can lay your hands on. . . . Get some notion of people and ideas.' "

Inspired by this advice, as severely as it has been worded, Ingeborg quickly subscribes to a number of British reviews, and "whatever books she read about she immediately bought." Unhappily, her continued pregnancies exhaust her cultural intentions. "Gradually sinking away more and more from energy as one child after the other sapped her up, she left off reading, dropping the more difficult things first." Instead, she takes to a kind of private religion. "The more anaemic she grew the easier religion seemed to be. It was much the least difficult thing to be passive, to yield, not to think, not to decide, never to want explanations." But after her sixth child is born dead, it occurs to Herr Dremmel that "an atmosphere of *chapelle ardente*" is pervading his house, and he consults the local doctor. As a result, Ingeborg is sent off with a nurse to the seaside resort of Zoppot, near Danzig, in the hope that fresh air and freedom from household cares and further pregnancies will restore her health and diminish somewhat her inclination to be religious.

Two and a half months later, on the day when Ingeborg, outwardly much restored, returns, her husband gives up his afternoon in the fields and in his laboratory to meet her train, waiting "on the platform with an impatient expectancy he had not felt for years." She arrives sunburned, freckled, very youthful and rounded, and in Herr Dremmel arises the expectation of many more children. But Ingeborg's doctor is less pleased with her progress, despite the seeming physical improvement, and forbids further sexual encounters. At first, Ingeborg "spilt over like a brimming chalice of gratefulness for the great common things of life—sleep, hunger, power to move about, freedom from fear, freedom from pain." But this new freedom soon palls: "She hovered uncertainly round the edges of life, fingering them, trying to feel the point where she could best catch hold and climb into its fulness again." Worse still is Robert's indifferent attitude toward her. "He had loved her. She knew he had. . . . Now nothing fetched him up. He was quite unresponsive. . . . She had never felt so far away from him. He was not angry evidently; he was quite kind. She could not guess that this steady unenthusiastic kindness was the natural expression of a fraternal regard."

In the chill that settles over her life, Ingeborg turns to the children for solace and occupation, but they are as phlegmatic as their grandmother. "What would make Robertlet and Ditti lissom, quick, interested, and gay?" She decides on a spirited combination of education and play, and spends hours over the *Encyclopaedia Britannica* in search of information that may interest the little boy and girl. She becomes "heavy with facts" about flies and stars and distances, but she alone ends up possessing the information. She tries dancing and gymnastic classes, and a conversational hour at bedtime that quickly transforms itself into a monologue. " 'What are you thinking of?' she would ask them sometimes, disturbing their dreamless dream, their happy freedom from thought. And then together they would answer, 'Nothing.' " On the whole, they are immensely patient with their mother. "When . . . in spite of discouragements [Ingeborg] went bravely on, so did they. When out of doors she snowballed them they stood patiently till she had done. She showed them how to make a snow man, and they did not complain." Eventually, reaching school age, the children are removed from their parents' care and settle with their grandmother, who lives near the school they are to attend, and at this point in the narrative the children fade away.

Utterly deserted now, Ingeborg wakes to the fact that "after all, there's still me. . . . Nobody can take that away. . . . Whatever happens, I've still got my own inside." She takes up the sort of reading that Ingram had recommended to her long before. By the end of the following year she has read a mass of unrelated books sent her from London by a news agent who is evidently in his dotage, for what she mostly gets from him is "mid, early, and pre-Victorian literature" which rubs shoulders oddly with the books she sends for on her own. "Ruskin jostled Mr. Roger Fry and Shelley lingered, as it were, in the lap of Mr. Masefield." One day she is in the "placid arms of the Lake Poets," and on another "caught in the exquisite intricacies of Mr. Henry James."

But her enthusiasms focus increasingly on the literature of travel. She, who has been almost no place at all, begins to dream of the cathedrals of France, of the lagoons of Venice and all of Italy. In these empty days of reading and dreaming she achieves a measure of solitary happiness, and it is at this point that Ingram reenters her life, having returned to the Glambecks for a few days in the futile hope of escaping the boredom that everywhere pursues him.

There can be little doubt that Edward Ingram is a thinly disguised portrait of H. G. Wells. Lovat Dickson, in his recent book *H. G. Wells: His Turbulent Life and Times,* remarks that in 1912 Wells was infatuated with Elizabeth, who was by then a widow and living in England. She "was an attractive woman with a sharp wit and a very wide circle of friends in the literary and social worlds. She had taken a house in London, and here she entertained a great deal, flirted furiously, wrote busily, and was the centre of a little maelstrom of activity." Dickson adds:

> Wells fell under her spell, and one sees why. She represented the aristocratic disdain—which can be melted, and then what fire!—discernible in Beatrice in *Tono-Bungay* and the girl on the wall who captivated Mr. Polly's imagination; as a type, she reappears under one name or another in many of the novels he was to write long after the painful episode of his experiences in 1912. . . . He bombarded her with letters, telegrams and protestations of love; she seems to have enjoyed humiliating him and using him for her own convenience.

Wells was later to portray her more or less literally as Mrs. Harrowdean in *Mr. Britling Sees It Through,* but that book was not begun until 1915 and not published until 1916. In the meantime, Elizabeth had got in her own licks (*The Pastor's Wife* came out in 1914 and presumably must have been started at least a year earlier). Why, when in her relationship with Wells she was so clearly the victor, she draws a rather severe picture of him in her novel isn't clear, unless, as Swinnerton says, it is because her judgments of people were always unsentimental. There is one other possible reason, however. When, in 1911–1912, she built the Châlet Soleil and moved there in October of the latter year, Wells must have been one of her first visitors. They then began an affair in earnest. At some point Wells told Swinnerton, "when you've had her for a week you want to bash her head through the wall." He may have conveyed this feeling to her, and in addition told others besides Swinnerton.

Edward Ingram encounters Ingeborg one day when she is out in her punt and he is sketching on the shore. Later he speaks of her Scandinavian coloring, and determines to do her portrait. He deserts the Glambecks, to their rage, and to their humiliation takes a room in the squalid Kökensee inn, "to paint the hair of the pastor's wife." A portrait will have to be prefaced by a series of sketches, and soon Ingeborg and Edward are together every day. "Hardly ever did he do more than her head and throat, and sometimes the delicate descent to her shoulder. The day she saw his idea of her neck she flushed with pleasure, it was such a beautiful thing." For Ingram, at first, these are blissful days. "From this remoteness . . . he looked at his usual life as at something entirely foolish, hurried, noisy, and tiresome. All those women . . . who collected and coagulated about his path, what terrible things they seemed from here! . . . Women who had claims on him—claims on him! on him who belonged only to art and the universe. And there was his wife—good heavens, yes, his wife."

Ingram's seduction is unsuccessful. At first he finds Ingeborg's naïveté charming, "but to persist in it was tiresome. Nothing he could say . . . brought the faintest trace of self-consciousness into her eyes." To Ingeborg, part of the delight of Ingram's company lies in the fact that he talks to her. "She was interested in Ingram . . . and she was not interested in Robert. Perfect love . . . cast out a lot of things besides fear. It cast out, for instance, conversation. And interest, which one couldn't very well have without conversation."

After the third week of sketching, when the weather changes and becomes wretched, Ingram tells Ingeborg that she must come with him to his studio in Venice, so that the portrait can be done. "She laughed. 'How I wish I could!' she said. 'I ache and ache to see things, to go to Italy—' " (This penultimate movement of the narrative may have been inspired by Wells's once having almost persuaded Elizabeth to go to Ireland with him, and to the fact that later they did go to Italy together. "It was," says Elizabeth's biographer, "his excessively trying behavior on one of those journeys that decided her to break away at last.")

Ingram finally convinces Ingeborg that it's outrageous she should be stuck in Kökensee for the rest of her life, and that the portrait, plus the coming and going, will take at most ten days. When it becomes clear to the startled lady that Herr Dremmel is not to be of their company, Ingram talks to her "of the folly of conventions."

It is "wonderful," Ingram thinks with some impatience, how much trouble a man takes at the beginning over a woman. He also thinks—indeed, it's seemed obvious to him all his life —"that when it came to the supremest things not only did one give up everything oneself for them but other people were bound to give up everything, too. The world and the centuries were to be enriched—he had a magnificent faith in his position as a creator—and it was the duty of those persons who were needful to the process to deliver themselves, their souls and bodies, up to him in what he was convinced was an entirely reasonable sacrifice."

Still Ingeborg, unconvinced, hovers on the edge of decision until Ingram reminds her of her one other impulsive adventure—that which brought her, eventually, to Kökensee. She can tell her husband that she has some long-delayed shopping to do in Berlin; he need never know of the Italian trip. She is finally persuaded, but at the last moment she is invaded by conscience and leaves a note for Robert confessing the truth.

The trip south is a leisurely one—the ten days indeed

seem to be passing without much progress toward Venice and the great portrait. But Ingram's expectation of an affair still fails to materialize. "The first step, the process of the actual removal from Kökensee to Berlin, from legality to illicitness, had in its smoothness been positively glib; and he had supposed that, once alone together, lovemaking, which was the very marrow of running away—else why run?—would follow with similar glibness." But Ingeborg continues to consider her trip a holiday filled with "frank companionship" and much conversation and sightseeing. At last, in despair, Ingram determines to take her somewhere ugly—to Milan (for "who would not be galled by the discovery that he has become a background?"). Another threat to further sightseeing is that when they finally get to Venice Ingeborg will find the city enchanting, as she has found every other place enchanting, unless she has learned "to blot out everything in the world with his image alone. This blotting out, he perceived, would have to be achieved in Milan, and quickly."

Milan is, in every sense, Ingram's ultimate mistake. Ingeborg adores looking at its buildings—all the worst ones, in Ingram's view—-and she is indifferent to the awful food. What finally rouses her sense of guilt is the realization that the ten days are passing; that this kind, thoughtful man has devoted a large number of them merely to giving her a view of Italy. "Why, of course—the picture. Why—incredible, but she had forgotten it. Actually forgotten it in the wild excitement of travelling."

Encouraged by her penitence, Ingram at last declares his love. He compares Ingeborg to " 'the light on crystals' " and " 'the clear shining after rain,' " and she interprets his declaration in an innocent fashion. Robert couldn't possibly mind her being "loved" in this wholesome way. But as Ingram continues she finds her response "tinged with a faint uneasiness. . . . Pastors' wives didn't give love except to their pastors. Friendship, yes . . . but love? She had supposed love was reserved

for lovers. Well, if he liked to call it love . . . one must not
be missish . . . it was very kind of him." But before the day
is over it at last becomes clear to her that in Ingram's view she
has " 'completely and gloriously burned [her] ships. . . . Little worshipful thing . . . did you really think you could go
back? . . . After that letter [Robert] couldn't [let you].
And Kökensee wouldn't and couldn't. And Glambeck
wouldn't and couldn't. And Germany, if you like, wouldn't
and couldn't. The whole world gives you to me. You're my
mate now for ever.' "

Ingeborg realizes she must run away—that very night,
even though Ingram has taken all her money for safekeeping.
There is no alternative, however vigorous the rejection of her
both by Robert and by Kökensee. Yet she also knows, misera-
bly, that she is leaving "something she would never find again
. . . a light and a warmth, however fitful, and a greatness."
She is now, if belatedly, becoming an adult, feeling "the acute
desolation of life, the inevitable hurtings, the eternal impossibility, whatever steps one took, of not treading to death something that, too, was living and beautiful."

When she believes that Ingram is asleep that night, she
slips into his room to retrieve some of her money. There is a
train to Berlin at 1:30. She finds his wallet in the drawer of a
table—"Italian notes, the first she found, a handful of them"—
but when she turns to leave the room she finds that Ingram is
looking at her. " 'Ingeborg?' he said in a sleepy wonder, still
half in the deep dreams he had come up out of. 'You? My little
angel love—you? You've come?' " With the ingenuity of
panic, she assures him that she has indeed come to share his
bed, but must return briefly to her own room. " 'I—I've forgotten my toothbrush—' "

Two days later, minus luggage, she is almost home, exhausted, dirty, and dilapidated. Penniless, she walks the distance
from the railway station to Kökensee, observed by many disapproving people, including her own children, her mother-in-

law, and the Baroness Glambeck. To all of them, the explanation for this creature in tatters is *"Engländerin."* By the time she has reached the steep part of the road just before the village she is crawling "like a hurt insect," and she is in tears. "It was the thought of having ruined Robert that clove her heart in two. To have ruined him, when all her ambition and all her hope had been to make him so happy . . ."

Inexplicably, Robert is not in his fields but in his laboratory—"still going on doggedly among the ruins she had created." As she enters his room, he doesn't look up, and when he does he expresses no surprise at her appearance. He merely inquires whether she has managed to obtain the boots for which, ostensibly, she went to Berlin. At first Ingeborg believes he is playing a particularly cruel cat-and-mouse game with her, but then, to her incredulity, she discovers that he has never got round to reading her letter. When she refers to it, "Herr Dremmel wore a slight air of apology. 'One omits, occasionally, to notice,' he said." He then asks for his tea, and bending over his work begins to write again. Ingeborg retrieves the unopened letter, and then hovers uncertainly. "Tradition, copious imbibing of the precepts of bishops," impel her to persuade him to read the letter now, but her voice fails, as do "the precepts of a lifetime." As she goes slowly toward the door, she hesitates and looks back. " 'I—I'd *like* to kiss you,' she faltered. But Herr Dremmel went on writing. He had forgotten Ingeborg."

And so, with these words, Ingeborg's story reaches its finish. Some readers will feel that Elizabeth has abdicated responsibility with this wryly "happy" ending, but my own feeling is that the unread letter is entirely consistent with all we have seen of Robert's conduct since his return to Kökensee after the wedding. A more valid criticism, I think, is that his character throughout the narrative, except for the courtship period and the unlikely fact of his being on a conducted tour at all, is too unvarying. He is not quite a Forsterian "flat" creation, but except when he relegates Ingeborg to the role of sister we see little of his inner workings.

Ingeborg is a far more completely realized character (the story is, after all, about the pastor's *wife*). But it is a bit difficult to believe that even a girl as thoroughly sheltered as she could be so entirely unaware of Ingram's real intentions. Still, one must, I suppose, remember that the action takes place prior to 1914—no dates are ever given—and women, even married women of at least a certain class, were far more ignorant then than they would be today. And that would be especially true of a bishop's daughter in whose home neither love nor marriage was ever mentioned.

We all know that many authors, especially best-selling ones (Edna Ferber is perhaps our prize American example), "get up" a book by saturating themselves in a particular background or way of life. A situation, usually not very interesting, is then imposed on the material. It has always seemed to me a sad thing that John Marquand, whose early (nondetective) novels have genuine literary quality, ran out of material after, let's say, *Wickford Point*—or, at a pinch, *H. M. Pulham, Esq.* —and subsequently had to dig around not just for theme and subject but for backgrounds to put them in. A remarkable thing about *The Pastor's Wife* is that one has no sense of a writer desperately consulting notes about an unfamiliar or alien way of life, and then sticking details willy-nilly into the manuscript. Yet, Elizabeth lived most of her life among the rich or at least the prosperous famous. Nor had she married above her station, since her father, Henry Beauchamp, was a rich man, and Elizabeth had grown up in Australia with all the amenities. No doubt as a result of all this she usually wrote about the rich, or the well-to-do, or the more prosperous clergy —and on one occasion about royalty. When she decided before the First World War to move from England to Switzerland, she constructed the Châlet Soleil near Randogne-sur-

Sierre in the southwest corner of Switzerland because the site, according to her biographer, had a "truly glorious view across the Rhône Valley to the Pennine Alps, the Weisshorn, Rothorn, and the Mont Blanc range and to the east to the Simplon." On the first page of *In the Mountains,* which as I have indicated is an account of her recovery from her marriage to Francis Russell, Elizabeth writes: "I crawled up here this morning from the valley like a sick ant, struggled up to the *little house* on the mountain side that I haven't seen since the first August of the war." She adds: "Here I am once more, come back alone to the house that used to be so full of happy life that its *little wooden sides* nearly burst with the sound of it." (All italics mine.) Yet Hugh Walpole, while visiting the châlet in 1914, wrote Henry James of the house's "splendour" and added that the experience there was "like staying with Queen Mary at Windsor." James, in his reply, says that Walpole's letter "presents little Elizabeth to me . . . like some small shining quartz-crystal set in the rock to which she is kindred and yet hard enough to break by her firm edge the most geological hammer." Elizabeth's biographer calls these references to a "little" house "an inaccurate endearment," and this is nothing if not a spectacular understatement. The châlet had sixteen bedrooms on its two top floors; passing travelers, charmed by the house and the site, often mistook it for a hotel. In her autobiography, Elizabeth herself wrote ruefully of what social constrictions life in the Schloss at Nassenheide imposed on both her and her husband.

Elizabeth's biographer gives us some idea of how she came by the material she used in *The Pastor's Wife.* In doing research for that earlier novel, already referred to (*Fraülein Schmidt and Mr. Anstruther*), she hired herself out in 1905 to a university professor in Jena. She called herself "Miss Armstrong," explained that she was a governess in the Arnim household, and that during her vacation she wanted to improve her German. In return for her lessons, she would help the lady of the house with domestic tasks. The arrangement didn't last long. According to Fräulein Backe, a governess who remained a friend of Elizabeth and her children long after the Nassenheide years had come to an end: "To her consternation she found that she was not only expected to live in an unheated attic room, but that she had to do the marketing— herself carrying her purchases home and up many flights of stairs—to brush the family's clothes and do the household mending." So ended, rather rapidly, what could be called Elizabeth's "descent to the lower-middle classes," resulting, writes her biographer, "in some unexpected physical disciplines that she often spoke of with amusement, much insight into lives very different from her own that would come in handily not only for the contemplated book, but for a later one, *The Pastor's Wife*."

As to the amount of farming information in the latter book, one assumes that Elizabeth picked this up from her husband. Henning von Arnim had been an urban dweller all his life until Elizabeth persuaded him to move to Nassenheide, but once there he became a passionate farmer until his health failed him.

In her journal, only a few months before her death, Elizabeth wrote: "Read Hugh Walpole's *Roman Fountain*. The archness and gush and female skittishness of it! Mixed up with the most uncomfortable-making elementary philosophising. And also a great gift for slap-dash journalism. Poor Hugh. He so longs to be a great writer. I blushed for him, reading the stuff."

As I've said, Elizabeth herself is not entirely free of "archness and gush and female skittishness," but as a philosopher, at least of the mentality and sensibility of a certain class of woman, she has few peers. And because she had, I suspect, no profound ambition to see her books last beyond their time, they may have a better chance of doing so than any of Walpole's. At the end of her autobiography, speaking of one of her pets, she says, "Wise and sensible dog; making the most of what he has, rather than worrying over what he hasn't. . . . Ruminating . . . it occurred to me that it would be very shameful if I were less sensible, less wholesome, and less sturdy of refusal to go down before blows, than Chunkie." She concludes, "So I made another vow."

It seems to have been a vow, despite the misfortunes of her life that included exile, illness, and death in this country during the Second War, that she kept.

# BRAINARD CHENEY

## ON

## CAROLINE GORDON'S

# The Malefactors

---

### BRAINARD CHENEY

BRAINARD CHENEY *was born in 1900 in Fitzgerald, Georgia. He attended Vanderbilt University during the days of the Fugitive-Agrarian group of writers, and he was especially influenced by their leader, John Crowe Ransom. Mr. Cheney is the author of four novels:* Lightwood (*1939*), River Rogue (*1942*), This Is Adam (*1958*), *and* Devil's Elbow (*1969*). *He has also contributed to many magazines and has received a Guggenheim fellowship. He lives in Smyrna, Tennessee, with his wife, Frances Neel Cheney, the eminent librarian, and is at work on a new novel.*

∽

### CAROLINE GORDON

CAROLINE GORDON *was born in Trenton, Kentucky, in 1895. In the early twenties, she worked as a reporter on the* Chattanooga News. *She has taught at Columbia and at the Woman's College of the University of North Carolina; she has been writer-in-residence at Purdue and several other universities and has lectured on writing at many universities and writers' conferences. She has received a Guggenheim and a National Institute award. Her first novel,* Penhally, *appeared in 1931. Then came* Aleck Maury, Sportsman (*1934*), None Shall Look Back (*1937*), The Garden of Adonis (*1937*), Green Centuries (*1941*), The Women on the Porch (*1944*), The Strange Children (*1951*), *and* The Malefactors (*1954*). *She has published two volumes of short stories,* The Forest of the South (*1945*) *and* Old Red and Other Stories (*1957*). *Her works of criticism are* The House of

232

Fiction *(1950), written with her former husband, Allen Tate, and* How to Read a Novel *(1957). Caroline Gordon lives in Princeton, New Jersey, and is working on a long novel set in Biblical times.*

---

*The Malefactors,* fifteen years after its publication, is here recommended to your discovery, or rediscovery, not merely for the durability of its art, but also because of its prophetic relevance for this day. For you of that small company of its earlier readers, I urge that the turn of events has given this novel a new importance. Not that it then went utterly without appreciation.

The *Collier's Encyclopedia Yearbook* for 1956—after listing the best sellers of the year, among which *The Malefactors* was not numbered, and devoting two paragraphs to comment on the novel recognized as the year's most popular, *The Last Hurrah,* and going on a little later to announce *Ten North Frederick* as the recipient of the National Book Award and *Andersonville* as the Pulitzer Prize winner—had this to say: "Caroline Gordon's *The Malefactors* was probably the finest novel of the year—in certain respects, at least, if not in all."

It then quotes the realistic if appreciative reviewer for the *New York Times,* Arthur Mizener: " 'She [Miss Gordon] is not simply a gifted novelist; she is one with the intelligence to discipline and cultivate her powers so that her books have grown more skillful with time and her perceptions have not dried up as gifted writers' so often have in our time.' But, he went on to observe, 'not many people seem to notice. The decades go on tossing up their temporary immortals to fill the journals with their reputations, and Miss Gordon goes on being unnoticed.' "

His implications for *The Malefactors* could hardly have been carried out more fully in the succeeding years. It had but a small first printing, no reprinting, and it is now out of print.

Perhaps we don't have to go far to explain why it didn't become popular. It didn't have a chance. Three of the New York literary world's most influential journals, the *New Yorker, Time,* and the *Saturday Review,* all panned it. The New York *Herald Tribune* treated it respectfully, but coldly. The *Yale Review* was annoyed that "Miss Gordon pulls no punches in making reverence realistically difficult." Kirkus, the rating service important to libraries and book sellers, called it "a strange book, dealing as it does with spiritual and emotional deviates who have found little incentive or purpose to their lives, bemused, and for some it will also be bewildering."

The "strange book" is summarized on the jacket as the "story of a man of the world who finds the lost meaning of his life in conversion to Roman Catholicism."

This is, in various ways, a formidable theme. Perhaps one to hold at bay? The *Time* reviewer went virtually berserk over it. Under the derisive headline "Ode to the Expatriate Dead," he would commit it to the ashcan as "the spiritual hangover of the Lost Generation," which he complains "has gone on for a quarter of a century now, and the pain is beginning to settle in the neck of the reader."

His next tactic is to attribute his own irresponsible malice to the book: "In keeping with its semi-autobiographic overtones (Author Gordon and her poet-critic-novelist husband, Allen Tate, are recent Roman Catholic converts), this book is one of those Mary McCarthy-like exercises in intellectual cattiness in which one claws one's literary coterie in public."

In hostility no less obvious, he concludes, "Apart from such embarrassment as it may cause the author's immediate friends, the moral and intellectual striptease is a legitimate novelistic device for baring some universal truth. In *The Malefactors,* it becomes an end in itself, exposing only cliquish gossip. Written with sensibility, if debatable sense, the novel inadvertently reveals that the Lost Generation may not have been lost at all, just born to be led astray and taken in. Was its christener, Gertrude Stein, its patron saint after all, or was it P. T. Barnum?"

Characteristically, the anonymous *New Yorker* reviewer dismissed *The Malefactors* with a modulated sneer: "Miss Gordon's tone is earnest and provokes echoes that sound as though they ought to be significant, but there is always the possibility that she intended her work to be taken as satire."

*The Malefactors,* "like incest," made Rosemary Benét, in the *Saturday Review,* "nervous."

Perhaps it should be observed for what it is worth that for this year in which *The Malefactors* got the hatchet, *Collier's Encyclopedia* also announced an all-time high in church membership in this country, announced that more than 60 percent of all Americans professed a formal religion and that the Roman Catholic church had made the largest percentage of gain among the Christian denominations. Also, that the craze of the year was the literary hoax of the present reincarnation of a medieval servant girl, *Bridey Murphy.*

Even *The Malefactors*'s admirers, for the benefit of their secular, Protestant, and anti-Christian readers, put the warning label on it. Said Arthur Mizener: "The life of *The Malefactors* is in its observed detail and in its fine structure. . . . But she is not creating this world for its own sake; it exists to give authenticity to her perception of its meaning, a perception which controls every detail of the novel. . . . The perception is Roman Catholic, but it is a perception, not an argument, and only by absorbing the book's life can the reader see how it accounts for everything in Tom Claiborne's experience."

Willard Thorp, in the *New Republic,* wrote: "I know of no modern novel in which this polyphony of present, past, and future is so skillfully composed," and he hailed it as Miss Gordon's finest novel, yet felt it necessary to identify the viewpoint as Roman Catholic.

But the Roman Catholics didn't take it up, either. With one exception, the topical Catholic press did not review it, I believe. At least I don't find reviews listed. The exception is a notable one—the review by the Reverend John W. Simons, in *Commonweal,* which wasn't officially Catholic but secular. How do I account for the Catholics? I can't. There are some obvious assumptions to be made. It was perhaps too strong meat for the conventional Catholic press. Then the novel's medieval (I suppose they would call it) romanticism, put off liberal Catholic journals.

The Lost-Generation-hangover brand that *Time* would put on the book, of course, misrepresents it. But it may be recalled that immediately after World War II and perhaps first articulated by literary men, there developed a revival of interest in the twelfth century, the traditional Catholic church, Thomism. This found intellectual leadership in this country in the philosophers, Jacques Maritain and Étienne Gilson. It involved, notably, conversion to the Catholic church of literary men, artists, intellectuals, some of whom had previously been secular, materialistic, even Marxist. It was wider in its intellectual focus than this, including in its early leadership the poets T. S. Eliot and W. H. Auden, who became Anglican. But the movement back to the Middle Ages went far beyond the literary.

The Trappist monastery at Gethsemane that had held on in the Kentucky hills for a century by virtue of support from its European order suddenly blossomed forth with, I believe, five daughter houses scattered over the country. This new population—at least my own sampling so indicated—was made up considerably of World War II fliers and other war veterans, dentists, accountants, mechanics, Negroes, Riffs, Chinese, and, to be sure, at least one poet, Thomas Merton.

Perhaps this is the point at which I should announce that I am a Catholic convert, too. And one on whose coming into the church Caroline Gordon had considerable influence, both as a writer and as a friend.

Soon after *The Malefactors* was published (I had just

read it and was excited over it) my wife and I accompanied Miss Gordon on a visit to one of Dorothy Day's farms in New Jersey, and on another occasion, to Hospitality House, her place on the Bowery. Without attributing the story, I will say I think it reliable enough to repeat. Miss Gordon intended to dedicate *The Malefactors* to Miss Day. But Miss Day demurred, because she felt that the novel would be taken by the literal-minded as literally biographical in its account of the fictional Catherine Pollard and her Mary farm. It was the literal-minded that Miss Day had daily to deal with, and she felt that the open avowal that would be implied in a dedication might give her added difficulties in mediating her hospitality houses and her Christian Worker movement.

This was, perhaps, sound common sense. And Miss Gordon, I think, understood it.

The *roman à clef* aspect of a piece of fiction has no direct literary or artistic importance. And there is no such thing as a biographical or an autobiographical novel, in the strict meaning of the words. But journalistic reviewers make much of the *roman à clef,* usually with invidious implication.

And in another way, publishers make what they can of it, too. It was said that the decision, just before publication, to eliminate the dedication, gave the publisher cold feet and that the novel was shelved, rather than promoted: that, if true, could have had considerable to do with its small sale.

But that was fifteen years ago! When all of us converts were young in the church and sainthood was a romantic, if not immediate, prospect, and the new Thomism buttressed us against scientific nihilism. And a man could hang a Saint Christopher's medal on the rear-view mirror of his car with some assurance of driving to church in safety, there to hear, in the ancient and universal tongue of the church, a mass chanted Gregorian and, at the sound of the bells, the body of Christ elevated, in all its medieval mystery. That was before

Pope John XXIII opened the window to let a little fresh air
into the church and in came the Vatican Councils. That was
before the computer had brought the prospect of peace (and
priests) to married life, without of course abolishing the di-
vorce courts; and the pill had removed the prospect of marriage as a necessity altogether. And before the DNA code
had become our new language of life, before cybernetics had
robbed it of its last alternative, and before the test tube had
replaced the womb and cryogenics had put heaven on ice.
That was before Teilhard de Chardin and his "cosmic Christ"
had raised anew the issue of God's free gift of grace.

Then why am I recommending this novel—reflecting as it
does a Catholic neo-medievalism of a generation ago—now
that the generations have been shortened? Why do I speak of
discovery and intimate prophecy in a story that the literary so-
phisticates of Boswash, of megalopolitan America, couldn't
stomach even when it was published? That, to be sure, is the
point of this piece, and I will withhold my answer yet a little,
against a fuller view of Caroline Gordon's accomplishment.

*The Malefactors* was Miss Gordon's eighth novel. And,
as Ashley Brown says in his fine essay "The Novel as Christian
Comedy," it is "the culmination of her work." Seven years ago
I reread all of Miss Gordon's fiction, and, like others—Mr.
Brown, perhaps her closest student; Andrew Lytle; the late
Vivienne Koch; Frederick P. W. McDowell—I found that
collectively it added up to considerably more than had appeared in the reading of each book as it came along. To quote
Mr. Brown from "The Achievement of Caroline Gordon":
"Her eight novels and her short stories and even her critical
essays compose a genuine *oeuvre*. Using the materials accessible to her (her own life, the history of her family, the history
of her region) she has built up an impressive image of Western
man and the crisis which his restlessness has created."

In a piece I wrote for the quarterly *Renascence* at that
time, I found in her fiction, not merely dramatic sequence in

her successive pieces, but the composition of an epic ordeal—
an ontological quest of thirty years that had taken her from the
heartland of economic absolutism to Christian mysticism.

Thus it was, and first in a prefatory novel called *The
Strange Children,* she came upon that theme "peculiarly in-
tractable, or inaccessible to the modern novelist: the actual experience, not the mere fact, of religious conversion," as Mr.
Brown has put it.

But this introduction has gone on surely as long as it
should without a synopsis of the story. *The Malefactors* opens
on the day of a fete, a sort of Bucks County fair, privately
sponsored by the Claibornes and held on their luxurious farm,
Blenker's Brook, on the anniversary feast of Saint Eustachius,
who, it may be recalled, was converted when he saw a vision of
Christ between the antlers of a deer. Claiborne, protagonist
and husband to Vera, who has the money and raises blooded
cattle as a hobby, is the central intelligence of the novel.

Very skillfully Miss Gordon uses this fete to introduce
her controlling symbol, Bud, Vera's prize bull. But as a double
symbol, he too signifies the brass bull, in which Saint Eustachius and his family were burned to death. The legend becomes
the theme of the novel. All the main actors come to the party.
With Tom Claiborne at breakfast, as the novel opens, is Max
Shull, friend of his Paris days, painter, homosexual, and permanent guest at Blenker's Brook. Along comes George Crenfrew, Tom's cousin and lifelong friend and neighbor, who
early failed as a painter and husband, but has now remarried
and is a successful psychiatrist. A little later, there is Catherine
Pollard, the girl who left Crenfrew in their wild Paris days, but
who in middle life now appears as a Catholic lay worker operating a haven on the Bowery and a farm in the country for
derelicts, and who is to be instrumental in Tom's conversion.
Meanwhile Tom's background is filled in: a casually educated
Tennessean who ended his study of law in Nashville to become
a poet, spent five years in Paris editing a successful literary

magazine, and marrying there. His problem: he was once a
first-rate poet, but his inspiration has dried up. At his wife's
request, Tom goes to the train to meet her distant cousin Cynthia. There is a marital aspect to Tom's dryness and Cynthia
turns out to be the siren who takes him away from Vera. All is
underway by the end of the day.

Tom's affair with Cynthia not only moves him to promote
her literary career in the days that follow, but also bestirs him
to a revival of sorts of his own. An open breach develops between man and wife; Tom, who has been living off Vera for
twelve years, now has to get a job, and so accepts the editor-
ship of a new literary magazine.

No intellectual, Vera is nonetheless a woman of intuition
and prescience and she had long been aware that her relationship with her husband was under a blight. But she is still deeply
in love with him. She is so distraught over the breakup that she
attempts suicide.

Already Tom has discovered that his mistress, Cynthia, is
more concerned with what he can do for her than with their
love affair. And when, because of their ambiguous relationship, his new employer, head of a publishing empire and
one of the Claiborne social set, doesn't invite them to a big
party and Cynthia quarrels with him about it, his infatuation
begins to evaporate. He learns of his estranged wife's desperate
act, is greatly upset, and sets out to locate her.

Already he has come under Catherine Pollard's influence
indirectly. At her instance and at her Bowery establishment, he
meets a nun–English teacher, engaged in a fantastic literary
exploration, which she calls "Companions in the Blood." Sister
Immaculata has found a metaphoric and spiritual analogy between the *Divino Dialogo* of Saint Catherine of Siena and the
poem *Pontifex,* by Horne Watts, a debauched drunkard homosexual poet and friend of Tom's Paris days, who had drowned
himself. Watts, a major poet and the first to recognize Tom's
own poetic talent, had been a profound literary influence in
his life, although Tom had been repulsed by Watts's depravity.

Tom is incredulous, indeed enraged, over the nun's insistence that Watts's poem is proof that he was blindly seeking God, that he and Saint Catherine were companions in the Blood.

In his disturbed state Tom is pursued by dreams and visions. He first calls on his friend George Crenfrew, who interprets them for him and manages, while ostensibly withholding the secret of her whereabouts, to send him off after Vera. Already under Catherine Pollard's wing, Vera (who was baptized a Catholic in childhood) is tending pigs and a mindless old man and a deformed child on the Mary farm. But when Tom finds her, she will not leave with him. He discovers then that he hasn't yet really found himself.

This occurs a little later, when he enters a church to which he had been directed by his dead friend Horne Watts, in a dream, to discover there Catherine Pollard praying for him, and he joins finally the companionship in the Blood. At Catherine's request he sets out again for the Mary farm, in quest of Vera.

With fine perception, Mr. Brown, in his essay on *The Malefactors* to which I have already referred, delineates in detail the parallel between Caroline Gordon's novel and Dante's *Divine Comedy*. Thus, through symbolism, structure, and other correspondence, Miss Gordon has given her novel added dimension and significance, and her theme traditional Christian enunciation. Father Simons brings expert knowledge to his appreciation of her accomplishment, pointing out that from the point of view of art, what happens to Tom Claiborne "is less important than the strategy by which it is accomplished."

A conversion is admittedly a special invasion of Grace into a particular life. If the artist, in his effort to summon the mystery, gives a maximum plausibility to the motives and conditions leading up to conversion he risks an attenuation of the essentially free character of Grace. If he gives a maximum permissiveness to Grace he risks making his character seem the puppet of Grace. In this case it is the art which seems implausible, for God becomes an almost literal *deus ex machina.* Highly endowed artists from Corneille to Graham Greene have either foundered on the rocks or been sucked into the whirlpool. Only Bernanos, for all his *gaucherie,* has come close to accomplishing this miracle.

After surveying in considerable detail the "resources" Caroline Gordon calls into play to bring Claiborne through the hazardous *passage* for her readers, Simons concludes: "When I had finished the history of Tom Claiborne—obviously and not too implausibly in the toils of Grace—I was more than ever in admiration of a novelist who had not only avoided with her usual consistency the clichés of her craft but had come closer than any vernacular writer to accomplishing the elusive miracle."

Let me repeat for the sake of my argument: the elusive miracle is the dramatic presentation of the freedom of God's grace. But that is only half the measure of the stature of this book, and the paradox of its prophecy.

The *Time* reviewer's frivolous charge that *The Malefactors* is a *roman à clef* exposing literary gossip for the sake of gossip, becomes ironic indeed as we see Miss Gordon's real purpose. There is about the novel an obvious aspect of *roman à clef*. Factual parallel has been used by many novelists, and great ones, to dramatic purpose: Dostoevsky in *The Possessed,* for instance. Though I would prefer to cite here a recent play as a better comparison: *Sunrise at Campobello.* The impact of Dore Schary's drama lay in the image of President Franklin Roosevelt that each spectator brought with him to the theatre.

Father Simons says he cannot escape equating the novel's *Pontifex,* by Horne Watts, with *The Bridge* by Hart Crane. In my view, he couldn't be more right. Indeed, Miss Gordon obviously intended this equation. Therein lies, not only the book's great drama (its Christian irony), but its prophecy. I don't know why Father Simons fails to find a parallel between *The Bridge* and the *Divino Dialogo;* but Sister Bernetta Quinn, in her essay on Eliot and Crane ("The Metamorphic Tradition in Modern Poetry"), very persuasively sets it forth. He might have carried his transposition to "real life" on to identify the fictional work of Sister Immaculata with that of Sister Bernetta, who says: "Whether consciously or not, Crane presents his Bridge as a concretization of God considered in terms of the Incarnation—an idea at least as old as the Thirteenth Century when St. Catherine of Siena used it as the focal symbol of her Dialogues."

After developing the parallel, she concludes: "All this is not to say that in 'Proem' Crane deliberately selected Jesus Christ as the tenor of his metaphor, or (what is less likely) that he had read St. Catherine of Siena, but rather that his mind, hungry for the Absolute, reached out to Roebling's triumph of engineering as one way of expressing the means of union with his Creator, so passionately and blindly desired under all his excesses."

Sister Bernetta Quinn attributes her realization of the parallel between the *Divino Dialogo* and *The Bridge* to the suggestion (in a letter) of Miss Gordon. By leaving *Pontifex* a blank label, Miss Gordon intended surely to suggest to the reader the substitution of Hart Crane's "Epic of America"—in all its richness, its power, and its weakness. Perhaps no other poem, no other poet could so well represent the liberal voice of this country. Saying that "some of the best poetry of our generation is in *The Bridge*," Allen Tate (in his 1937 essay on Crane) goes on: "Its inner confusion is a phase of the inner cross purposes of the time. Crane was one of those men whom every age seems to select as spokesmen of its spiritual life; they give the age away."

But Miss Gordon, I say, is not yesterday's prophet, but tomorrow's. My belief in her prophecy rests then, not only in my sharing her interpretation of the significance of *The Bridge,* but her vision, too. Let me then, with a few tags, characterize this hour of the Age. The hour of behaviorism's ambiguous triumph; the incoherent climax of the adolescent existentialism of our universities. The hour when our shrill and raucous ghetto rhetoric is answered by Little Sir Echo; when

God is dead and his incarnation has reached the limits of scientific and vulgar speculation. It is my guess, the eleventh hour of our interregnum. That hour when (as viewed by Science's most viable theory: an evolution envisioned in man's historical consciousness) man again comes to recognize his fallibility, and his potentiality, and the guidance of God's grace. That hour, let me say, when man, in his prolonged revolt against the human predicament, begins to find his way once more back toward maturity.

Another essay, indeed a whole book would not suffice the argument. But, within behaviorism's framework, I will suggest it by reminding us that man's idiosyncratic distinction among the animals is based on his reflective realization of death, natural death—by deduction, his own death. All of his peculiar monuments, institutions, dreams are characterized by this realization. And its mystery. When he looks upon this mystery, in the fullness of maturity, he realizes that only God can make his predicament bearable, that is, intelligible, and free him of it. But in maturity he realizes that through no stratagems nor structures, no imprecations nor pleadings, no pretensions nor deceits (and, to be sure, the only deceits he can devise are self-deceits) of his own, can he impress God into his service. He realizes that God's grace is essentially a free gift. And the measure, the very definition of maturity, are the supernatural virtues of faith, hope, and charity that dispose him to the gift.

If one reads *The Malefactors,* along with *The Bridge* and Sister Bernetta Quinn's essay, he will surely perceive this intuition in the action of Caroline Gordon's story. Better still, if he will read in sequence all eight of her novels, he will need no key to come to a full perception of this, their climax.

Ah, bitterly, let me rephrase my invitation: if one *could* read her eight novels! For, they are, all of them, out of print. My protest is implicit in this piece.

# FRED CHAPPELL

## ON

## RICHARD YATES'S

# Revolutionary Road

## FRED CHAPPELL

FRED CHAPPELL *was born in the mountains of western North Carolina in 1936; he lives now in Greensboro, North Carolina, and teaches at the university there. The* Paris Review, Sewanee Review, Transatlantic Review, Renaissance Papers, *and other periodicals have published his stories, poems, and scholarly essays. He spent 1967–1968 in Florence, Italy, on a Rockefeller grant. His novels are* It Is Time, Lord *(1963),* The Inkling *(1965), and* Dagon *(1968). In the fall of 1971 he will be bringing out two more books,* The World Between the Eyes *(verse) and* The Gaudy Place, *a novel.*

⤙⤚

## RICHARD YATES

RICHARD YATES *was born in Yonkers, New York, in 1926. He graduated from the Avon School in 1944. Until 1952 he worked at a variety of jobs, ranging from newspaper rewrite man to free-lance ghostwriter to publicity writer. He has taught at the New School for Social Research and at Columbia University; in 1963, he was special assistant in the United States Attorney General's office. Following publication of his first novel,* Revolutionary Road, *in 1961, Mr. Yates received Guggenheim and National Institute of Arts and Letters grants. He has written stories for* Esquire, Paris Review, *and* Atlantic Monthly, *and a volume of his stories,* Eleven Kinds of Loneliness, *appeared in 1962. He has also written a screenplay from William Styron's* Lie Down in Darkness. *Mr. Yates now teaches at the Writers Workshop at the University of Iowa.*

245

It seems to me one of the handsomest and most useful vocations a man could take for himself, this rediscovering of books; one hopes to prevent the forgetting of them by a new crowd of readers; and one hopes even more to attract for them some fresh critical attention. When I heard about this projected volume of essays a whole class of titles sprang to mind; I thought of G. K. Chesterton's *The Man Who Was Thursday*, of Sedagh Hedayat's *The Blind Owl*, of Erskine Caldwell's *Poor Fool*. But I would have had to think a long time before fastening on to Richard Yates's *Revolutionary Road*.

Because it was so highly improbable that this fine novel would ever need to be rediscovered. If I thought about its reputation I would imagine it securely ensconced somewhere near the center of American literary consciousness, standing at ease beside *The Great Gatsby, Appointment in Samarra, The Middle of the Journey,* and any of W. D. Howells's best work. This is the kind of novel our critics—such as Alfred Kazin and Malcolm Cowley—used to cry out for: it examines the broadest literate segment of American society, the suburban middle class; it is masterfully written in a conscientiously unfancy prose style; and it accomplishes what is probably the hardest task for the novel, the giving of solid life to characters who are always recognizable types. I should have expected that the critics would break out flags and rockets whenever they remembered *Revolutionary Road*.

But ten years have passed since its publication, and I have no notion how this book is regarded now. Since 1961 Jorge Luis Borges has been recognized, Kurt Vonnegut, Jr., has made his way with two brilliant fantasies, and the *New Yorker* has been hawking shamelessly the work of a sophomoric surrealist, Donald Barthelme. So that it's at least possible that one of the books we needed most and which appeared at the time we needed it most has been obscured, if not forgotten.

If this is true, it's probably not merely because of changing tastes. Fads are inglorious little things; there are surely enough clear-eyed people to ensure that any book escapes an undeserved fate. That's what I hope. But my optimism gets a bit lessened every time I pick up a volume of, say, movie reviews. Maybe Randall Jarrell has voiced my suspicions in the most disheartening form: "It is hard to write even a competent naturalistic story, and when you have written it what happens? —someone calls it a competent naturalistic story." And what if you have written a brilliant, even a great, naturalistic story? Is it possible to dismiss it by saying, "This is a great naturalistic story, if you really care for that sort of thing"?

No, goddamnit, it's not possible. My own predilection is for the metaphoric, even the hyperbolic, novel. If I have a choice between rereading *A Voyage to Arcturus* and *The Rise of Silas Lapham,* I will unfailingly choose David Lindsay; but I will give 8–3 odds that most readers, no matter what current fashion dictates, will pick Howells. If there is lack of regard for *Revolutionary Road,* it is likely not caused by changing fashion, but by the fact that the book strikes too close to home. It is so relentlessly honest and so embarrassingly personal that any critic who tries to take the customary view-from-above, the "superior" stance (which is probably necessary, after all, in order to judge), has got to feel hypocritical and obtuse.

You see yourself here. When you have an argument with your wife, or with someone who is a bit less articulate than you, or with someone over whom you imagine yourself to have a slight edge socially or economically, you begin to hear Frank Wheeler standing inside your voice, expostulating with false earnestness. A glib pompous fat voice with an undertone of hysteria, and it echoes hollow and ridiculous in the most comfortably furnished room. In the bathroom mirror when the party is at its loudest his face appears in your face: flushed with bourbon and with the excitement of hearing itself talk, the eyes slightly glazed and at the same time unnaturally clever,

the lips twitching with the reckless sophisticated phrases that
almost but didn't quite get said at the exact dramatic moment.
And if you are dressing for an appointment and have a sudden
vision of Mr. Yates's protagonist dressing, well. . . . It's
enough to make you swear off clothes forever.

But of course you don't. And why? Because you lack the
nerve.

We are hindered by social pressures, we like to say, refus-
ing to recognize that social strictures are part of the strictures
of being human. We are troubled and attracted by an ideal
impossible to define, a fuzzy dream of freedom and "self-
realization," a dream which can't be realized because the self it
projects is not a true self. It's a weird kind of intellectual pride,
and though it is prevalent all over suburbia, I can't help thinking that it is a highly specialized hubris which could come into
being very rarely in history. The conditions in which this
opium vision can operate upon a man's destiny are occasional
indeed: plentiful money is required and an easy ignoble means
of acquiring it, a good spotty liberal education is needed, and
there must be a lack of strong ties to family or even to place. If
we look only at European history we can see that these requi-
site conditions are rarely, if ever, fulfilled. It is an American
dilemma, but—God help us!—it is a *characteristic* American
dilemma.

And it's all the more embarrassing and frustrating because this glossy Technicolor fantasy we carry in our heads is so
easy to refute. "If only I didn't have to"—that's probably the
commonest excuse we give ourselves. Richard Yates points out
quite simply that we *don't* have to; we have the means and
opportunity to do what we damn please, if we have the courage to please ourselves. His Frank and April Wheeler want to
go to live in Europe (to them a sort of Land of Oz), and while
it is a moral certainty that they wouldn't be happy in Europe
either, they never get up the courage to leave. Or even to take
out the passports.

Please notice in these paragraphs that it is I who moralize. *Revolutionary Road* isn't moralistic, is no sermon. It is rigorously—almost doggedly—all story, so completely dramatized that not even Henry James could find fault with it on that score. This being so, it becomes that much more difficult to praise the distinctly moral thinking that went into the conception of the novel. The morality is dramatically implicit in the situation. We can say the same thing of the *Divine Comedy;* although Virgil and Beatrice are moralizing personages, their moralizing is built into their dramatic roles as characters. There is in fact a figure in *Revolutionary Road* who corresponds to Dante's Virgil; his name is John Givings and he sees through the sham and pretense that make up the lives of the Wheelers. He asks a few awkward questions when Frank and April reveal that they have decided not to go abroad after all:

"What happened? You get cold feet, or what? You decide you like it here after all? You figure it's more comfy here in the old Hopeless Emptiness after all, or—Wow, that did it! Look at his face! What's the matter, Wheeler? Am I getting warm?"

Givings's parents try helplessly to hush him up, but the Spirit is with him: "Boy! You know something? I wouldn't be surprised if you knocked her up on purpose, just so you could spend the rest of your life hiding behind that maternity dress."

Not even Frank Wheeler is spineless enough—or should we say, courageous enough?—to stand still for this kind of insult; he loses his temper and (more or less—all his actions have to be qualified) ejects the outrageous Givings from his house. But this is a John of revelations, and he has the last word:

> But John wasn't finished yet. "Hey, I'm glad of one thing, though," he said, stopping near the door and turning back, beginning to laugh again, and Mrs. Givings [his mother] thought she would die as he extended a long yellow-stained index finger and pointed it at the slight mound of April's pregnancy. "You know what I'm glad of? I'm glad I'm not going to be that kid."

Glad he ought to be. April aborts the child and kills herself in the process.

You can tell when we have hit a bad patch of contemporary history. We begin to describe excellences in negative terms. As far as writing goes the last five years and the next ten appear to me as a thousand miles of potholes and detours. *Revolutionary Road* is not a hysterical novel, it is not turgidly symbolic, it hasn't a complex plot, it is decidedly not clever. But if I try to recommend the book to a younger reader—to a college student, say—I can almost hear his mind translating my positive words out of what he considers academic bullshit. If I praise Mr. Yates's control, my student will take it to mean that the book lacks intensity; if I speak of meaning dramatized rather than symbolized, he will take it that the book has no "profound" meaning; simplicity of construction means to him simplemindedness; a strict avoidance of the clever signifies humorlessness. If this were merely a case of the young having been corrupted, I should go looking for someone to dose with hemlock and feel satisfied that I was in the right. Unfortunately these prejudices are not merely widespread but rampant among people who ought to know better.

Of course, part of the trouble is inherent in the subject. It is traditional that the virtues of a good novel do not call attention to themselves. A good plot has a "natural" feeling about it, a good prose style is unobtrusive, a well-drawn character is one whom you do not have to struggle and suffer to understand. (How odd, at this moment, these verities sound!)

Well, let's look at a paragraph:

Now, as the house swam up close in the darkness with its cheerful blaze of kitchen and carport lights, they tensed their shoulders and set their jaws in attitudes of brute endurance. April went first, swaying blindly through the kitchen, pausing to steady herself against the great refrigerator, and Frank came blinking behind her. Then she touched a wall switch, and the living room exploded into clarity. In the first shock of light it seemed to be floating, all its contents adrift, and even after it held still it had a tentative look. The sofa was here and the big table there, but they might just as well have been reversed; there was the wall of books, obediently competing for dominance with the picture window, but it might as well have been a lending library. The other pieces of furniture had indeed removed the suggestion of primness, but they had failed to replace it with any other quality. Chairs, coffee table, floor lamp and desk, they stood like items arbitrarily grouped for auction. Only one corner of the room showed signs of pleasant human congress—carpet worn, cushions dented, ash trays full—and this was the alcove they had established with reluctance less than six months ago: the province of the television set ("Why not? Don't we really owe it to the kids? Besides, it's silly to go on being snobbish about television . . .").

It's just about perfect, as far as I can tell. Frank and April are returning home after one of their frequent and terrifying marital fights, and though they come in from the darkness to a "cheerful blaze" of light, they enter this spot of civilization like animals, "in attitudes of brute endurance," unseeingly wrapped in themselves, April "blindly," Frank "blinking." When she turns on the living room lights the room, surcharged with the tension of their desperate lives, "explodes." It is merely a lair for animals, "obediently competing for dominance." This miserable pair has established, has accomplished nothing; they might as well be camping out naked under the sky. Part of the trouble between them is unrecognized avarice (we have the lending library and the auction block), but mostly it is hypocrisy doing them in. Those parenthetical scraps of dialogue have the queasy oiliness of coins too-much-handled. It was a minor fashionable lie of the 1950s ("I don't watch television, but the other night I was passing through the living room while the thing was on and . . ."), and now one is hard put to remember why that sort of lie was important enough to be told. But Richard Yates captured it, and it might almost stand as epitaph for a whole class and generation. Who utters these sentences, anyway? They sound like Frank, but April might as easily have spoken them. So completely mutual has the poisoning of their lives been that this transparent apology could belong to either. The sentences are not set dramatically, but are included as part of the furnishings of the room; the lie is as familiar a part of the furnishings of their existence as the carpet, the cushions, the ashtrays.

Perhaps the most important thing about the paragraph is that it is not unusually good. If a brilliant novel can be said to contain typical paragraphs, this is a typical one, standing not on the virtues of itself, but abetting the development of theme.

A truly admirable book. Not to say that it's a likable one. When I try to recall admirable novels that are also likable I come up with the picaresque (*Don Quixote, Huckleberry Finn*) or children's books (*The Wind in the Willows*) or farces (*Cranford*) or fantasies (*Childhood's End*). But I don't *like* many of the novels I revere most: *Anna Karenina, Miss Lonelyhearts, Lost Illusions, L'Assommoir, The Idiot, Invisible Man, Wise Blood*. All these latter volumes, along with many others, are books which impose themselves on the consciousness by sheer force of honesty and intensity; if I had to choose a single word to describe them, I should probably say "unsparing." This is the quality *Revolutionary Road* shares with them, and the means by which it classes itself among them.

And I suspect that it is this quality which has cost Mr. Yates's book a fair number of readers. I know for a fact that the tributes most of my friends and colleagues pay to Balzac and Zola are only lip service. At some point in their lives they have felt they needed to know *Père Goriot* or *Nana,* but having experienced these, nothing on earth will persuade them to open another by the same authors. It's an understandable reaction. Reading the first forty or so pages of *Cousin Bette,* I too experience a sinking feeling; I know all too well what I'm in for, and it's only a momentary effort of will that propels me further into this harrowing milieu.

But this is the traditional employment of the novel, to awaken awareness to evil in its audience, and of all current literary forms the novel—particularly the American novel—is the one most bound to tradition. Probably the readers of a few generations ago were compounded of sterner stuff than we are. The audiences that appreciated *The Scarlet Letter* and *Vanity Fair* and the stories of Chekhov would have no trouble discerning the bitter virtues of *Revolutionary Road*. But even merely as readers, most of us now share the faults of the Wheelers: we are cowardly, self-indulgent, and, worst of all, irresponsible. The central justification for the novel as a work of art, its fibrous angular morality, we would like to avoid, or at least to consider as secondary.

Morality isn't secondary to a novel. Likableness is. Likableness is a secondary quality in all forms of art. And though a literary critic is usually deceived by its presence, and readers can be deceived by the critic's acclamation of it, a writer is not deceived. If likableness were a quality of primary importance to novelists, they would all be producing sheerly verbal confections like the Firbank novels or intellectual puzzles like detective stories or simple kitsch like *Gone With the Wind*. Someone once remarked that every age gets the art it deserves, and this is probably true at the time because popular taste becomes a condition which the artist has the choice of working within or against. But finally it is not true. Augustan Rome did nothing so wonderful as to deserve the *Aeneid,* nor did Elizabethan England in any sense "earn" the plays of Shakespeare. In Calvinist terms these are rewards that are achieved through God's grace rather than through good works. Hell, even when we had Melville, the best American novelist, among us we didn't recognize him, much less deserve him.

I have suggested that the book appeared at the time it was most needed, but there is also the angering possibility that the right time for it is just now upon us. If I were Cleaver or Chavez or Aptheker I think I might prescribe *Revolutionary Road* as the best handbook about the character of the enemy.

Frank and April Wheeler are—whoopee!—liberals, precisely the kind of white liberals black leaders complain that they most often encounter. Not merely impotent but apathetic, not merely hollow but crumbling. The luminous ideals they claim to profess have sundered their lives, not because the ideals are necessarily bad in themselves, but because these two have failed to acknowledge the simple scary fact that ideals demand not profession but adherence, not speech but action. Mouthed ideals quickly become blasphemy. One of the recurrent strands of action in the novel is Frank's fitful (and usually hung-over) building of a stone pathway that will connect his front door to Revolutionary Road running along, significantly, below his house. He never gets very far with it.

   *Lord Jim* is a book that condemns idealism or, at least, false ideals. Richard Yates doesn't condemn idealism, but instead the claiming of ideals not truly possessed. When we recognize this attitude in one of our cheaper politicians we are quick to label it "opportunist" or "cynical." How then do we excuse it in ourselves and our friends? We may as well honestly admit that "moderate" or "academic" liberalism is the most cynical of all political stances because in 1971 it takes as its *first* premise the political powerlessness of the private individual and attempts to add tenuous platitudes about racial equality and economic justice as viable pieces of the syllogism. Cynicism clothes *Revolutionary Road* as neatly and fastidiously as a Saville Row tuxedo, but the cynicism doesn't proceed from the novelist.

In fact, looking back over this bit of an essay, I fear I have talked entirely too much about Mr. Yates's attitudes, ideas, and purposes. To attract readers to the book—which I will unabashedly admit as my purpose here—I should probably have spoken more about technical triumphs, about the sharpshooter's eye for detail, the unfailing ear for dialogue and the exact English sentence, the improbably taut construction of scene and transition. But after all: first things first. In this era of elaborately technical criticism, possibly attitudes, ideas, and purposes go unrecognized more often than anything else. At least I won't cop out in a servilely fashionable way.

That would be committing the sin *Revolutionary Road* is committed against.

# DANIEL STERN

## ON

## WILLIAM GOYEN'S

# The House of Breath

*DANIEL STERN*

DANIEL STERN, *once a cellist with the Indianapolis Symphony Orchestra, was born in New York City in 1928. He has written reviews and criticism for the* New York Times Book Review, *the* Nation, Life, Commonweal, Harper's *magazine,* Book World, *the* Saturday Review, *and others. In 1969 he was a visiting fellow at the Center for the Humanities at Wesleyan University; he has also lectured at Notre Dame, Russell Sage College, and the Poetry Center of the YMHA in New York. He is the author of several novels:* The Girl with the Glass Heart (*1953*), The Guests of Fame (*1955*), Miss America (*1959*), Who Shall Live, Who Shall Die (*1963*), After the War (*1967*), *and* The Suicide Academy (*1968*). *His latest novel,* The Rose Rabbi, *will be published in 1971.*

✒

*WILLIAM GOYEN*

WILLIAM GOYEN, *born in Trinity, Texas, in 1915, attended Rice University. He became a critic for the* New York Times, *taught writing at the New School for Social Research, and is now a senior editor at McGraw-Hill. He has been awarded two Guggenheim grants and a Ford Foundation residency in playwriting at the Lincoln Center Repertory Theatre. Three of his stage plays, including his adaptation of his novel* The House of Breath *in 1956, and two of his television scripts have been produced; he is a member of Actors Studio.* The House of Breath (*1950*), *his first work of fiction, won the MacMurray Bookshop Award.*

*His other works include* The Faces of Blood Kindred *(1960)
and* Ghost and Flesh *(1962), short stories;* In a Farther Country *(1955) and* The Fair Sister *(1963), novels. Mr. Goyen lives
with his wife, the actress Doris Roberts, in New York City.*

---

In order to speak of a deep reconsideration of a book one
must, I believe, have had a personal as well as literary experience. I encountered *The House of Breath* when segments
of it were published in a magazine in 1949. I was not yet a
writer but was in the subtle stage of collecting literary loves—
not influences; those were longer in coming. But in the months
or years before one sits down to write for the first, serious,
time, the writers that give one a sense of the value of a grave
address to the problems of language, character, nuance, and
theme are of crucial importance. I collected one from each
quarter: from England, Henry Green's *Loving,* from France,
Camus's *The Stranger,* from Italy I recall a now-forgotten
book, *In Sicily* by Elio Vittorini. And from that other foreign
country, the American South, *The House of Breath* appeared.
Those four books may not give one a full sense of the literary
forties; but they were very much my forties. Metaphysical yet
strangely realistic, and stringently concerned with "language
as gesture."

Other candidates from the South had already been in the
air. It must be remembered that in the forties the South of
Faulkner, of Thomas Wolfe, and of Carson McCullers was
much more dominant than it is today. On the face of it
Goyen's book seemed to embody all the then fashionable qualities of southern Gothic. It was rural, being set in the tiny town
of Charity in East Texas. It was written in a sibling style to the
richly veined language half out of the King James Bible, half
out of Shakespeare, that served Faulkner so well and Wolfe
less reliably. It dealt with the grotesque. And it possessed an
ingrained sense of an almost proto-Catholic vision of original

sin—of doomed people against a doomed and shrinking landscape.

In the intervening years when I've discussed the book
with friends who did not know it, the one unique element that
keeps presenting itself is: language. *The House of Breath* tells
the truth that we live in language as we live in a place. The
South has, of course, been America's language-place for generations. Its thought-place may be New England, its concept-
places may be on the West Coast, but our sense that experience
may be dealt with and invoked in the richness of metaphoric
juxtaposition, that a time and place may be captured by certain rhythms and not by others, that richness of language and
sensibility are on a one-to-one basis, that sense is, to a great
degree, a southern one.

It seems to me that a prime source of this is the great
wave of fundamentalist religion that swept over the South and,
receding under the drying pressures of modernity, left the language of King James's Bible translators like a permeating silt
over the expressive style of the entire area. The Bible is as
central a presence in the life of the South as it is in the life of
the Jews, who (along with the Irish), are the other great lan-
guage-people. Goyen's language trembles with Old Testament
rhythms—the dactyls and spondees of singing that invoke Ec-
clesiastes or Isaiah. Like the authors of those two great books,
Goyen is given to incantation to evoke both actual scenes and
prayerful visions. In the first chapter the narrator Berryben, to
prepare for the backward-looking technique of the novel says:
"Yet on the walls of my brain, frescoes: the kneeling balletic
angel holding a wand of vineleaves, announcing; the agony in
the garden; two naked lovers turned out; and over the dome of
my brain Creations and Damnations, Judgments, Hells and
Paradises (we are carriers of lives and legends—who knows
the unseen frescoes on the private walls of the skull?)."

The ambitions of this slender book are thus announced
on the first page: nothing less than a new Passion—extending

backward to and forward from Eden. It will be borne out. The agony in the garden will take place in Bailey's Pasture; the two naked lovers may be, instead of Adam and Eve, in this case Adam and Adam in slightly incestuous and polymorphous perverse experimentation, but the intent is both memory and metaphysical symbolism. Rarely has language woven such a perfect thread through the homely personal detail of country life to end in an evocation of Berryben's "lover" and would-be saviour, Christy as Christy-Christ, in the magnificent final incantation that ends the book (and with which I will end this personal appreciation, as the only appropriate way).

Along the journey the double- and triple-textured language is used to evoke forgiveness, in the guise of understanding, for such lost people as old Malley Ganchion; mad Folner Ganchion, who fully lives out the grotesque passion play that Ben only touches at the edges; restless Sue Emma Starnes (*Swimma, Swimma, come in 'fore dark*). And of course for the spirit who broods over the entire book: Christy.

I will give no summary of the plot. Say only that it is incredibly dense and deals with a ruined family in a ruined house in the town of Charity, with nothing to offer except a place for old people to die in. There are the Ganchions but there are also half relations and the eternally southern involvement with shadowy blood connections.

There is no Faulknerian nobility to draw upon here (unlike, say, *Lie Down in Darkness,* another novel of the period). This is the end of a tradition, not the continuation of one. A personal proof of this occurred when I saw an excellent production of Goyen's own dramatization of the novel in Providence. In that version the characters were interchangeably whites and Negroes. The fact that it worked, and it worked handsomely and movingly, demonstrates that the South of *The House of Breath* is terminal to the southern myth. The whites have no more power and the blacks reproach what the whites have done to themselves as much as any other injustice. The grotesquerie of a life in which the old roles are no longer clearly defined spills over classic boundaries and affects everyone.

The character most dramatically touched on in this vein is Folner Ganchion, the doomed, gay, fantastic Follie. (Names in Goyen's book carry the appropriate weight of their implications—the passages on Folner are in praise of folly, as the treatment of Christy justifies the theological overtones, but always with the lightest of touches.)

*"Folner was sad and cheap and wasted, a doll left in the rain, a face smeared and melted a little, soft and wasted and ruined."* Everyone who yearns, yearns to run from Charity. (*Swimma, Swimma, come in 'fore dark* poor Granny Ganchion keeps crying long after Sue Emma has run away to *her* disappointing freedom.) Folner runs away from the role-confusion of his life to a life that is all roles: "Of all the ways and things in the world, he chose a show, with acrobats and lights and spangles."

After he dies and is brought back home to be buried in Charity, there is an extraordinary scene in which Berryben wanders through the attic where Folner's relics are stored. All the costumes of a boy who retreated into fantasies so powerful that he had to act them out, eloquent or tawdry as they might be, and carried them from the inside of his brain to the traveling stage. There ensues the catalogue of a fantasy-life—as it could only be experienced by a strange boy who did what boys have threatened to do for centuries, but almost never do: he ran away with the circus. He is the artist as freak, as he has always had to be. *"They blamed it on my mother, your Granny Ganchion, because she dressed me like a girl when I was little, and called me 'Follie'."* Of such are artists made: the strange child playing forbidden games in his head, who finally runs away to play them in the world. In Follie's aborted escape one can see the later game-players of Truman Capote and the restless boy/girls and girl/boys of Carson McCullers.

But, more, one can see the exhausted religious vision of

the South at the final end—beyond which the world is nothing but a spectacle, a circus from which nothing definitive can be inferred. Against the doomed and shrinking reality of Charity, no real city can effectively be placed. Only extreme gestures of imagination (the circus) will suffice. In this universe there are only two kinds: those who escape and are finally destroyed for it; and those who do not, and are condemned to spend their lives mourning their untaken opportunities.

Thus, in this slender book, all the great themes of modern literature find their echoes. Hunting birds with Christy, one day, Berryben is accidentally bloodied by contact with them. It is a kind of sacrament, ambiguous in content—as a religious tradition grows less vital, its sacraments grow more and more ambiguous. Yet, even as in occupied but unbelieved-in churches, they can be moving. (There are numerous references to sacraments in the book. Wafers on the tongue, and body and blood are not far off.) Christy, too, remains ambiguous until the end. Felt as a kind of saviour figure throughout, he becomes so, concretely, at the end.

> Something called, something hovered, hard and real and whole as a soaring bird. O Christy, our great lover! Reach down your birdbloodied hand to me, you who decorated me with your garland of news, crowned me with your birdbays of love . . . bless me now, unclaim me, haunt me, bless me now who led me away, broke my seal of secrets then left me—violated and ready again: pattern of all the journeys I would ever make, bird-enchanted, bird-shadowed, bird-tormented . . .

The aim is personal but universal. Each man who has been a child, has undergone initiation, has escaped what Yeats called the Country of the Young, and has tried to make some sense out of the broken puzzle of the past can find a responsive tremor on some page of this book, if not every page. As ever, the wound is life; as ever, the salve is language. And it gives if not the assurance then the hope of meaning. As, on the last page, Berryben calls for *"a language within language, responding each to each forever in the memory of each man."*

# WALKER PERCY

## ON

## WALTER M. MILLER, JR.'S

# A Canticle for Leibowitz

### *WALKER PERCY*

WALKER PERCY *was born in Birmingham, Alabama, in 1916 and now lives in Covington, Louisiana. His philosophical, literary, and medical essays have appeared in numerous journals, and he is working on a book on semantics. His first novel,* The Moviegoer, *received the National Book Award in 1962. His second novel,* The Last Gentleman, *was published in 1966, and a third,* Love in the Ruins, *was published in 1971.*

⌁

### *WALTER M. MILLER, JR.*

WALTER M. MILLER, JR., *has written television scripts, short stories, and science fiction.* A Canticle for Leibowitz *was published in 1959; his other novels are* Conditionally Human *(1962) and* The View from the Stars *(1965). Mr. Miller lives in Daytona, Florida.*

This book is recommended, but not without certain qualifications. That is to say, I would not want my recorded enthusiasm for it and the fact that I have read it several times to be taken as a conventional literary ploy to call attention to an underrated work of literature. Thus I am not setting up as a Malcolm Cowley rehabilitating a neglected Faulkner. For the

262

fact is, the peculiar merit of this book is traceable to virtues which are both subliterary and transliterary. For one thing, it is science fiction—parts of it appeared in the *Magazine of Fantasy and Science Fiction,* which I take to be a high-class sci-fi pulp—and its prose while competent is not distinguished. So it is not as "good" as, say, Katherine Mansfield. Yet it is of more moment than Katherine Mansfield. It is also of more moment than the better known sci-fi futuristic novels, *1984* and *Brave New World.*

Another reason for not recommending it is that it is not for every reader. *A Canticle for Leibowitz* is like a cipher, a coded message, a book in a strange language. From experience I have learned that passing the book along to a friend is like handing the *New York Times* to a fellow passenger on the Orient Express: either he will get it altogether or he altogether won't.

Like a cipher the book has a secret. But unlike a cipher the secret can't be told. Telling it ruins it. But it is not like giving away a mystery by telling the outcome. The case is more difficult.

A good indication of the peculiar nature of the secret is that the book cannot be reviewed. For either the reviewer doesn't get it or, if he does, he can't tell. My first inkling of this odd state of affairs occurred when I read a review of *Canticle* after receiving a review copy. I had read the book with the first of the pricklings of excitement I was to feel on successive readings. But I could not write the review. Why? Because when I tried to track down the source of the neck-pricklings, my neck stopped prickling. Then I read the review, which was written by a smart man, a critic. It dawned on me that the reviewer had *missed* it, missed the whole book, just as one might read a commonplace sentence which contains a cipher and get the sentence but miss the cipher.

To say that the book is a cipher and that some readers have the code and some do not makes it sound like a gnosis, something like Madame Blavatsky's *Secret Doctrine*, which only an elect lay claim to understanding. But it's not that either.

Rather has the mystery to do with conflicting anthropologies, that is, views of man, the way man is. Everyone has an anthropology. There is no not having one. If a man says he does not, all he is saying is that his anthropology is implicit, a set of assumptions which he has not thought to call into question.

One might even speak of a consensus anthropology which is implicit in the culture itself, part of the air we breathe. There is such a thing and it is something of a mishmash and does not necessarily make sense. It might be called the Western democratic-technological-humanist view of man as higher organism invested in certain traditional trappings of a more or less nominal Judeo-Christianity. One still hears, and no one makes much objection to it, that "man is made in the image of God." Even more often one hears such expressions as the "freedom and sacredness of the individual." This anthropology is familiar enough. It is in fact the standard intellectual baggage of most of us. Most of the time it doesn't matter that this anthropology is a mishmash, *disjecta membra*. Do you really mean that God made man in his image? Well hm, it is a manner of speaking. If he didn't and man is in fact an organism in an environment with certain needs and drives which he satisfies from the environment, then what do you mean by talking about the "freedom and sacredness of the individual"? What is so sacred about the life of one individual, especially if he is hungry, sick, suffering, useless? Well hm, we are speaking of "values"; we mean that man has a sacred right and is free to choose his own life or, failing that, a creative death. And suppose he is incompetent to do so, may we choose it for him? Well—

So it goes. At the end of an age and the beginning of another, at a time when ages overlap, views of man also overlap, and such mishmashes are commonplace. We get used to a double vision of man, like watching a ghost on TV.

Or, put mathematically, different ages locate man by different coordinates. In a period of overlap he might be located by more than one set of coordinates. Culture being what it is, even the most incoherent anthropology seems natural, just because it is part of the air we breathe. The incoherence is revealed—and the reader experiences either incomprehension or eerie neck-pricklings—only when one set of coordinates is challenged by the other: look, it is either this way or that way, but it can't be both ways.

The anthropology in *A Canticle for Leibowitz* is both radical and overt. Accordingly, the reader is either uncomprehending, or vaguely discomfited—or he experiences eerie neck-pricklings.

The time is c. 2600 A.D. The place is Arizona perhaps, or where Arizona was. Brother Francis Gerard is making his Lenten fast in the desert. Far away, on the broken interstate, a stranger appears, a pilgrim. Brother Francis, unused to strangers, hides and waits for him in the rubble of some ancient buildings left over from the holocaust of the twentieth century. Brother Francis belongs to the Albertian Order of Leibowitz, whose abbey is close by. The stranger approaches, speaks to the novice, writes two Hebrew letters on a rock and goes his way. The rocks cave in and Brother Francis falls into an ancient fallout shelter. There he finds an old toolbox and a memo: "Pound pastrami, can kraut, six bagels—bring home." He also finds a circuit design with the signature, I. E. Leibowitz.

Could it be a relic of the Blessed Leibowitz, founder of the order? And who was the old pilgrim who wrote the two letters, which read from right to left, *ZL?*

So opens *Canticle,* and already the reader, if he is going to, shall have experienced the first of his agreeable-eerie pricklings. It is a cross-vibration. These good vibes come from two directions.

First, Miller has hit on the correct *mise en scène* for the

apocalyptic futuristic novel. The setting is the desert. An old
civilization lies in ruins. There is silence. Much time has
passed and is passing. The survivor is alone. There is a secret longing in the reader either for the greening of America,
vines sprouting on Forty-second Street, or for the falling into
desert ruins of such cities as Phoenix. Phoenix should revert to
the lizards.

Such is the ordinary stuff of good end-of-world novels, a
sense of sweeping away, of a few survivors, of a beginning
again. Here is the authentic oxymoronic flavor of pleasurable
catastrophe. Shiva destroys, but good things come of it.

But the neck-pricklings, the really remarkable vibes,
come from another direction in *Canticle* and set it apart from
every other novel in the genre.

For the good vibes here are *Jewish*. The coordinates of
the novel are radically Jewish-Christian. That is to say, the
time-line, the $x$-coordinate, the abscissa runs from left to right,
from past to future. But the time-line is crossed by a $y$-axis, the
ordinate. What is the $y$-axis? It is Something That Happened or
Something That Will Happen on the time-line of such a nature
that all points on the time-line are read with reference to the
happening, as before or after, minus or plus. The Jewish coordinates are identical with the Christian save only where $y$
crosses $x$.

To apply Jewish-Christian coordinates to a sci-fi novel is
almost a contradiction in terms. Because all other sci-fi novels,
even the best, *1984* and *Brave New World,* are written on a
single coordinate, the time-line. There is a Jew in *Brave New
World*, Bernard Solomon, but his Jewishness is accidental. He
could as easily have been a Presbyterian or a Sikh.

In all other sci fi, the abscissa extends infinitely in either direction and is not crossed by a $y$-axis. When a starship
lands on a strange planet and intelligent beings are encountered, one's questions have to do with the other's location on
the time-line. Have you split the atom yet? Can you demate-
rialize? What is the stage of evolution of your political system?

For Jewish coordinates (I say Jewish because for our purposes it doesn't matter whether the coordinates are Jewish or Christian, since both have an intersecting y-axis, and after all the Jews had it first) to be applied to the sci-fi genre is a radical challenge of one set of coordinates by another. It is either absurd—and some reviewers found it so—or it is pleasantly dislocating, setting up neck-pricklings. It is something like traveling to a habitable planet of Alpha Centauri and finding on the first rock: Kilroy was here. Or it is like turning on a TV soap opera and finding that the chief character is Abraham.

In *Canticle* the great Fire Deluge fell upon the earth in the ancient twentieth century and the maimed and misbegotten survivors were so enraged by the scientists who encompassed their destruction that they set in motion the Simplification: the complete destruction of technology, books, and whatever. An order of monks was founded to save what they could of the ancient twentieth-century civilization, and they did, as they did in another dark age. They became "bookleggers" who either rescued books from the bonfires of the Simplification or committed them to memory. If a booklegger was caught, he was strung up on the spot. So indeed was Blessed Leibowitz martyred. Here for one thing was an alliance that baffled some reviewers: Jews, Catholic monks, and atomic scientists.

So passed the years and the abbey of the Albertian Order of Leibowitz kept its little hoard of precious documents out in the desert. In one of his best strategies, Miller shows how it is that keeping a few books is not enough to save a culture. When one age dies, its symbols lose their referents and become incomprehensible. The nicest touch of all: the monks copy blueprints, illuminating them with gold leaf, scrolls and cherubs, filling in most of the space with ink "—even though the task of spreading blue ink around tiny white letters was particularly tedious."

At length, in another six hundred years, the thirst for

knowledge revives and the new savants (from Texarkana Empire!) come to visit the abbey to see what can be salvaged from the wisdom of the ancients.

Miller uses this new renaissance adroitly to dramatize the perennial conflict, not between science and religion, but between the new adherents of x-axis, the single time-line, and the keepers of the old coordinates. The hot-shot physicist addresses the monks on the subject of the new science.

> After some discussion of the phenomenon of refraction, he paused, then said apologetically: "I hope none of this offends anybody's religious beliefs," and looked around quizzically. Seeing that their faces remained curious and bland, he continued for a time, then invited questions from the congregation.
>
> "Do you mind a question from the platform?" asked the abbot.
>
> "Not at all," said the scholar. . . .
>
> "I was wondering what there is about the refrangible property of light that you thought might be offensive to religion?"
>
> "Well—" the thon paused uncomfortably. "Monsignor Apollo, whom you know, grew quite heated on the subject. He said that light could not possibly have been refrangible before the Flood, because the rainbow was supposedly—"
>
> The room burst into roaring laughter, drowning the rest of the remark.

But the abbot has a sinking feeling about the thon. My God, he asks, are we destined to repeat the same cycle of renaissance, triumph, cataclysm?

The peculiar virtue of the novel lies in the successful marriage of a subliterary pop form with a subject matter of transliterary import. Literature, in one sense of the word, is simply leapfrogged. Katherine Mansfield is bypassed.

*Canticle* is an agreeable battle of coordinates. The eerie neck-pricklings derive from the circumstance that the uni-axis time-line of futuristic fiction has never been challenged before and so has become one of those unquestioned assumptions that form us far more firmly than any conscious philosophy.

Miller lays the old coordinates over the uni-axis—like one of those clear plastic overlays in mathematics texts—and the reader experiences a slight shiver, or annoyance, or nothing at all.

When Miller's starship, which leaves the earth in the second holocaust, reaches Alpha Centauri and discovers intelligent beings there, most of the astronauts will ask the strangers the usual uni-axis time-line questions: What is the state of your agriculture? Have you split the atom yet? What about your jurisprudence? Etcetera.

But at least one of the astronauts will be a fellow like Walter Miller and he will ask a different set of questions—questions that, oddly enough, the strangers may understand better than his fellow astronauts: "How is it with you? Are you yourself? Or did something go wrong? Was there a disaster? If so, where do you presently stand in relation to a rectification of the disaster? Are you at a Time Before? Or a Time After? Has here been a Happening? Do you expect one?

When he finishes *Canticle,* the reader can ask himself one question, and the answer will tell whether he got the book or missed it. Who is Rachel? What is she?

# BENEDICT KIELY

## ON

## FRANCIS MACMANUS'S

# Watergate

### BENEDICT KIELY

BENEDICT KIELY, *born in County Tyrone, Ireland, in 1919, has been writer-in-residence at Hollins College in Virginia, Emory University in Atlanta, and at the University of Oregon. He has worked for various periodicals in Ireland and has contributed stories to the* Kenyon Review, New Yorker, *and other American magazines. He has written several studies of Irish literature and eight novels, most of which have been published in the United States, including* In a Harbour Green (*1948*), Call for a Miracle (*1949*), Honey Seems Bitter (*1954*), *and* The Captain with the Whiskers (*1960*). *He has a novel and a historical work in progress.*

❧

### FRANCIS MACMANUS

FRANCIS MACMANUS *was born in Kilkenny, Ireland, in 1909. After completing studies at University College, Dublin, he taught at the Christian Brothers' Synge Street school. Some of the plays he wrote and produced for the students have been given productions by the Abbey Theatre. From 1949, Mr. MacManus was director of talks and features for Radio Eirann. Among his critical and miscellaneous works are* After the Flight (*1938*), Pedlar's Pack (*1944*), Boccaccio (*1947*), Seal ag Rodaiocht (*1955*), *and* Columbanus (*1963*). *Perhaps his best-known novels are* Flow on Lovely River (*1941*), Watergate (*1942*), The Fire in the Dust (*1950*), *and* An American Son (*1959*). *Francis MacManus died in 1966.*

270

Francis MacManus was, like Eugene O'Neill's father, a Kilkennyman, and Kilkenny City is still a medieval city that smells of Norman stone.

The house of the medieval witch Dame Alice Kyteler has but recently been turned—but not by witchcraft—into a rather good restaurant. Dame Alice was well and episcopally related, so instead of burning her they burned her maidservant, Petronilla.

Jonathan Swift went to school in the city, across the river from the great castle of the Butlers, the earls of Ormond. In a theatre on the other side of the castle Thomas Moore of the Melodies did a lot of singing.

For a while during the Cromwellian wars the city was almost the capital of Ireland: the Confederation of Kilkenny met there in a hopeless effort to find some unity against Cromwell's iron men.

The great river that flows between Swift's school and the castle of the Butlers, now a center for industrial design, is the Nore. It goes on to the southeast to join the Barrow and the Suir, and the sea. The fertile valleys of those three rivers gave the Normans their first gateways into Ireland.

MacManus was born in Kilkenny City in 1909. He taught school for a while after he left college in Dublin, then went into sound radio as controller of features in the Dublin station. Therein he was a civilizing influence, and that influence is still felt. His most notable achievement was the establishment on radio of the still-continuing Thomas Davis lectures—a series of lectures by the best people in their own fields, on history, archeology, literature, music, and cultural matters generally. The series takes its name from the man who was the cultural and inspirational center of the Young Ireland revolutionaries of 1848.

MacManus died suddenly five years ago.

He had published eleven novels, studies of Boccaccio and Saint Columbanus, a book of Irish historical eyewitness sketches in the Bellocian fashion, a book of miscellaneous pieces (stories, sketches, verse), and a book in Gaelic about a journey he made in the United States.

Regularly I return to read a novel of his because he was a good writer and a careful craftsman and also, let me admit it, because he was a friend of mine. But mostly I'd reread *The Fire in the Dust,* generally accepted as his best novel; or *The Wild Garden* or *Flow on Lovely River,* for both of which I have a particular regard; or *The Greatest of These;* but never until quite recently *Watergate,* which, when I first read it, I regarded as defective because of reservations and the pulling of punches.

Was the shambling farmer a quiet man with moments of violence, or was he not, bedding down with the gypsy woman, who had practically taken over his rich but unkempt farmhouse by the river Nore? Twenty-eight years ago I thought with impatience that MacManus should have told us, and in some detail—or have allowed some of the people in the novel to tell us. Now, having, I hope, grown a little more mature, I realize that one of the qualities that places the novel among the best he wrote is the restraint, the suggestion, the half-hint that was typical of MacManus. He was a Prosper Mérimée man.

The novel is about a returned American, a description that with the coming of the jet age and the crossing of the Atlantic in a few hours and by installment payments, will soon come to mean little or nothing. Generations will grow up for whom the old heartrending songs of exile will have no significance. Before 1939 in the Irish countryside a distinction was made between a "returned" American, an Irish-born person who had lived and worked in the States and come back to settle down in Ireland, and a "born" American, who would normally only be in Ireland to see the relatives of a father or mother, or a homestead or a townland that a parent had mentioned. Born Americans weren't all that plentiful. Hitler changed all that.

Seamus O'Kelly, the Abbey playwright who wrote *Mead-owsweet* and *The Bribe* and who wrote that masterpiece of a story *The Weaver's Grave,* had written, in a novel called *Wet Clay,* about an idealistic young born American trying to settle on the land in Ireland among his people's people—and failing tragically. Shan F. Bullock, the Fermanagh novelist, had in *Dan the Dollar* written the best novel about the returned American. Both novels still have their meaning. George Fitz-maurice had been very comic about the returned American on the Abbey stage in *The Country Dressmaker,* and others, including George Moore in one story in *The Untilled Field,* had touched on the topic. As I said, before 1939 the happenings and the people that brought it to mind were common enough in Ireland.

But MacManus did something more, a lot more. At a time when a bloody war was crowding the roads of the world with displaced persons, he wrote this novel about homelessness and loneliness, about, in fact, displaced persons: two very different women who are to fight like savages over a home, a place to live in. One of them fears to return with her imbecile child to the homeless roads of Ireland. The other fears to return, childless as she is, to the great American cities.

Alice Lennon had left Ireland, in an unprosperous time, a lonely girl wandering mournfully around the streets of Cobh, the point of embarkation, on her last night in her native land. Her strong farming family—they drew lots to see who would go away so as to ease the economic strain—hadn't had the time to leave her all the way to the tender. She comes back much as she had departed, alone, except that she is no longer a girl but a woman with bleached hair, and a life of hard work and a sort of a marriage about which we are never to be told much, behind her. Her girlhood had had its hard days too: "the patched and broken shoes and bare feet, the lined strained

harsh face of her father, the endless trudging for water, pota-
toes and bread and scant meat, the early rising and the
chapped hands and the east wind blowing into the cowsheds."

Comparatively prosperous in the States, and as happy as
that prosperity could make her, she dredged those unpleasant
things up out of her memory. But she was still homeless and
what she really kept remembering were "the serene happiness
and the stored warmth of the valley." To all that and to her
own people she is returning, as she thinks, and in the train
going north from Cork, through the rich lands of Munster and
Leinster, she looks out of the window and sees the idyllic thing
that she had dreamt of for years: "Controlling her restlessness
she gazed at the fields swinging past the window, Ireland sliding under a clear sea-depth of sunlight. Thin smoke coiled upward slowly like stirred chalk ooze above trees petrified in the
stillness; the hedges were ridges of brilliant white hawthorn;
along a road a cart drifted, moving at an imperceptible gait
that would lodge it finally in some deeper sundrowned valley
among limewashed lost houses."

That was MacManus in the mood in which he wrote one
of his few poems, an interesting resonant sort of liturgical
chant called: "Praise God for Ireland." But he goes on: "Her
restlessness was dissolved. It was so good to be home again."

Fair enough, there's a devil's advocate, or a skeleton at
the feast, or a skull in the house of prayer, or a serpent in the
garden, or whatever you like to call it, in the very train with
her. An old priest, who shares her compartment, mutters
through the smoke of his pipe as paradise parades past the windows: "You Americans could have ruled the world after the
war—but ye preferred the bit of business." The novel, remember, was published in 1942.

And: "Aye! America seems to keep people young to a
certain age, and then they go old of a sudden, and dry. It must
be the air. There's no twilight. Just day and night over there,
summer and winter."

The simplicity of his ideas does nothing either to comfort

or amuse her. She begins to dislike the old man, "in whom the almost childish softness seemed a disguise for a hard, calculating, disillusioned nature." She was afraid of him, afraid that the first person to whom she had really talked since her return would be a sign of what was to come: "They, too, would be inquisitive, prying from her answers she thought securely held, sizing her up, her age, her life, treating her casually as if thirty years spent abroad should signify nothing new for them. But hadn't he said that home was the best place in the latter end? The hawthorn would be in bloom around Watergate as well, down to the river banks; but would she know the house, know it like an old dress long laid by or a comfortable pair of shoes?"

By a series of accidents, there are none of her people to meet her at the small wayside halt. She has returned as she went forth—alone.

There is worse to follow, even if the farming community to which she has returned is a sight more prosperous than it was when she left. Neither is there any east wind blowing: because, full of hope for the future, she has come back in the spring to stay forever, and the dark savage struggle of the novel, not only between two women but between two worlds, goes on with brutal incongruity through an indolent summer —an Irish summer at its best, which, in spite of all the talk about Irish weather, can be very lovely; and summer by the deep-grassed banks of the river that meant so much to Mac-Manus. The Nore flows through several of his novels and the sun-warmed stone of the old Norman city rises nobly above it.

Even when, as in *Flow on Lovely River,* he borrows, ironically, a title from a ballad written about the Suir, he still writes about the Nore. He was one of those men who know that every river is a different river. Remembering Dante, whom he was reading with great devotion when he wrote *Flow on Lovely River,* he makes of the seaward movement of the Nore that symbol of life and eternity that men have always seen in rivers and the sea:

I coursed on with the current, sliding between clay banks and the thick, marshalled spears of the reeds and rushes. Spray leaped in delight from the boiling whirls in the arrow-pointed weirs, flecking the waters and dissolving again, momentarily refreshed, into the broad humdrum sweep that moved along by mills, houses, towns, Kilkenny, Bennettsbridge, Thomastown, Inistioge, to open out free at last for the inrolling surge, salt and cold and redeeming: poor human folk muttering their own fragments of a vast story on their short, broken, inevitable journey to the sea. And in His will is our haven. It is that ocean to which all things flow.

In those two novels—and they are quite closely linked—he has studied every mood of the river. Walking out in the evening, Mr. Lee, the schoolmaster in the little village of Drombridge—he also reads Dante and has the narrow Dantean face, and is the chief character in one novel but just a narrow Dantean face, briefly glimpsed, in the other—sees the Nore as the loveliest of rivers, like glass flushed faintly: "in which the reeds, the sky and the willows, and even a sloping field of wheat-stooks swayed gently, a rosy lost world that a few scudding swallows pretended to reach by diving among the swarms of midges." Somewhere, the still mirror of the waters seems to suggest, there exists the ideal and the unalterable.

By moonlight the bleached woman who had returned from the States, and her young nephew, and Lee the schoolmaster look down on the river "lurking between lines of trees and breasting meadows." When she cries out to them to look at the river, you'd think it was on fire, Lee sourly advises her to try getting into it, that it would cool the poetry in her. The poetry in himself has long been cooled by hopeless love; and what Alice Lennon encounters when she finally gets to Watergate—the very name of the house is part of the river—is enough to cool in her all the sentimental poetry of homecoming.

The life of her people centers on two houses: in one, her brother John Lennon, his wife and family, and the young visiting nephew with whom she looks down on the river under the moon; in the other, which is Watergate, the home place, her hypochondriacal sister and her husband, Martin Brunton of Windgap, an easygoing giant of a man given once in a blue moon to a drunken fit of violence. But also in Watergate are the gypsy woman and her imbecile child, brought in to house-keep by Martin Brunton as an act of charity, but intending apparently to stay on forever, seemingly sinister, and with designs on the ailing woman, the place, and the weak husband.

The most sinister thing about the gypsy woman is her silence. Her dark face smolders like the face of a Spaniard set in a portrait. In the summer dusk with the stars coming out over the valley and a swallow chirping in the rafters of an outhouse, "adding its feeble nest-warm piping to the steady, sibilant settling down of the night among the dew-drenched fields," she sits with her child apart from the happy family party by the river and plays on a concertina her slow uncanny music:

> It tensed you oddly that music, which had begun again to unwind and insinuate and uncoil like the slow insatiable wailing of a child that yet knows no words, nothing except hunger, cold, pain, and awful lonesomeness. It was in league with the chittering swallows nesting in old verminous mud-pouches plastered on rafters, with the birds fluttering among the entwined wild growth of the ditches, with the desolate fields, as empty as water. That was one way of listening to it. You could hear it, too, as patient malignity, resentment, that made you hate that woman sitting on the tailboard of a tilted cart that pointed its shafts like guns at the stars, and the child quiet beside her, listening.

Apart from the uncanny music, the lonely voice of a hostile wilderness that threatens to eat up the house, the gypsy woman, you might say, speaks only once, when she cries out on the road to John Lennon's wife: "Ever since the American woman walked into the house, they have been stirring against me, and as God is my judge, Mrs. Lennon, I intend no hurt or harm to anyone. It's terrible, Mrs. Lennon, and I sit out there in the yard, for they don't want us beside the bit of a fire while she's there, and I lie awake in the nights wondering and worrying, seeing myself without a roof again or a bite to eat or a bed to lie on."

But around them Watergate is going to ruin. There can be no end, except in the destruction of one of them, to the struggle—it even goes to a dark night of violence—between the two women and the two worlds: the world of bright modern American efficiency and the shambling aimless world of a secret people who may never have known what a rooftree was or who may simply have been driven to the roads by the Great Hunger of the 1840s.

The victory is to be with the American woman. But in the end, we, and perhaps she, are left to wonder who was the real destroyer. Afterwards, she never speaks again of the days of squabbling and the night of violence that brought her to victory and a home to live in. "She put it from her," the favorite nephew says, "like some of her time in America." For the gypsy may only have been, as I have said, seemingly sinister. I must confess that when I first read the novel I got it wrong, and thought that MacManus meant us to think that the victory of the goodhearted, bleached, efficient woman, and the defeat and the driving back to the homeless roads of the dark woman and her child, was a good thing. Now I feel that he meant something else—and a lot more. A little dirt and slovenliness and laziness never really threatened to destroy the world. But here and now in the 1970s it appears that efficiency may very well manage that destruction. *Watergate* remains the most enigmatic of his novels, and I wish he were alive today so that I could argue the matter with him.

Sometime in the 1940s, in my native town of Omagh, in the County Tyrone in the north of Ireland, I saw two old crones cross themselves when they saw another younger woman approaching. She was a dark gypsy type who had come to the town from somewhere in the south. She lived in a small house in a side street, and her only company was a half-witted daughter who did odd things: like strangling one afternoon the seven or eight chickens her mother kept on a grassless, wire-netted plot behind the house. Because, oddly enough, I distributed in that part of the town the coy little envelopes for the parochial monthly collection—the John the Baptist of Planned Giving—I got to know her and became one of the few people who drank tea, strong as tar, in her house.

She was gentle and well spoken and, to a young northern boy, her accent was fascinating. She thought the little envelopes were very funny—and so did I.

Often in those hazy moments between sleeping and waking she comes back to my mind and I feel, against all reason, that she could have wandered north from Watergate.

# MILLEN BRAND

ON

## HENRY MYERS'S

# The Utmost Island

*MILLEN BRAND*

MILLEN BRAND, *born January 19, 1906, is a graduate of Columbia College and taught ten years at New York University, at the Writing Center. He is at present senior editor at Crown Publishers and lives in New York City. His books include* Savage Sleep *(1968),* The Outward Room *(1957), and other novels;* Dry Summer in Provence *(1966), poetry; and* Fields of Peace *(1970), history and reportage.*

∽

*HENRY MYERS*

HENRY MYERS *was born in Chicago and now lives in New York City. He refuses to give his age, believing that time is a mistaken concept. He has been a theatrical press agent, an accompanist for concert singers, a teacher, a film writer, a dramatist, and a chess player of some note. His books, besides* The Utmost Island *(1951), include* Our Lives Have Just Begun *(1939),* O King, Live For Ever *(1953),* The Signorina *(1956), and* Winner of World War III *(1966).*

North of Göteborg in Sweden, two years ago, I visited the small town of Grebbestad with my son and his wife and my two half-Swedish granddaughters, Ulrika and Jenny. While there, we looked at a nearby petroglyph, a big boulder at the edge of the woods with shields, spears, and a viking boat clearly drawn on it, and Jenny impulsively slid her cute bottom down it—it formed a natural slide—as we stepped rather more respectfully in and out among the early raiders.

Grebbestad is on a long, calm, shadowy inlet. The root meaning of *viking* is "inlet-people" and, going down Grebbestad's million-pointed rippling channel to the sea, the boat of this petroglyph might have set forth to raid England and the other coasts of Europe.

Grebbestad is only a few kilometers from Norway, the home of Norsemen. Not too far over the horizon is Iceland, to which the vikings had spread well before the year 1000, and from which they enthusiastically contributed to viking raiding and enslaving—their slave-grabbing ranged from Ireland to Hungary. And here, around the turn of the millennium, with fateful sureness the sign of the cross began to show itself and to contend with the sign of Thor.

It is this moment that Henry Myers selected for his novel, *The Utmost Island* (Iceland), and he had an unerring instinct, for this is a key moment in history, at least as a symbol in small for some of the larger controlling and hopeful (and despairing) movements of our existence.

Since I'm to write about a novel by a person for whom I have a great personal affection, I had better admit it and work with whatever advantages it gives me. Henry Myers is shy and good-humored, with some strange likenesses to Bertolt Brecht: not much care for his clothing and a technique of making attacks on society while seeming to be laughing at it and even liking it. Liking human beings, at any rate.

His mother wanted him to be a concert pianist. He evaded that, but it left him some talent as an accompanist of singers, and in the late thirties when, via the Nibelungen saga, he found himself passionately interested in the Icelandic voyages to Vineland, he had the thought of doing a musical about them. The musical eventually became a novel bearing traces of its origin, both in a number of attractive lyrics and in a well-shaped structure. This is the story of its writing:

In the late forties, he and his wife had a chance to go to Europe and they wound up in the village of Ascona, in a Swiss-Italian canton off Lake Maggiore. Here he planned to write his "new novel." It was new because he had in 1939 published a moving and imaginative short first novel, *Our Lives Have Just Begun,* about the Children's Crusade, a small masterpiece that was turned down by thirty-five publishers and that sold less than a thousand copies. Undiscouraged, he now wanted to start his viking novel in the soft mists of Lake Maggiore, but there was a difficulty. He lacked a copy of Paul du Chaillu's *The Viking Age,* which he needed for background material. Now he discovered something nice about continental library methods. He inquired in nearby Lugano about the Du Chaillu book and they got it for him, in English, and told him that to return it, all he had to do was drop it in the nearest mailbox.

He wrote his novel and it was published in 1951, and, to his amazement, it was a Book-of-the-Month Club selection. This was then a not-gigantic club, of better-than-average taste, for in 1951 it also chose a Thomas Mann, Salinger's *Catcher in the Rye,* and a Nancy Mitford. I don't know what its distribution was then, but not too many years earlier, when it had as co-selections William Maxwell's *They Came Like Swallows* and my own *The Outward Room,* the club sold only 80,000 copies.

At any rate, *The Utmost Island*'s trade sale was only about 6,000 copies in excess of its Book-of-the-Month Club distribution; Henry Myers continues to be not highly marketable, but he is one of the finest writers of his time, steadily and ceaselessly interesting and entertaining. His *The Winner of World War III* was published abroad, and he is currently at work on a novel based on the life of George Smith, the first translator (and partly the discoverer) of the Gilgamesh Epic.

All this by way of preface to *The Utmost Island.* The

story begins with six-year-old Eric, named for his grandfather Eric the Red, being told by his father, Leif Ericson, about the sky. "The sky rests on the shoulders of four dwarfs. They stand at its corners, holding it up, and their names are Nordri, Sudri, Ostri, and Westry—" And he learned from his father about Odin and Thor and Loki and Frey and Freya, and Thor was real because it (he) was a gleaming greased chunk of wood that stared down at him from a nearby hill.

And this rather happy boy made the sign of Thor.

Now in the year 977 arrived a priest from Norway, Theobrand, the brand of God. This was a different Theobrand from Longfellow's Thangbrand in *Tales of a Wayside Inn*. Longfellow made him squat, repellent, a drinker and quarreler, putting down the skalds, but Henry makes him attractive, tall, and skilled in manipulating an unprepared people, able to attack the visible gods with the True God who is behind the clouds. The likelihood is that he was this kind of priest.

Christianity had been slow coming to Norway and now, close to the year 1000, to Iceland. Its advance had a kind of descending (or ascending geographical) symbolism. But a consistent form. The basic form goes back to Constantine (and don't think Constantine wasn't much in the consciousness of later would-be emperors, like Charlemagne). In the fourth century, Constantine, just before the battle of the Milvian Bridge, had the thought of taking over the rising force of Christianity as a means of unifying his rule. The legend is that he saw the flaming words in the sky: IN THIS SIGN CONQUER. What he undoubtedly did was put the sign of the loving and nonresisting Christ on his soldiers' shields, and he did conquer. And kill. And he made Christianity the state church.

The point of this momentous change is often overlooked, or at least not looked at head on. A state church is something everybody is forced to join. This was its historic meaning, and this still tends to be its meaning. Pre-Constantine Christians were a persecuted minority. The only reason anybody belonged to the Christian religion was conviction. They belonged from a belief in Jesus' goodness so profound that if they fell short and sinned, they were sorry and honestly tried to strengthen their hearts until their conduct was consistent and good. But with Constantine everything changed. Since everybody was forced in by mass conversion, there was no longer any difference between Christians and "other people." Belief didn't matter and conduct was leveled out. The false-swearer, the drunkard, the soldier became Christian. Banker, general, trader, slave-trader, everybody became Christian. And the Christian was now a different person.

Of course the body of the church still contained some good, incorruptible people who tried to live by Christ's teaching, but they were likely not to be popular, even to be hunted down as heretics. Or they were used, on the edge of empire, as the secret allies of those looking for power. So in Iceland, the Irish slaves were secret Christians or ready for Christianizing. And the other slaves too.

But the figure of Christ set before the Norsemen was that of a hero, the conqueror of enemies. A runic inscription, probably from Cynewulf's *Dream of the Rood,* exalted Christ's heroism: "Stripped Himself, God Almighty, when He wanted to mount the cross, courageously in the sight of all men."

And early in *The Utmost Island* is this passage:

The guardian sea let an occasional ship steal in, which, amid an innocent cargo, carried rumors of a change, a change, a change. . . . King Harold Bluetooth had tried to bring Christian Bishops into Norway, but Earl Haakon killed him and put everything back the way it was, for which he was affectionately called Haakon the Good. For a while the ancient ways resumed their comforting way, then the evil came again. King Olaf, who was thought dead, unaccountably returned with an armed host, and with a Christian Priest beside him who carried a sword and used it too; together they hunted the good Haakon to a filthy death in a pit beneath a pigsty where he was hiding. Now Olaf ruled Norway as a baptized Christian, followed to the font by men with neither shame nor honor. They said he ruled by a Divine Right. Divine, by the word of a strange Divinity, not chosen by Bonders equal to himself.

So it was that when Theobrand arrived in Iceland, he had supporting him the threat of an invasion by Norway's King Olaf if the island didn't listen to his preaching. And his preaching was skillful. He told how he had been prepared to convert King Olaf. Bishop Sigurd "told me how Olaf envied and admired the two great Kings, Constantine and Charlemagne . . . How great is the power of prayer, how boundless! The thoughts I had hoped to implant in his mind were already there." After a short, inconsequential talk, Olaf agreed to be baptized. Then he made his first convert, Bolli, seizing him by the throat and drawing his sword.

> Bolli swore fealty to Olaf. This he did in the names of both his old Gods and his New and gave his word besides, which I knew he would never break, because he was a Bonder. He rose to his feet and drew a breath down into his very toes, as if he had not expected to taste air again. "Is it not a great comfort to have eternal life?" asked Olaf. "Any kind will do," answered Bolli, feeling his windpipe where Olaf had squeezed it, "but I would feel more comfort still, when I return home, if a few others shared this eternity with me." "That is easily managed," said Olaf.

And so mass conversions began.

And now it was Iceland's turn. The people were to vote in a Thing, their communal meeting, but in advance of this Thing, Leif knew that the vote would go against the Gods, and he decided to choose six utterly dependable Bondsmen and emigrate to a new land, Greenland, carrying the Gods, especially Thor, with them.

Theobrand smelled this non-Christian plot going on, and although he couldn't stop it, at the last minute he detained Leif's son Eric, hoping that that would bring Leif back. And it did. Theobrand also got a slave, Turker, to join the expedition as his secret agent.

So the single large boat, with obviously long-term

supplies of food and even live cattle, set off for Greenland. There the Skraelings (Eskimos) were waiting for them. Skraelings had been treated thirty-two years before to the Icelandic vikings' courtesy. They had welcomed a boatload of them, fed them, and given them their wives for the night, and in the morning the Icelanders tried to kill them and steal their wives —the usual "superior race" treatment of "savages." Now the Skraelings, in kayaks, attacked Leif's boat, screaming and yelping like a pack of wolves, and Leif and his people were lucky (Lok-y) to get away.

They escaped in a storm and the only alternative left them was to go west. They persisted and after a long and troubling trip and much rowing, reached the coast of a new continent. At Vineland (to them an idyllic spot) they dropped old Thor into the water, to see if he wanted to stop there. "To their immense satisfaction, he did. The tide was moving in, toward shore, and he let it bear him straight into one of the inlets. The ship followed where he floated, through that safe, pleasant harbor flanked by clean-looking sand-spits."

The Vineland stay was a delight. The only drawback was that there were only five women along, and though Leif himself managed to get a Wampanoag Indian girl, to symbolize the union of the Old World and the New ("All primeval places from which the Gods have not yet been driven are, in spirit and atmosphere, alike"), Turker kept reminding the other men of their need for women, and he maneuvered their thoughts toward home, on the lure of at least a raid on Iceland to get themselves wives.

And meantime, while all this was going on, something else had occurred back home of the utmost importance, something that remains legendary and luminous to this day. (A good account of it is that of the thirteenth-century historian Snorri Sturluson.) King Olaf assembled a fleet of dozens of ships along with three of the largest ever known in northern waters, the *Crane,* the *Little Serpent,* and the *Long Serpent.*

And while pretending he was going to invade Iceland, he smartly turned south, intending to make himself emperor of all the Scandinavian countries, and attacked the Danish and Swedish fleets, which were supported by some ships of his own anti-Christian compatriots. In the battle of Svold, he was beaten. But now comes the legend. Driven to the prow of the *Long Serpent,* he raised his shield over his head and jumped into the water. The shield floated on the water, but when it was lifted, Olaf wasn't under it. The story was that he had swum to safety, but Snorri says "he never returned to his kingdom in Norway."

And so Leif, on his return home to raid his island, found Theobrand killed (Longfellow merely chased him back to Norway) and the old gods restored. So the Vineland settlement was abandoned. America went on untroubled by white men for another half-millennium.

Leif's return home is supposed to please us, but although we have no feeling for the Christians in *The Utmost Island,* I doubt that we do well to nourish our childhood admiration for the vikings and their gods, either. Henry leans fraternally toward them, but Brechtian humor keeps him from sentimentalizing. He ends his book with a moving and honest passage:

> [Leif] could not foresee what we would be like, having no way of imagining the transformed world that was to mold us. By the same token, he may have reasoned that we would scarcely be able to imagine him, even if we should want to take the trouble. However, there is a way by which we can evoke this brother of ours out of his distant century. If we put some armor from his grave together with some Runes from his Sagas, he will thereby have a sort of life again for a little while, in the faulty glimpse we get of him. Someone may do as much for us.
>
> Good Lok be with you.

*The Utmost Island* then is a novel of substance about a crucial moment of history, but it would not be well to leave it without some discussion of its qualities. I mentioned the

Brechtian light touch and the lyrics. Here's an example. The Icelanders are on their way west, trying to believe it's not the end of the world, the jumping-off place. "Everybody did all they could . . . singing to encourage the others. The Sea-King [Leif] sang . . . The song had a good lilt and rhythm for rowing. You could scarcely call it a cheery song—what song could be, with that darkness about and that surge beneath?—and this was about a man's grave. But it cheered nonetheless, because it reminded them that there was land as well as water.

> I shall not die at sea;
> There is a house ashore, awaiting me.
>
> That house is very small,
> No broader than myself, from wall to wall,
>
> Not long, nor wide, nor high,
> But room enough wherein a man can lie,
>
> It has not any door,
> But once inside, I shall come out no more.
>
> I shall escape the deep;
> There is a house ashore, where I shall sleep.

At another moment, Leif the Sea-King, who had left his wife behind, said "he meant to live without women from then on, but he would help the other men to get some for themselves. The two wives and three daughters" on board "thought privately that this mood would pass and presently they would see what they could do about it."

The writing has occasional tenderness, but for the most part content dictates bluntness, a content that, in another connection, Friedrich Engels called "robust vandalism." A thousand years later, much of the irony is undated and the problems continue. Like Leif, some of our younger activists are trying to find communes and hostels where they can reconstitute values they still cherish. Like Theobrand, we have persons in high office, on both sides of today's ideological fence, defending "means justified by the great good end." And even today we find echoes of "Here, for the first time, because he [Leif] was thinking of making Turker an ally, he wondered for an instant—oh, for the merest brief fraction of an instant—whether there was any way at all of enslaving a man that could make his slavery less bitter. At once he reproved himself for such an impious thought, remembering that a slave must not receive any sympathy, as if he were a man."

For a passage like this, we have an American precedent, *Huckleberry Finn*. And since we are dealing with "the utmost island," Iceland, a passage in another modern novel about that country (also a Book-of-the-Month Club selection), *Independent People* by the 1955 Nobel Prize–winner Halldór Laxness, comes irresistibly into my mind. Its hero, or antihero, Bjartur of Summerhouses meets some strikers and listens to them, and entrusts his son to them and tries to sleep:

> It seemed as if he would never get to sleep; this night's lodging put him in too great a quandary. Was it a gang of thieves he had fallen in with? Of hooligans and robbers who intended to beat up the authorities and pillage the country? Had he not gone too far when he had decided that his son should remain here in the company of thieves? What had he, the free man, or his children, in common with such a crew? . . . Or was it, on the other hand, possible that these were the just men? If such was the case, they were the only just men he had ever met. For there were only two things to choose from now; either the authorities were the officers of justice and these men criminals, or these men were the officers of justice and the authorities criminals. It was no easy problem to solve in the space of one short night.

This is a statement of the universal problem behind the problem, for Henry's slaves and honest Christian converts, for the pre– and post–King Olaf Norsemen, for the Anabaptist heretics of the Reformation, for the Lollards who "sang their 'heresy' into men's hearts," for many Czarist and Soviet writers, for many active dissidents in today's difficult, polarizing world.

It may be meaningful to mention that when Halldór Laxness's *World Light* was published here in 1969, in a translation sponsored by the Nordic Cultural Commission of the governments of Denmark, Finland, Iceland, Norway, and Sweden (a beautiful translation by Magnus Magnusson), I tried to interest a leading New York literary medium in reviewing it. I was told there was no interest in Laxness.

Henry Myers is in good company.

# DAVID MADDEN

## ON

## WILLIAM GADDIS'S

# The Recognitions

*DAVID MADDEN*

DAVID MADDEN, *writer-in-residence at Louisiana State University, was born in Knoxville, Tennessee, in 1933. A former assistant editor of the* Kenyon Review, *he has edited three volumes of essays on the tough guy and the proletarian writers of the thirties and on the theme of American dreams and nightmares; his own works of criticism are* Wright Morris (*1964*), The Poetic Image in Six Genres (*1970*), *and* James M. Cain (*1970*). *His poems, essays, and stories have appeared in a wide variety of publications. A collection of stories,* The Shadow Knows (*1970*), *was a National Council on the Arts selection. In 1969, his second novel,* Cassandra Singing, *was published, and he received a Rockefeller grant to work on a new novel,* Bijou.

*WILLIAM GADDIS*

WILLIAM GADDIS *was born in New York City in 1922. After receiving a degree from Harvard, Mr. Gaddis worked as a writer for corporations and for film studios; he also worked on magazines and taught for brief periods. In 1955, his complex and controversial novel* The Recognitions *appeared. A new novel,* J.R., *is in progress. Mr. Gaddis has received grants from the National Institute of Arts and Letters and the National Endowment for the Arts.*

Even the most indulgent well-wisher is likely to pick up any novel, especially a first novel, three hundred pages longer than *Ulysses,* with reluctance and read it to the end only with stalwart perseverance, even if stimulated, as in Gaddis's novel, by excellence in conception and execution. Stretches of vexation, frustration, *déjà vu,* and frank boredom make the first reading sluggish; but I read it a second time much more willingly and have perused it again and again eagerly.

Near the end of *The Recognitions,* "the stubby poet" points to a book the "hunched critic in the green wool shirt" is carrying and asks, "You reading that?" The critic replies, "No. I'm just reviewing it. . . . all I need is the jacket blurb." The "stubby poet" himself has bought the novel on the advice of his analyst, who has suggested that he count the letters to induce sleep. "It was in fact quite a thick book," says the omniscient author, describing *The Recognitions* itself. Gaddis is not pictured on the jacket; *Time* unmasked him by printing a photograph—a handsome young man of thirty-three. Only a few ads announced *The Recognitions,* but there was a sufficient number of reviews, mostly hostile or condescending; an underground reputation has kept it on the brink of oblivion, and Harcourt, Brace has faithfully kept it in print.

Gaddis has published no other novels; but a chapter from a new one appeared in the fall of 1970 in *Dutton Review,* No. 1. At forty-nine, Gaddis is a classic example, apparently, of a young writer of genius shooting the works in his first novel— equal in length, range, and complexity to five novels. Appalled by the disconnectedness of time, Stanley, a character in the book who has devoted his life to finishing a massive composition for the organ, makes a statement that describes *The Recognitions* itself: "It's impossible to accomplish a body of work without a continuous sense of time, so instead you try to get all the parts together into one work that will stand by itself and serve the same thing a lifetime of separate work does, something higher than itself."

I'm tempted to risk weaving a tangled web by trying to lure you into this difficult novel through a description of the character relationships and of the story that gradually evolves from those relationships. Readers who stop too early miss contemplating one of the richest tapestries of character relationships in modern literature. But while it's not impossible to disentangle the numerous nexuses of relationships among the more than fifty characters, ten of whom are major, and to trace and link up the disconnected strands of narrative, the novel's genius derives partly from a form that defies the kind of plot parsing one must do in discussing a book few people have read. Extracted out of Gaddis's carefully prepared contexts, the episodes make little sense. A brief look at Wyatt Gwyon, forger of classic paintings, on whom the first fourth of the book focuses, should suffice.

Wyatt grows up in a small New England village, shaped mind and soul by his father, a Calvinist minister; his father's sister, Aunt May; and his mother's father, The Town Carpenter. When she sees his first drawing—a robin—Aunt May, a barren woman who often admonishes, "No cross, no crown," accuses Wyatt of trying to take God's place as creator; thereafter, he draws as if he is damned. He feels secure in the house, "saturated with priesthood," but constantly watched. All his life, the ghost of his mother, which he sometimes sees, haunts him. Having quit his training for the ministry, Wyatt goes to Paris to paint. Then he marries Esther, a novelist, and settles in New York. The mysterious fever he had as a child still burns in his eyes; in nightmares, his hair catches fire; he sleeps on his face, both hands to his throat. His torment, manifested in his unfinished paintings, is more spiritual than artistic. In a novel of brilliant talk, Wyatt stutters; sometimes men who *see* the most are the least articulate, breaking through now and then fluently with lucid insights.

From page 222 until near the end when he renames himself Stephen, Wyatt is nameless; enough confusion ensues to make many readers put the book aside until much later, but the device is thematically expressive and, on second reading, the experience is profound. The figure of Wyatt looms over the intertwining stories of four other characters in segments that focus alternately on each: Basil Valentine a spoiled priest, now an art critic involved in forgery schemes with Wyatt, aspires to protect the world's rare and beautiful things from the vulgar masses; Esme, Wyatt's model and mistress, is a schizophrenic, heroin-addicted poetess; Otto, probably Gaddis's most fully realized character, is a young playwright, a parody of Wyatt, his hero; Stanley is a simple, intensely devout Catholic, whom Gaddis places, in a seriocomic, sometimes almost farcical spectrum, between tortured Wyatt and ridiculous Otto. The reader is made to perceive—at once emotionally and intellectually—the ways in which Wyatt affects each of these characters.

Five other characters counterpoint aspects of those five: Sinisterra, a master counterfeiter, thinks of himself as an artist, and cherishes, like Wyatt, the medieval concept of the anonymity of the artist. Otto's father, Mr. Pivner, a victim of diabetes, is a sentimental true-believer; although Gaddis analyzes his character severely, as a creature programmed by Madison Avenue, Pivner elicits our compassion. Gaddis puns raunchily in naming Recktall Brown, who markets Wyatt's forgeries, but Recktall earns his name; his money touches most of the main characters. Agnes Deigh, a literary agent who has undergone analysis, regards herself as a betrayer betrayed. Anselm talks and behaves out of a conviction that, in life and in art, God has become a sentimental figure, a melodramatic device; he obsessively uses perverted sex and obscene blasphemies to disrupt Stanley's spiritual serenity and to distract himself from an absolute spiritual trauma.

Galaxies of minor characters cluster around and enhance

the major figures, providing a many-faceted series of parallels and contrasts: characters associated with religion; the variegated group of Greenwich Village artists, writers, editors, intellectuals, impostors who hang out at the Viareggio Bar; "queers and lesbians," who throng every avenue of the novel. And Gaddis turns loose in his demonic world several innocent half-wit women and hapless children. Numerous characters wander in and out of the book with no direct relationship to the others. *The Recognitions* is probably a *roman à clef*, but I don't recognize anyone except myself (though not literally, I hope).

Wyatt leaves Esther and becomes a forger of old masters; possessed by an image of himself as a master painter in the Guild in Flanders, working "in the sight of God," he says, "I don't live, I'm lived." Seeking renunciation, Wyatt returns home to New England to work with his father in the ministry, but Reverend Gwyon has become obsessed with Mithraism; he worships the sun and thinks Wyatt, too, is a pagan. Realizing that "no one knows who I am," Wyatt returns to New York; having gone "back," he now goes all the way "down." Resolved to claim as his own work the paintings he has forged, Wyatt interrupts a big party at his estranged wife's apartment to retrieve a long unfinished portrait of his mother; then he goes raving into the apartment of Recktall Brown, interrupting another party, trying to retrieve other paintings. Brown, wearing some ancient armor (his favorite possession) falls down the stairs and is killed. Basil Valentine tells Wyatt that now there are just the two of them; sensing mutual spiritual depravity, Wyatt now sees that Basil has been a "luxury," enabling him to postpone self-knowledge. Wyatt stabs Basil, and flees to San Swingli, the little Spanish town where his mother is buried.

Anonymous throughout most of the middle of the novel, Wyatt is reborn as Stephen. At his mother's tomb, he meets Mr. Yak, who is, we gradually perceive, Mr. Sinisterra, whom we met at the start of the book; impersonating a doctor on a ship at sea, Sinisterra had operated on Wyatt's mother, who was suffering an acute case of appendicitis, accidentally killing her (Wyatt never learns this). As they travel to Madrid, Sinisterra persuades Wyatt to become his assistant in preparing a counterfeit mummy to sell to an Egyptologist (who we know is an international espionage agent working with Basil). They return to San Swingli where they dig up a body and, disguising it as an old woman, take it back to Madrid on a train.

Then Wyatt stays in the monastery at San Swingli, working patiently with a knife to restore old masterworks that have been painted over. He and the old man who rings the bells are friends, penitents for murder (Wyatt doesn't know that Basil survived) and rape (the old man raped an eleven-year-old girl here, and now the girl is being canonized). Wyatt reveals to a popular religious novelist a revelation he has had: that the old man stays as close as he can to his victim as a way of atoning; he is living through his guilt. And Wyatt has seen that that is what *he* must do. So he goes back to America, to "live it through." As he leaves, he yells back at the religious novelist (who wants easy answers): "Now at last, to live deliberately. . . . No, there's no more you and I. . . . We'll simplify? Hear?"

Despite its geographical range (New England, Paris, Spain, Italy, but mostly New York), *The Recognitions* often induces a feeling of claustrophobia, for much of it is set in rooms: "They arrived at a room full of people who spent their lives in rooms." And we experience time in fragments that are in the process of being ordered by the mind—Gaddis's, ours.

Like *Ulysses, The Recognitions* is an encyclopedic novel, full of expertise on a wide range of subjects, many of them obscure. I suppose some readers got mired down in the surface *stuff* of the novel. But possessing this expertise, Gaddis was naturally impelled to create characters who use it; as the godlike creator, he dispenses a great deal of it himself. His omniscient commentary (sometimes as aggressive as Thackeray's or Fielding's) enables him to suggest the pagan origins of modern

Christian beliefs and to evoke every major era of man's history, with an emphasis on medieval times. There are numerous anecdotes of the customs, past and present, of foreign places; he occasions quotations from most of the major languages; a list of historical personages, secular and ecclesiastical, alluded to would take ten pages.

Gaddis omits no kind of sex, normal or perverted. "Someone else suggested using a duck, putting its head in a drawer and jamming the drawer shut at the critical moment." Anselm suggests a scheme for selling the semen of movie stars to young girls—advertising in the fan magazines. Every kind of narcotic is used (this subject matter is handled with restraint). Many kinds of crime are committed; but there are more instances of suicide (about ten) than of murder. "If you really believed what you wrote there," someone tells a novelist, "you'd be morally obliged to blow your brains out."

In the course of the novel, the reader becomes intricately involved with all the arts. Wyatt and others discuss the old master painters and a few of the moderns at length: Bouts, Memling, Van der Goes, Fra Angelico, Van Eyck, Van der Weyden, Tintoretto, Caravaggio; Cézanne, Juan Gris, Van Gogh, Uccello. Just before Wyatt stabs him, Basil says, "Flanders in the fifteenth century, do you think it was all like the Adoration of the Mystic Lamb?" They weren't all masterpieces; what about the trash that disappeared? Van Eyck lived in a loud, vulgar court. Bouts, with his realistic details, was bourgeois. Detail in painting betrayed a terror of emptiness, space, a profound mistrust of God. Everything was done then for the same reason as now: avarice, lust, vanity. Vulgar ostentation, then as now, stifled beauty everywhere. Painters hired out to paint the fine altarpieces that glorified the vulgar men who commissioned them. "Everything was so afraid, so uncertain God saw it, that it insisted its vanity on His eyes." Then as now, fear, pessimism, depression, were everywhere. "Maybe God *isn't* watching."

Gaddis's *Recognitions* swarms with references to books, including "the first Christian novel," Clement of Rome's *Recognitions*. "Mostly talk, talk, talk," says Basil. "The young man's deepest concern is for the immortality of his soul." Today's novelists, says Wyatt, "write for people who read with the surface of their minds," people who were brought up reading for facts, who want to know what's going to come next." Some of the books Gaddis and his characters refer to are actual, some are not: *Toilet Training and Democracy;* Djuna Barnes's *Nightwood; Can Freaks Make Love?; The Razor's Edge* (a middlebrow parallel to Gaddis's novel); *Walden* (which Wyatt is reading); *Uncle Tom's Cabin* (which Esme is reading); Mother Goose (which someone is psychoanalyzing); *Imitation of Christ* (which someone is plagiarizing). Even—or especially—very literate readers may retch, mistaking Gaddis's many allusions and epigraphs for literary ostentatiousness, but for this novel they function lucidly and are absolutely appropriate, if not essential.

Incongruously juxtaposed, popular and classical music assault the characters—a confusion of "Yes, We Have No Bananas" (which someone announces was lifted from the *Messiah*), Purcell, Bruckner, "White Christmas," "Let's Do It." The Department of Sanitation Band plays "The Bells of St. Mary's," and in Paris, Hollanders in native dress sing "Red River Valley." Long before Susan Sontag or Dwight Macdonald, Gaddis demonstrated ways in which popular culture intersects high culture through camp and parallels serious and avant-garde culture.

In the course of the four very different parties, Gaddis examines closely the folkways of partygoing. I am seldom convinced in a novel by depictions of parties, but Gaddis has a distinctive talent for evoking their special reality. The partygoers are mostly those who create, foster, or frustrate the arts, and they get off some very funny jokes and witty one-liners—fringe items of our intermingling popular and highbrow cultures.

In America, it is business that keeps art and literature going. "Business is co-operation with reality," Recktall Brown lectures. "Money gives significance to anything." And business controls and thrives on the mass media. "This is the age of publicity," an advertising man proclaims, and Basil laments that you can sell neither a painting nor a laxative without publicity. Anselm torments Stanley with an ad: "THROW AWAY THAT TRUSS! Here's your peace and salvation . . . literally *thousands* of Rupture sufferers *have* entered this Kingdom of Paradise Regained." Along with the ads, *The Recognitions* is loaded with signs, symbols, and graffiti: JESUS IS A COMMUNIST. HITLER WAS RIGHT.

Wherever they go, most of the characters carry either a book or a magazine. Newspaper headlines and stories graphically reflect the world in which the characters live and commit various kinds of suicide. "Ashamed of the world," a man electrocutes himself in a homemade death chair. For Otto's father, Mr. Pivner, the newspaper externalizes in "the agony of others the terrors and temptations inadmissible to himself"; the radio offers him something free, then a sermon, then a deodorant, and reminds him constantly that he "is under absolutely no obligation." Before turning off his radio, Pivner, even when he is being unjustly arrested, waits courteously for the announcer to finish speaking. Pivner's omnivorous craving for information allows Gaddis to compose medleys of newspaper items and radio voices; in my opinion, he handles this pastiche technique as adroitly as Dos Passos.

Gaddis exposes the reader to critics in all the arts, especially to the pronouncements of the "hunched critic in the green shirt," who ends up in bed with Esther, begging her to watch him masturbate. But Wyatt is convinced that "criticism is the art we need most today. . . . a disciplined nostalgia, disciplined recognitions."

For all its sophistication and aura of ostentatious genius, Gaddis's novel has, like Pound's *Cantos,* a redeeming air of naïveté and faith. And it is a prophetic book, depicting horrors of the fifties that, rooted in the past, anticipate realities of the seventies. Describing the superficial religious novelist near the end, Gaddis parodies the serious experience some of his major characters, and perhaps the reader, have been undergoing: "he . . . glimpsed a man having, or about to have, or at the very least valiantly fighting off, a religious experience."

*The Recognitions*'s main theme is religion. The superficial "revival of religion" in the early fifties only increased church attendance, one of the payoffs of the "age of publicity." In constant contrast to religion today, the novel is full of ancient Christian lore, each item as relevant in one place as in another. The question "Is God watching?" haunts the book. Gaddis deliberately exaggerates the Christ symbolism, which was at the height of popularity in the fifties; it is complex, pervasive—he gives even minor characters the "Christlike" tag—and deliberately arbitrary. There are many instances of superstition, too. "Do you know why nuns must have their ears covered? My dear, so they won't conceive!" says a homosexual. More seriously, Wyatt covers all mirrors in his apartment. "There are evil mirrors where he works," says Esme, "and they work with him, because they are mirrors with terrible memories." He uses them in his forgery process, to capture, for instance, a memory of Bouts.

Valentine, artist and priest, critic and criminal, tells Wyatt (who is all these, except critic) that "the priest is the guardian of mysteries. The artist is driven to expose them." Earlier, a dishonest art critic reminded Wyatt of Degas's statement: "The artist must approach his work in the same frame of mind in which the criminal commits his deed." The artist as criminal, the criminal as artist, is one of the most fascinating concepts dramatized in the novel.

But Wyatt wants neither money nor praise from critics and the public. He wants approval from "the thing itself," wherein value resides. He tells the religious novelist that one must suffer beautiful things. "The arch never sleeps." When he reaches a spiritual nadir, Wyatt's talismanic saying is an exultant "Thank God there was the gold to forge!"—amid all the dross. Paraphrasing Saint Paul's exhortation, Wyatt says, "A work of art redeems time."

Painting forgeries is one way of trying to redeem time. The technical and philosophical conversations between Wyatt and Basil about forgery are extremely absorbing. Wyatt regards magazine reproductions of his forgeries as a "calumny," like plagiarism. But in another sense, the notion of originality is "a romantic disease. . . . all around we see the originality of incompetent idiots"; they can "draw nothing, paint nothing, just so the mess they make is original. . . . Even two hundred years ago . . . to be original was to admit that you could not do a thing the right way, so you could only do it your own way. . . . you do not invent shapes, you *know* them." Forgery is a futile attempt, Wyatt finally realizes, to recapture the past, to live and create in the present, an attempt made out of impotence, on the assumption that the past was closer to origins. By the end, he has gone the gamut, from abortive or unfinished originals, to almost perfect copies, to deceptive forgeries, to restorations in the monastery at San Swingli.

The final futility of forgery as a means of "recognizing patterns already there" and redeeming time is demonstrated in life as well as in art. The saints are counterfeits of Christ, who is God forged. Imitative, forged, counterfeit people, impostors, populate Gaddis's novel. At Max's party, someone quotes de Maupassant, "I mask myself among masked people." *The Recognitions* reverberates with hundreds of voices that reek of corruption. "Everything's sort of contraceptive," someone says. Emotions are so "cultivated that the only aberration was normality." "Do we only know things in terms of other things?" The kinds of synthetics and falsifications are multitudinous. Brown uses a pulpit as a bar. "I got a friend he's got a glasseye with the American flag on it." A convent is refurbished as a madhouse. "Science cut open Caruso's throat to see

what made him sing." "Keep Tabs on Mystery!" says an ad for
a machine that records one's repetitions of the rosary. But such
things existed in the past, too; the hermit Paul used pebbles to
keep count of his daily three hundred prayers.

Delusions, mistaken identity, masquerading result in *sep-
aration:* "everything in its own vain shell, everything separate," says Basil, "withdrawn from everything else!" One of
Gaddis's emptiest characters is tormented by the concept of
vacuum, "where a handkerchief and a cannonball fall at the
same God damn speed." Another character echoes this cry of
despair: "And every God damn place you go, and every God
damn thing you do, it's still this same God damn handkerchief
and this same God damn cannonball falling in this same God
damn vacuum." This description of theme also describes form:
god-Gaddis throws fragments out into the vacuum and they
rush at us randomly at the same speed and may have an effect
later in his creation, or an immediate effect now, a different
one later.

Chance, coincidence, accident, and repetition reign in
Gaddis's field of vision; eventually each of the characters, with
the "unswerving punctuality of chance," encounters or un-
knowingly crosses paths with most of the others. Acts of a supposed great magnitude recur on a minor scale, and minor acts
are enlarged, in a new context, to a scale of great magnitude,
with seeming comic absurdity. Civilization is composed of
trivia. Both fascinated and repelled himself, Gaddis makes us
feel the mystery of the ordinary. He stresses the triviality of the
present by juxtaposing great insights and extraordinary events
from the past with the mouthings and the random pseudo-
events of today. Simultaneously, he implies the existential absurdity of *all* culture. Nothing in *The Recognitions* is gratuitous, because the abstract terror of gratuitousness is, as in Gide,
one of the major experiences this novel induces. Still, this is
not a random book in the negative avant-garde sense; these
experiences are controlled, making the repetitions and returns

all the more exhilarating. Whether there is a specific cause or not, everything *seems* familiar; Gaddis demonstrates that we are damned to experience familiar patterns and people over and over.

The blessing is that all these coincidences and resemblances can result in *recognitions*—a word repeated endlessly, with every possible denotation and connotation, along with variants and puns. And grace comes when these recognitions result in *revelation,* a word seldom used, but always implied as the reader's responsibility. Vision is contagious, as in the instance of the lunatic's seeing Christ after resurrection; Gaddis implies that life (or perhaps just art) should be full of recognitions, visions, resurrections, and transformations—and that is what the reader's imagination, fed by *The Recognitions,* should achieve.

The high incidence of chance, coincidence, accident, and repetition in the book is a compulsive consequence of Gaddis's vision. The reader's attentiveness to the crossed-paths pattern, for instance, emphasizes simultaneously a primitive sensory delight and an intellectual excitement in these recognitions, and the reader finally comes to see that where he started—with the title—is where the theme is relentlessly going: the way of recognitions. With so many complexities thrown out into space, Gaddis leaves the time sequence chronological, though fragmented; always in the present, we move from episode to episode toward the future, assessing the past. In the method and organization of *The Recognitions,* Gaddis enables us to "redeem time"—if we will.

Gaddis's images assail the reader with "all the vivid insistence of those irrelevant details which crowd a memory being probed for some calamity." *The Recognitions* is both the genesis and the raw material of a memory or consciousness that the author and the reader co-create. The repetitions of images and motifs result in deliberate *déjà vu.* "This self-sufficiency of fragments, that's where the curse is, fragments that don't belong to anything. Separately they don't mean anything, but it's almost impossible to pull them together in a whole," says Stanley. Poetic juxtaposition is Gaddis's most effective technique, and with the reader's complicity, he comes as close as any writer ever has to pulling his fragments together, to shoring them against his, and our, ruins. The achievement of the orchestration of Gaddis's technical devices is the creation, for the most attentive reader, of a sense of simultaneity, cohering not, as for most works of art, in a compressed, poetic image, but in a mental, and perhaps spiritual, state of recognition.

*The Recognitions* is a perfect prototype of the neglected novel. Its very last words construct a metaphor for many of the works rediscovered in this volume. Ignorant of the warning given him in Italian not to play too loudly, Stanley at last performs, pulling out all the stops, his lifelong composition on the organ in the ancient cathedral at Fenestrula, Italy: "Everything moved, and even falling, soared in atonement. He was the only person caught in the collapse, and afterward, most of his work was recovered too, and it is still spoken of, when it is noted, with high regard, though seldom played."

# FICTION DISCUSSED*

HARRIETTE ARNOW. *The Dollmaker* (1954). New York: Collier, Macmillan Co. (P).

MARIANO AZUELA. *The Underdogs* (*Los de Abajo*) (1915). Translated by E. Munguia, Jr. New York: Signet Books, New American Library (P).

WOLFGANG BORCHERT. *The Man Outside*. Translated by David Porter. London: Calder and Boyars, 1952 (OP).

HUMPHREY COBB. *Paths of Glory*. New York: The Viking Press, 1935 (OP).

BENJAMIN CONSTANT. *Adolphe* (1815). Translated by L. N. Tancock. London: Penguin (P).

NORMAN DOUGLAS. *South Wind* (1925). New York: Reprint House International.

ELIZABETH (COUNTESS MARY ANNETTE BEAUCHAMP RUSSELL). *The Pastor's Wife*. Garden City, N.Y.: Doubleday and Page, 1914 (OP).

DANIEL FUCHS. *Homage to Blenholt* (1936). New York: Basic Books, 1961 (OP).

WILLIAM GADDIS. *The Recognitions*. New York: Harcourt, Brace, 1955.

JEAN GIONO. *The Horseman on the Roof*. Translated by Jonathan Griffin. New York: Alfred A. Knopf, 1954 (OP).

MARCUS GOODRICH. *Delilah*. New York: Farrar & Rinehart, 1941 (OP).

---

* For explanation of symbols, see page 309.

CAROLINE GORDON. *The Malefactors*. New York: Harcourt, Brace, 1956 (OP).

WILLIAM GOYEN. *The House of Breath*. New York: Random House, 1950 (OP).

KNUT HAMSUN. *Growth of the Soil* (1921). Translated by W. W. Worster. New York: Alfred A. Knopf, 1953.

MARIANNE HAUSER. *A Lesson in Music*. Austin: University of Texas Press, 1964.

JANET LEWIS. *The Wife of Martin Guerre* (1941). Chicago: Swallow Press (P).

ANDREW LYTLE. *The Long Night*. Indianapolis and New York: Bobbs-Merrill Co., 1936 (OP).

FRANCIS MacMANUS. *Watergate*. Dublin: Talbot Press, 1942 (OP).

WILLIAM MAXWELL. *They Came Like Swallows* (1937). New York: Vintage, Random House (P).

WALTER M. MILLER, JR. *A Canticle for Leibowitz* (1959). Philadelphia: J. B. Lippincott Co. (P).

HENRY MYERS. *The Utmost Island*. New York: Crown Publishers, 1951 (OP).

BORIS PILNYAK. *The Volga Falls to the Caspian Sea* (1931). New York: AMS Press, 1970.

MARIO PUZO. *The Dark Arena* (1955). New York: Dell Publishing Co. (P).

RAMÓN SENDER. *A Man's Place*. New York: Duell, Sloan, and Pearce, 1940 (OP).

MARY LEE SETTLE. *O Beulah Land; Know Nothing; Fight Night on a Sweet Saturday*. New York: Viking Press, 1956 (OP), 1960 (OP), 1964.

GERTRUDE STEIN. *Things As They Are*. Pawlet, Vermont: Banyan Press, 1950 (OP).

GLENWAY WESCOTT. *Good-Bye Wisconsin.* New York: Harper & Bros., 1928 (OP).

RICHARD YATES. *Revolutionary Road.* Boston: Little, Brown & Co., 1961 (OP).

# A PARTIAL LIST OF OTHER FICTION WORTHY OF REDISCOVERY

Although hundreds of hours of research, correspondence, and consultation have gone into this annotated bibliography, we feel it should be considered a mere beginning. It has not been a chore: It has been, on the other hand, a delight, a challenge—and a puzzle. Our contributors, other writers and critics, colleagues, students, and friends have all made passionate nominations. Consequently, it is extremely interesting that a great majority of these titles have come up again and again—or different titles by the same author.

After a while, it became apparent that we had embarked on a continuing—if not an endless—research project; moreover, one which, if done properly, should perhaps involve a committee of writers and scholars of various disciplines and tongues. We concede that Anglo-Irish novelists are shortchanged here, but we are appalled how much more so are those novelists in other languages. Yet such a study is clearly beyond the scope of this book.

From the very beginning, we were caught up by a most vexing question: Just how does one account for the neglect of good fiction? Some good books just never seem to get anywhere; others are victims of time, fads, and fashions; and still others were instantly popular but dropped quickly from public consideration, prizes, book club selections or quondam bestsellerdom to no avail.

Some few surface now and again, never to get much more than a tip of the critical hat. *Parade's End,* Ford Madox Ford's great tetralogy, is a classic example of this kind of neglect, for it has been in and out of print several times since it was published forty-two years ago.

And so it goes. We hope others will devote more time to this sad problem of neglect.

In the annotations, we have cited several books that devote a good deal of discussion to neglected writers:

JOHN M. BRADBURY. *Renaissance in the South: A Critical History of the Literature, 1920–1960.* Chapel Hill, N.C.: University of North Carolina Press, 1963.

ANTHONY BURGESS. *The Novel Now: A Guide to Contemporary Fiction.* New York: W. W. Norton & Co., 1967. Reprinted in paperback by Pegasus Press, 1970.

CHESTER EISINGER. *Fiction of the Forties.* Chicago: University of Chicago Press, 1963.

GEOFFREY GRIGSON, ed. *The Concise Encyclopedia of Modern World Literature.* New York: Hawthorn Books, Inc., 1963.

DAVID MADDEN. *Proletarian Writers of the Thirties* and *Tough Guy Writers of the Thirties.* Carbondale, Ill.: Southern Illinois University Press, 1968.

We have also cited the Autumn, 1956, and the Spring, 1970, issues of the *American Scholar,* which contained features on neglected fiction as well as nonfiction. In addition, the Summer, 1970, issue contains letters in which further recommendations are made.
The letters OP indicate books *out of print.*
The letter P indicates books *in print in paperback.*
Where none of these letters are used, the book is *in print in hardcover.*
Hoping that reading through this annotated list will be a pleasure, we have tried to keep bibliographic data to a minimum. The fact that we have listed only one title by each author does not, of course, imply that his other works are not often equally worthy of "rediscovery." Looking back, we find some patterns and interrelationships that, within the context of the entire book, are quite fascinating. We hope the reader will find his own. May there be good times in secondhand bookstores throughout the nation and vigorous activity among the publishers.

> David Madden
> David McDowell

CHESTER AARON. *About Us.* New York: McGraw-Hill Book Co., 1967. "Best Russian novel written in English by an American."—Edwin Honig.

CONRAD AIKEN. *Great Circle.* New York: Charles Scribner's Sons, 1933 (OP). See Grigson.

Anonymous. *Madame Solario* (1956). New York: Ace Books (P).—Mary Renault, *American Scholar,* 1970.

DOROTHY BAKER. *Trio.* Boston: Houghton, Mifflin, 1943 (OP). "An enormously readable book, swift and tight, polished to the point of brilliance, and plotted with the kind of dramatic suspense which makes it impossible . . . to put it down again without racing through to the end."—Diana Trilling, *Nation.*

DJUNA BARNES. *Nightwood* (1937). New York: New Directions (P). "To say that *Nightwood* will appeal primarily to readers of poetry does not mean that it is not a novel, but that it is so good a novel that only sensibilities trained on poetry can wholly appreciate it. . . . What I would leave the reader prepared to find is the great achievement of a style, the beauty of phrasing, the brilliance of wit and characterization, and a quality of horror and doom very nearly related to that of Elizabethan tragedy."—T. S. Eliot, Introduction to the 1937 edition.

PÍO BAROJA. *Red Dawn* (*Aurora roja*) (1929). Third part of a trilogy. Translated by Isaac Goldberg. New York: French & European Publications (P). See Grigson.

WALTER BAXTER. *Look Down in Mercy.* New York: G. P. Putnam's Sons, 1952 (OP).—Henri Peyre, *American Scholar,* 1956.

THOMAS BEER. *Mrs. Egg and Other Americans.* Edited by Wilson Follett. New York: Alfred A. Knopf, 1947 (OP). "Mr. Beer's stories are as pleasantly entertaining as stories of this sort can be . . . a more polished, a more dexterous O. Henry."—Hamilton Basso, *New Yorker.*

YVES BERGER. *The Garden.* Translated by Robert Baldick. New York: George Braziller, 1963 (OP).

WENDELL BERRY. *A Place on Earth* (1967). New York: Avon Books (P).

ANDREY BIELY. *St. Petersburg* (1913–1916). Translated by John Cournos. New York: Evergreen, Grove Press (P). See Grigson.

JOHN PEALE BISHOP. *Act of Darkness* (1935). New York: Avon Books (P). Afterword, Leslie Fiedler.

LEONARD BISHOP. *Down All Your Streets*. New York: Dial Press, 1952 (OP). "You may not like it—you may find it positively unpleasant—but the chances are you will go on reading it, as I did, to the bitter end."—Maxwell Geismar, *Saturday Review*.

ISABEL BOLTON. *Many Mansions*. New York: Charles Scribner's Sons, 1952 (OP).—Babette Deutsch, *American Scholar*, 1970.

ROBERT O. BOWEN. *The Weight of the Cross*. New York: Alfred A. Knopf, 1951 (OP). See Eisinger.

JANE BOWLES. *Two Serious Ladies* (1943) in *The Collected Works of Jane Bowles*. New York: Noonday, Farrar, Straus & Giroux (P). "Both her language and her themes are sought after along tortured paths and in stony quarries: the never-realized relationships between her people, the mental and physical discomforts with which she surrounds and saturates them—every room an atrocity, every urban landscape a creation of neondourness. And yet, though the tragic view is central to her vision, Jane Bowles is a very funny writer, a humorist of sorts."—Truman Capote, Introduction.

PAUL BOWLES. *The Spider's House*. New York: Random House, 1955 (OP). "As writing, it is powerful and moving. As reporting, it goes far beyond what correspondents see or write. Few Americans have understood the forces at conflict in Morocco as well as Paul Bowles has done."—Ralph de Toledano, New York *Herald Tribune*.

GERALD WARNER BRACE. *The Garretson Chronicle* (1947). A trilogy. New York: W. W. Norton & Co. (P). Introduction, C. Hugh Holman. See Eisinger.

MILLEN BRAND. *The Outward Room*. New York: Simon & Schuster, 1937 (OP). "A brave novel about a woman who escaped from the fogs of today's misery into the sun of normality and happiness; a story as devoid of sentimentality as a blizzard, and yet a great love story—a real love story. I don't know that I have ever seen a more exciting first novel, and to Millen Brand, of whom I know nothing whatever, I present my most earnest greetings."—Sinclair Lewis.

HERMANN BROCH. *The Sleepwalkers* (1932). A trilogy. Translated by Willa and Edwin Muir. New York: Grosset & Dunlap (P). "The story of the Romantic who believes in honor, of the Anarchist who seeks a new faith, and of the Realist who destroys them both." "At its end [it] breaks into lyricism on one side and philosophy on the other."—Hannah Arendt, Introduction.

RICHARD BROOKS. *The Brick Foxhole*. New York: Harper & Bros., 1945 (OP). "I doubt whether any other book will catch so well the jittery rhythm of a world finishing a war and guessing at peace."—Niven Busch.

HEYWOOD BROUN. *Gandle Follows His Nose*. New York: Boni & Liveright, 1926 (OP).

HARRY BROWN. *A Walk in the Sun*. New York: Alfred A. Knopf, 1944 (OP). "This short novel describes a few hours with a few men on a beachhead in Italy. The book is by a soldier who is also a poet, and it is very good indeed."—John Hersey.

FREDERICK BUECHNER. *A Long Day's Dying*. New York: Alfred A. Knopf, 1950 (OP). "A novel of sheer magic. The richness of the prose, the delicacy in handling situations belong to a more refined era of American fiction. I think the book will be read by anyone curious as to what a wonderful novel can and does do."—John Horne Burns.

JERRY BUMPUS. *Anaconda*. Western Springs, Ill.: Special issue of *December,* 1967 (P). "Shook me more than any other piece of student work I've ever had. I can't forget it and I can't understand why it has never been published before."—Vance Bourjaily, quoted in the afterword by Curt Johnson, editor of *December.*

JOHN HORNE BURNS. *Lucifer with a Book*. New York: Harper & Bros., 1949 (OP). "Perhaps the most savagely and unjustly attacked book of its day."—Gore Vidal in "The Revelation of John Horne Burns."

JAMES M. CAIN. *The Butterfly*. New York: Alfred A. Knopf, 1947 (OP).

ITALO CALVINO. *Cosmicomics*. New York: Harcourt, Brace, 1968 (OP).—Dwight Macdonald, *American Scholar,* 1970.

ELIAS CANETTI. *Auto-da-fé* (1935). New York: Stein & Day (OP). See Grigson.

JOHN STEWART CARTER. *Full Fathom Five*. Boston: Houghton Mifflin, 1965.

BRAINARD CHENEY. *This Is Adam*. New York: McDowell, Obolensky, 1958. "This is by no means just another Southern book. Nor is it one about 'the problem.' It is not a book about the race question, save that the symbolism is an inescapable part of any such problem. Nor is it a book about 'the South.' It is a book about life and the part man played in it. I assuredly recommend it."—Ralph McGill, *Atlanta Constitution*.

G. K. CHESTERTON. *The Man Who Was Thursday* (1908). Capricorn, G. P. Putnam's Sons (P).

KATE CHOPIN. *The Awakening* (1899). New York: Capricorn, G. P. Putnam's Sons (P). *"The Awakening* was the most important piece of fiction about the sexual life of a woman written to date in America."—Larzer Ziff, *The American 1890s*. Also Stanley Kauffmann, *American Scholar,* 1970.

ELEANOR CLARK. *The Bitter Box*. Garden City, N.Y.: Doubleday, 1946 (OP). "A serious, funny, and truthful picture of Communist doings in this country, and therefore a work of courage . . . a work of unquestionable moral-political taste."—Diana Trilling, *Nation*.

WALTER VAN TILBURG CLARK. *The Watchful Gods and Other Stories*. New York: Random House, 1950 (OP). "One of the few distinguished 'first collections' to appear in our time, comparable with such volumes as Hemingway's *In Our Time,* Faulkner's *These Thirteen,* Caroline Gordon's *A Forest of the South,* and Eudora Welty's *A Curtain of Green.*"—Ray B. West, *Saturday Review*.

WALTER CLEMONS. *The Poison Tree*. Boston: Houghton Mifflin, 1959.

ROBERT COATES. *The Eater of Darkness* (1929). New York: Capricorn, G. P. Putnam's Sons (P). See Eisinger.

JOHN COBB. *The Gesture.* New York: Harper, 1949 (OP). See Eisinger.

CYRIL CONNOLLY. *The Rock Pool* (1936). New York: Atheneum, 1968. "The story, which owes something to *South Wind* and Compton Mackenzie's novels of Capri, differs from them through its acceleration, which has something demonical about it."—Edmund Wilson, *New Yorker.*

JACK CONROY. *The Disinherited* (1933). New York: Hill & Wang (P). Introduction, Daniel Aaron. See *Proletarian Writers of the Thirties.*

ALBERT COSSERY. *The House of Certain Death.* Translated by Stuart Kayser. Norfolk, Conn.: New Directions, 1949 (OP). "In *The House of Certain Death* the super-content is clear and obvious. We are all living in this house which the author writes about and which he has placed for convenience in Egypt. . . . It is a house which has a crack in it, and this crack has now spread through every country in the world. . . . It is the sort of house which, if the powers that be persist in ignoring the crack, can be transported by its real owners to 'the dear government' itself for inspection."—Henry Miller, in an Open Letter to American Critics.

JAMES GOULD COZZENS. *Castaway* (1934). New York: Harvest, Harcourt, Brace (P). "A modern Gothic novel set in a department store in a large American city." Written in the midst of the Depression, it "caught perhaps better than any other single work (being untroubled by ideology) the mood of the times."—Leslie Fiedler, *Proletarian Writers of the Thirties.*

HUBERT CREEKMORE. *The Chain in the Heart.* New York: Random House, 1953 (OP). "Written with power and a healthy amount of bitterness, and also with a good deal of pride. . . . It is a convincing story about people who come to life as we read and continue to interest us after the book ends."—*New Yorker.*

RAYMOND DE CAPITE. *A Lost King.* New York: McKay, 1961 (OP).

JOHN WILLIAM DE FOREST. *Miss Ravenel's Conversion from Secession to Loyalty* (1867). New York: Harcourt, Brace and World (P).

FLOYD DELL. *Moon-calf* (1920). New York: Hill and Wang (P). "Moments of unexpected loveliness . . . in the story of Felix Fay's childhood, after which the author writes carefully until adolescence with all its terrors sets in. . . . The author has surprised his enemies. . . . *Moon-calf* . . . has the importance of showing how serious and how well-composed an American novel can be. . . ."—Ezra Pound, *Dial*.

NIGEL DENNIS. *Cards of Identity*. New York: Vanguard Press, 1955. "I have read no novel during the last fifteen years with greater pleasure and admiration."—W. H. Auden.

G. V. DESANI. *All About H. Hatterr* (1948). New York: Farrar, Straus & Giroux. Introduction, Anthony Burgess.

MARGUERITE DORIAN. *A Ride on the Milky Way*. New York: Crown Publishers, 1967 (OP). "This is a lyric, impressionistic, yet fearfully accurate writing in that tradition which might be called the dynamics of delicacy—that of such distinguished writers as Walter de la Mare, Elizabeth Bowen, Anaïs Nin, John Updike, with their fusion of myth, psychology, poetry in every sentence. Miss Dorian belongs to this galaxy."—Marguerite Young.

COLEMAN DOWELL. *One of the Children Is Crying*. New York: Random House, 1968 (OP).

EDOUARD DUJARDIN. *We'll to the Woods No More* (1887). Translated by Stuart Gilbert. New York: New Directions, 1957. Introduction, Leon Edel.

HARRY STILLWELL EDWARDS. *Aeneas Africanus*. Macon, Ga.: J. W. Burke, 1927 (OP).

CARADOC EVANS. *My People: Stories of the Peasantry of West Wales*. London: A. Melrose, 1915 (OP). See Grigson.

WARREN EYSTER. *The Goblins of Eros*. New York: Random House, 1957 (OP). "Mr. Eyster is so sound, so preternaturally profound and penetrating about Mexican places and psychology, the looks and smells of one, the subtle gradations of the other—that the most exacting local reader has to wave his hat and shout *olé*."—*Mexico City News*.

RONALD FIRBANK. *Prancing Nigger* (1922). New York: New Directions (P). Edmund Wilson has called Firbank "one of the finest English writers of his period and one of those most likely to become a classic."

VARDIS FISHER. *Children of God.* New York: Vanguard, 1939. "Vardis Fisher has brought something approaching genius to [the Mormon story]. His novel has done the whole thing, from beginning to end, and with grace, and dignity and understanding and simplicity."—F. T. Marsh, *New York Times.*

ZELDA FITZGERALD. *Save Me the Waltz* (1932). New York: Signet, New American Library (P). Introduction, Harry T. Moore.

FORD MADOX FORD. *Parade's End* (1925). Tetralogy in two volumes. New York: Signet, New American Library (P). Afterword, Arthur Mizener. "It is easier now to read the Tietjens novels than when they were first written. It is becoming apparent that when he wrote them Ford was writing history."—Caroline Gordon, *New York Times Book Review.*

MICHAEL FRAENKEL. *Werther's Younger Brother.* Carrefour, 1930 (OP). "Novel of a young man's discovery of his inner death." —Howard McCord.

WALDO FRANK. *The Death and Birth of David Markand.* New York: Charles Scribner's Sons, 1934. "If he wrote poetry . . . we would take him as we take Robinson Jeffers, and never bother about any correspondence with material reality. As it stands, Mr. Frank's novel invites too obviously the scrutiny that fictional argument must undergo; and the poetry of it gets neglected."—Donald Davidson, *American Review.*

HAROLD FREDERIC. *The Damnation of Theron Ware* (1896). New York: Harvest, Harcourt, Brace, and World (P).

JOSEPH FREEMAN. *Never Call Retreat.* New York: Farrar and Rinehart, 1943 (OP). See Eisinger.

SANFORD FRIEDMAN. *A Haunted Woman.* New York: E. P. Dutton & Co., 1968.—Mark Strand, *American Scholar,* 1970.

MAX FRISCH. *I'm Not Stiller.* New York: Vintage, Random House, 1958 (P).

RENÉ FÜLOP-MILLER. *The Night of Time.* Indianapolis: Bobbs-Merrill Co., 1955.—Hiram Haydn, *American Scholar,* 1956.

WILLIAM GERHARDI. *Futility.* London: Duffield, 1922 (OP).—C. P. Snow, *American Scholar,* 1970.

LEWIS GRASSIC GIBBON. *A Scots Quair* (1932–34). A trilogy. London: Jarrolds, 1946 (OP). See Grigson.

BRENDAN GILL. *The Trouble of One House.* New York: Doubleday, 1950 (OP). "Not a false note is struck in this mature and honest novel. Although the book is beautifully contrived, there is no creak of machinery. Each person, down to the wry, engaging little son, is vivid, complex and always understandably motivated, and the style is consistently quiet and subtle."—Kate Simon, *New Republic.*

PAUL GOODMAN. *The Break-up of Our Camp and Other Stories.* Norfolk, Conn.: New Directions, 1949 (OP).

LESTER GORAN. *The Candy Butcher's Farewell.* New York: McGraw-Hill Book Co., 1964 (OP).

CAROLINE GORDON. *Aleck Maury, Sportsman.* New York: Charles Scribner's Sons, 1934 (OP). "At a time when topicality and innovation seem to be everything to many readers, some reminder should be given that such a masterpiece as Caroline Gordon's *Aleck Maury, Sportsman* still exists. Those who read it thirty years ago can hardly have forgotten the superb craftsmanship, the profound character drawing, the poetry the novel finally achieves in the meaningful relationship of all its elements."—Peter Taylor, *American Scholar,* 1970.

CAROL GRACE. *The Secret in the Daisy.* New York: Random House, 1955 (OP). "Often the simple language of this book achieves freshness and interest. The author has a genuine gift for the graphic phrase. . . . she has introduced us to a disarming personality, sophisticated and childlike, imaginative and skeptical."—Gene Baro, New York *Herald Tribune.*

JULIEN GRACQ. *The Castle of Argol.* Translated by Louise Varese. Norfolk, Conn.: New Directions, 1951 (OP). "Gracq's extraordinarily conscious art has already been likened more to the painter's than to that of the writer. And, indeed, Heide and Albert walking down the geometrically traced avenue of trees that closes behind them gives one the illusion of an animated Dali."—Justin O'Brien, *New York Times*.

JULIAN GREEN. *The Dark Journey*. Translated by Vyvyan Holland. New York: Harper, 1929. "The originality of the author's mind is more freely disengaged in this book than in previous ones. And the sombre power of the tragedy is . . . tremendous. Mr. Green is assuredly of the lineage of great novelists." —Arnold Bennett.

DAVIS GRUBB. *Night of the Hunter* (1953). New York: Avon Books (P). "A moving and darkly disturbing book. There is power, poetry, imagination . . . much achievement and great promise."—Walter Van Tilburg Clark.

ALBERT J. GUERARD. *The By-stander*. Boston: Little, Brown & Co., 1958. "An original work in its own right. . . . If the book's reverberations do not carry beyond the confines of its own small, decadent world, it nevertheless casts a strong spell . . . the style is virtually flawless."—Dan Wickenden, *New York Herald Tribune Book Review*.

JAMES B. HALL. *Not by the Door*. New York: Random House, 1954 (OP). "The primary virtue of this book is that it presents its subject clear and plain, and leaves him to us, as readers, to judge him without authorial labeling or interpretation. Implications of course abound, and they are often critical; and Howard suffers under them. Yet even under their weight he remains a real and understandable human being."—Richard Sullivan, *New York Times*.

OAKLEY HALL. *Warlock*. New York: Viking Press, 1958 (OP). "Hall's sense of unavoidable tragedy . . . holds *Warlock* together. . . . This is not only an important addition to the short list of serious novels about the Western frontier; it is on any grounds a solid and impressive piece of fiction, marking Oakley Hall's growth in imaginative grasp and in craftsmanship."—Granville Hicks, *Saturday Review*.

ELIZABETH HARDWICK. *The Simple Truth*. New York: Harcourt, Brace, 1955 (OP). "Elizabeth Hardwick is a crack shot, and in this book she doesn't miss any of us today. *The Simple Truth* is *An American Tragedy* NOW."—J. F. Powers.

ALAN HARRINGTON. *The Revelations of Dr. Modesto* (1955). New York: Avon Books (P).

L. P. HARTLEY. *Eustace and Hilda* (1947). A trilogy. Chester Springs, Pa.: Dufour. "Certainly Hartley's quiet, unpretentious fiction . . . deserves consideration as serious as that which should be given any written in our century. . . . Shows dramatically the possibility of individual salvation. . . ."— Harvey Curtis Webster, *After the Trauma.*

MILDRED HAUN. *The Hawk's Done Gone* (1940). Nashville, Tenn.: Vanderbilt University Press. "The human predicament done in terms of a natural world, which does not forbid the supernatural. Mildred Haun has the true sense of a certain people, removed from a (so-called) more advanced kind of society." —Andrew Lytle.

MARIANNE HAUSER. *The Choir Invisible.* New York: McDowell, Obolensky, 1958. "A novel of great literary and artistic merit, a novel with an exquisite prose style. . . . There are doubtless few readers who can fail to agree that Miss Hauser has made a genuine spiritual investment here, bringing light to the mysteries of human nature."—Marguerite Young, New York *Herald Tribune.*

JOHN HAWKES. *The Cannibal* (1949). New York: New Directions (P). "John Hawkes clearly belongs . . . with the cold immoralists and pure creators who enter sympathetically into all their characters, the saved and the damned alike. . . . to understand everything is to ridicule everything. . . . a total vision of horror."—Introduction, Albert J. Guerard.

WILLIAM HAY. *The Escape of the Notorious Sir William Hean (and the Mystery of Mr. Daunt): A Romance of Tasmania.* Melbourne: Melbourne University Press, 1955.

HIRAM HAYDN. *The Hands of Esau.* New York: Harper, 1962 (OP).—Anaïs Nin, *American Scholar,* 1970.

BASIL HEATTER. *The Dim View.* New York: Farrar, Straus, 1946 (OP). "No other piece of writing I know has so clearly and frankly caught the talk of fighting men . . . has told so moving and complete and satisfying a love story."—Merle Miller, *Saturday Review.*

CECIL HEMLEY. *Young Cranshaw*. London: Constable, 1963 (OP).

JOSEPHINE HERBST. *Nothing Is Sacred*. New York: Coward-Mc-Cann, 1928 (OP).

VICTOR ALEXANDER SERELD HEY. *Ferelith*. London: Hutchinson, 1903 (OP). See Grigson.

GRANVILLE HICKS. *Only One Storm*. New York: Macmillan Book Co., 1942 (OP).

ROY HORNIMAN. *Israel Rank*. London: Chatto and Windus, 1907 (OP). Novel from which the movie *Kind Hearts and Coronets* was made. See Grigson.

MAUDE HUTCHINS. *Victorine* (1950). Chicago: Swallow Press. "Without any use of explicit language, Maude Hutchins, who is the equivalent of Colette in descriptions of erotic relationships, describes vividly and cinematically love scenes which are far more effective than those of many plainspoken writers. She is one of our most aristocratic of writers. . . . Any of her books can be read for a lesson in style, in sensual grace." —Anaïs Nin, *The Novel of the Future*.

ILF and PETROV. *Diamonds to Sit On*. New York: Harper, 1930 (OP). See Grigson.

CHRISTOPHER ISHERWOOD. *Prater Violet*. New York: Ballantine (P).—Brian Glanville, *American Scholar*, 1970.

RANDALL JARRELL. *Pictures from an Institution* (1954). New York: Farrar, Straus & Giroux (P). "This is the most appallingly witty novel in years. . . . Here is a savagery of insight delicately restrained and a command of language that is gay, gruesome, and absolute."—Paul Engle, *Chicago Sunday Tribune*.

JOHANNES V. JENSEN. *The Fall of the King*. New York: Henry Holt, 1933 (OP).

GLYN JONES. *The Water Music and Other Stories*. London: Routledge, 1945 (OP). See Grigson.

MADISON JONES. *The Innocent.* New York: Harcourt, Brace, 1957 (OP). "A sureness of touch, a fullness of experience and somber currents of emotion distinguish this first novel by an able young Southern writer."—Walter Havighurst, *Chicago Sunday Times.*

ERNST JUENGER. *On the Marble Cliffs.* Translated by Stuart Hood. New York: New Directions, 1947 (OP).—W. S. Merwin, *American Scholar,* 1970.

I. J. KAPSTEIN. *Something of a Hero.* New York: Alfred A. Knopf, 1941 (OP).—J. H. Plumb, *American Scholar,* 1970.

VALENTINE KATAEV. *The Embezzlers.* New York: Dial Press, 1929 (OP).

THEODORA KEOGH. *Meg.* New York: Creative Age, 1950 (OP). "Meg herself is a coruscating thing, a denizen of that buried land of childhood which . . . claims the whole world for its precinct."—Patricia Highsmith.

GERALD KERSH. *Fowlers End.* New York: Simon & Schuster, 1957 (OP). "Mr. Kersh diagrams Laverock's adventures with great relish and with an infectious delight in the complete gaminess of the landscape . . . a generally entertaining escapade that is fun to read."—Martin Levin.

JOSEPHINE LAWRENCE. *If I Have Four Apples.* New York: Stokes, 1935 (OP). "One of the pleasures of settling down with literature of a time past is the joy of discovery. I had never come across any of Josephine Lawrence's books, and, since it is fashionable . . . to make a 'find,' I claim Miss Lawrence's novel."—Gerald Green, *Proletarian Writers of the Thirties.*

WYNDHAM LEWIS. *Revenge for Love* (1937). Chicago: Regnery, 1952 (OP). "A great novel . . . the almost perfect articulation of a vision, poised and paradoxically quiet, though the vision is what Lewis has elsewhere called 'the black material of social truth': Nietzsche's and Machiavelli's vision of the world as a void informed by mere power."—Hugh Kenner, *Wyndham Lewis.*

LUDWIG LEWISOHN. *The Case of Mr. Crump* (1947). New York: Noonday, Farrar, Straus & Giroux (P). "We have here a novelistic document of life, of the *inferno* of a marriage. That word exhausts the book's horrifying and infuriating subject matter—a marriage that should never have been contracted nor would have been save for the man's weakness and youthful inexperience."—Thomas Mann, Introduction.

DAVID LINDSAY. *Voyage to Arcturus* (1946). New York: Ballantine (P).

J. J. FERNÁNDEZ DE LIZARDI. *The Itching Parrot* (1816). New York: Appleton-Century-Crofts. "His one novel that he had never meant to write, which had got itself suppressed in its eleventh chapter, is without dispute The Novel of the past century, not only for Mexico but for all Spanish-speaking countries." "It is not his moral disquisitions, then, nor his portrayal of character, nor his manner of telling his story, that keeps *El Periquillo* alive after more than a hundred years: it is simply and broadly the good show he managed to get out of the sights and sounds and smells of his native town."— Katherine Anne Porter, Introduction to the 1942 Doubleday edition.

ROMULUS LINNEY. *Heathen Valley.* New York: Atheneum, 1962 (OP). "It is a pleasure to discover a book such as this: a first novel with a powerful original idea . . . beautified by a deep concern for positive morality and religion . . . a book to remember."—Gilbert Highet.

MARGARET LONG. *Affair of the Heart.* New York: Random House, 1953 (OP). "A warm engaging full-length portrait of a southern town."—Coleman Rosenberger, New York *Herald Tribune.*

ROBERT LOWRY. *Casualty.* New York: New Directions, 1946 (OP). "The most uncompromising indictment of the military system to appear since *The Brick Foxhole.*"—David Dempsey, *New York Times Book Review.*

PERCY LUBBOCK. *Roman Pictures.* New York: Charles Scribner's Sons, 1923 (OP).

ALISON LURIE. *The Nowhere City* (1965). New York: Avon Books (P).

ANDREW LYTLE. *The Velvet Horn*. New York: McDowell, Obolensky, 1957 (OP). "It tells a cunningly plotted story. It speaks with a radiant seduction of language, and the exalted lyric monologues of one of its characters, Jack Croplcigh, can stand beside those of *Nightwood*'s Doctor O'Connor. There is resonance and overtone everywhere, and its wild Cumberland woodlands are so shimmering with vision and 'correspondences' that their mighty white oaks seem like so many of Baudelaire's *vivants piliers*."—Robert Phelps, *National Review*.

JAMES McCONKEY. *Crossroads*. New York: Dutton, 1968.— Joyce Carol Oates, *American Scholar,* 1970.

VINCENT McHUGH. *The Victory*. New York: Random House, 1947 (OP). See Eisinger.

THOMAS MABRY and WARD DORRANCE. *The White Hound*. Stories. Columbia, Mo.: University of Missouri Press, 1959. Introduction, Caroline Gordon.

ROBIE MACAULEY. *The Disguises of Love*. New York: Random House, 1952. "Mr. Macauley, whose critical work on the fiction of Ford Madox Ford has served him well, has worked very commonplace materials into an extremely good novel through the exercise of an interplay of points of view, principally those of the three members of the family."—Frederick J. Hoffman, *Saturday Review*.

ALBERT MALTZ. *The Cross and the Arrow* (1944). New York: Pyramid Press. See Eisinger.

FREDERICK MANFRED. *Lord Grizzly* (1954). New York: Signet, New American Library (P). "Manfred has magnificent qualities as a novelist: a fine and basic honesty, tremendous power of observation, considerable knowledge both of nature and of humanity by which to direct his observation, a Whitman-like enthusiasm for life."—George R. Stewart, *New York Times*.

FREDERIC MANNING. *Her Privates We*. London: Davies, 1930 (OP). See Grigson.

OLIVIA MANNING. *The Great Fortune*. A trilogy. London: Heinemann, 1960. "The most important long work of fiction to have been written by an English woman novelist since the war . . . one of the finest records we have of the impact of that war on Europe."—Anthony Burgess.

PIERRE MARCELIN. *The Pencil of God*. Boston: Houghton Mifflin, 1951 (OP).

WILLIAM MARCH. *Company K* (1933). New York: Hill & Wang (P). "There is courage, there is terror; there is lust and cruelty and stupidity and affection."—Phyllis Bentley.

ROGER MARTIN DU GARD. *The Postman* (1933). Translated by John Russell. New York: Viking Press, 1955 (OP).

EDGAR LEE MASTERS. *Kit O'Brien*. New York: Boni & Liveright, 1927 (OP).

SILAS WEIR MITCHELL. *Hugh Wynne, Free Quaker*. New York: The Century Company, 1896 (OP).

ELSA MORANTE. *House of Liars*. New York: Harcourt, Brace, 1951 (OP). See Grigson.

CHRISTOPHER MORLEY. *Thunder on the Left*. Garden City, N.Y.: Doubleday, Page, 1925 (OP). "The chief person in the book, George Granville, is so immensely and vividly present as to appear a self-portrait—or, even more truly, a portrait of the reader's self, the funny tragic essence of our humanity, fumbling from brave immaturity toward the cruelties of spiritual adulthood. He alone would make this a fine book. And he is not alone."—Babette Deutsch.

WRIGHT MORRIS. *The Works of Love* (1952). Reprinted in *Wright Morris: A Reader*. New York: Harper & Row. Introduction, Granville Hicks. "A mystical epic about the 'blighting' effect of a single-minded pursuit of the American Dream of Success."—David Madden, *Wright Morris*.

ROBERT MUSIL. *The Man Without Qualities* (1930, 1933, 1943). New York: Capricorn, G. P. Putnam's Sons.

L. H. MYERS. *The Root and the Flower*. London: Jonathan Cape, 1935 (OP).—Paul B. Sears, *American Scholar*, 1956.

ROBERT NATHAN. *Portrait of Jennie* (1940). New York: Popular Library (P). "I doubt if anyone today could have told Mr. Nathan's story with greater tenderness or with quite the blend of humor and imagination which the book has on every page and which might serve almost as Mr. Nathan's signature."— William Maxwell.

P. H. NEWBY. *The Barbary Light*. London: Faber & Faber, 1962. "Newby's prose-style, with its hallucinatory concentration on detail, is the perfect medium for presenting life's fitful fever." —Anthony Burgess.

FLANN O'BRIEN. *At Swim-Two-Birds* (1939). New York: Compass, Viking Press (P). "If I were cultural dictator in England I would make *At Swim-Two-Birds* compulsory reading in all our universities."—Philip Toynbee.

TILLIE OLSEN. *Tell Me a Riddle*. Philadelphia: J. B. Lippincott Co., 1961 (OP). "These stories . . . are to be read, experienced, pondered. They go deep, perhaps because they are both deeply felt and controlled by a disciplined intelligence."— Gene Baro, New York *Herald Tribune*.

YURI KARLOVICH OLYESHA. *Envy*. Toronto: Longmans, 1936 (OP). See Grigson.

SHÔHEI OOKA. *Fires on the Plain*. New York: Penguin, 1957 (P). See Grigson.

GIL ORLOVITZ. *Milkbottle H* (1968). New York: Dell Publishing Co. (P). "Gil Orlovitz's first novel, *Milkbottle H* . . . didn't do well at all. American reviewers at best regarded it with grudging and tentative praise and at worst with snarling invective. . . . Orlovitz is fifty-one years old and for years has been highly regarded by the literary underground. . . . Gil Orlovitz's opinion of his own work is very high, and his utterances on the subject are often haughty. Self-indulgence is a mainspring and a motive of art—for both the artist and his audience. It is in the *evaluation* of art that excessive self-indulgence is a danger and deserves contempt."—Hale Chatfield, *Kenyon Review*.

KENNETH PATCHEN. *Journal of Albion Moonlight* (1941). New York: New Directions (P).

ELLIOT PAUL. *Indelible.* Boston: Houghton Mifflin, 1922. *"Indelible* is not a first novel remarkable for its freedom from obvious faults. But it is very truly remarkable for the positive qualities . . . there is a quite professional sanity on the whole subject of music and musicians."—Wilson Follett, *Atlantic.*

CESARE PAVESE. *The Moon and the Bonfire.* Modern European Library Service, 1949 (OP). See Grigson.

MERVYN PEAKE. *Titus Groan* (1946). New York: Ballantine (P). "Having become a coterie favorite, it may yet be confirmed as a modern classic."—Anthony Burgess.

ANN PETRY. *The Street* (1946). New York: Pyramid Press (P). "Mrs. Petry knows what it is to live as a Negro in New York city and she also knows how to put it down on paper so that it is as scathing an indictment of our society as has ever appeared. . . ."—Bucklin Moon, *New Republic.*

ROBERT PHELPS. *Heroes and Orators.* New York: McDowell, Obolensky, 1958. "Capote and Gore Vidal (as novelist rather than TV entertainer) have come to seem a little old hat, and even Paul Bowles begins to look like an enthusiasm of yesterday, while a serious new writer like Robert Phelps produces in *Heroes and Orators* a complex and troubling study of homosexual love that goes unnoticed."—Leslie Fiedler, *Love and Death in the American Novel.*

DAVID GRAHAM PHILLIPS. *Susan Lenox, Her Fall and Rise* (1917). New York: AMS Press.

ERNEST POOLE. *The Harbor* (1915). New York: Hill & Wang (P).

CRAWFORD POWER. *The Encounter* (1950). New York: Avon Books (P). Afterword, Irving Howe.—James Dickey, *American Scholar,* 1970.

T. F. POWYS. *Mr. Weston's Good Wine* (1927). New York: Reprint House International. "God comes as a wine-merchant (his good wine is death) to the village of Folly Down."—Anthony Burgess.

FREDERIC PROKOSCH. *The Asiatics.* New York: Harper & Row, 1935 (OP). "It is the work of a man of a deeply poetic nature possessed of an astonishing ability to describe in a few words a color, a scene, an odor, an emotional situation, an attitude of mind, an idea."—L. H. Titterton, *New York Times.*

RAYMOND RADIGUET. *Devil in the Flesh.* Translated by Kay Boyle. New York: Crosby Continental Editions, 1932 (OP). "The work of a boy who has lived through many of the experiences of manhood. . . . Radiguet set out in possession of those literary values with which most writers painfully end. . . . Radiguet was still a boy when he died."—Aldous Huxley, Introduction to the 1949 Signet edition.

PIOTR RAWICZ. *Blood from the Sky.* Translated by Peter Wiles. New York: Harcourt, Brace, 1964.—Theodore Solotaroff and Stanley Kauffmann in *American Scholar,* 1970.

HERBERT READ. *The Green Child* (1935). New York: New Directions (P). A political allegory that "is one of the most sustained products of conscious rapture in our literature."— Kenneth Rexroth, Introduction. T. S. Eliot called it one of the finest examples of English prose style of our century.

LUDWIG RENN. *War.* New York: Dodd, Mead, 1929 (OP). See Grigson.

EUGENE M. RHODES. *Beyond the Desert* (1934). Lincoln, Neb.: University of Nebraska Press (P). Introduction, W. Hutchinson. "This story of Shanc McFarland's adventures out West during the panic of 1893 is probably the last of Eugene Manlove Rhodes's superior historical cowboy romances."—Will Cuppy, *Books.*

JEAN RHYS. *The Left Bank.* Stories. New York: Harper, 1927 (OP). Introduction, Ford Madox Ford. See Grigson.

DOROTHY RICHARDSON. *Pilgrimage* (1938). A twelve-volume novel. New York: Alfred A. Knopf, 1967. "The most abominably unknown contemporary writer."—Ford Madox Ford. "Until Dorothy Richardson has been given her proper place, there will be a great gap in our sense of the growth of the English novel."—Elizabeth Bowen.

HENRY HANDLE RICHARDSON. *The Fortunes of Richard Mahony* (1917, 1929, 1931). New York: The Press of the Readers

Club, 1941 (OP). "The trilogy met with not one-tenth of the excitement it merited. But now, with *Ultima Thule* a little forgotten, we can start all over again . . . a book of certain greatness, of which you actually may use the ordinarily impertinent phrase 'you must read it.' . . . a truly major work of fiction of the twentieth century. . . . Americans, most of them, are going to be a little astonished by the parallel of our own pioneering, and the harsher places of our land, with those of Australia. . . . When it was published, it was ahead of its time. I believe that now it is just at its time."—Sinclair Lewis, Foreword.

CONRAD RICHTER. *The Awakening Land* (*The Trees, The Fields, The Town*). New York: Alfred A. Knopf, 1969.—Carlos Baker, *American Scholar,* 1970.

LAURA RIDING. *Progress of Stories.* New York: Random House, 1937 (OP).—Susan Sontag, *American Scholar,* 1970.

ELIZABETH MADOX ROBERTS. *The Time of Man* (1926). New York: Compass, Viking Press (P). "Ellen Chesser . . . struggles in the dire poverty of the poor white, in ignorance, in rejection by the world and by her first lover, toward her spiritual fulfillment." Beyond naïve wonder and the deeper wonder at the growth of selfhood, there is a sense of life as ceremony, as ritual even in the common duties, as an enactment that numinously embodies the relation of the self to its setting in nature, in the human community, and in time."—Robert Penn Warren, Introduction.

FREDERICK WILLIAM ROLFE (BARON CORVO). *The Desire and Pursuit of the Whole* (1913). New York: New Directions.

LOUIS D. RUBIN, JR. *The Golden Weather.* New York: Atheneum, 1961 (OP). "Mr. Rubin is a storyteller with a fine sense of mood and shadow, rather than a writer of clinical reports in fiction form, which puts him well in the lead among many contemporaries."—E. S. Miers, *Saturday Review.*

JAMES SALTER. *A Sport and a Pastime.* Garden City, N.Y.: Doubleday & Co., 1967.

GEORGE SANTAYANA. *The Last Puritan* (1936). New York: Charles Scribner's Sons (P).

MARK SCHORER. *The Hermit Place.* New York: Random House, 1941 (OP). "Its plot, highly intellectual and dramatically tense, might have come from the pen of Henry James. It derives its weighty rhythm and color from one brilliant central idea around which the story rotates in narrow circles. The idea is extraordinary and hot as a flame."—Marianne Hauser.

ANDRÉ SCHWARZ-BART. *The Last of the Just.* New York: Atheneum, 1960 (OP).—Henry A. Murray, *American Scholar,* 1970.

EVELYN SCOTT. *The Wave.* New York: Jonathan Cape and Harrison Smith, 1929 (OP). See Bradbury.

ALLAN SEAGER. *Equinox.* New York: Simon & Schuster, 1943 (OP). "A mad, bad, and dangerous book."—Diana Trilling, *Nation.*

JORGE SEMPRUN. *The Last Voyage.* Translated by Richard Seaver. New York: Grove Press, 1964 (OP). "Amid the many fictionalized reports of the Nazi concentration camps, only a work of art embodying the significant shape, essence, and meaning of that massive experience can ultimately concern us as both life *and* literature."—David Madden, *Kenyon Review.*

MATTHEW PHIPPS SHIEL. *How the Old Woman Got Home.* Stories. New York: Vanguard Press, 1928 (OP).

DAVID STACTON. *A Dancer in Darkness.* New York: Pantheon, 1962 (OP).

LEON STATHAM. *Welcome Darkness.* New York: Crowell, 1950 (OP). See Eisinger.

CHRISTINA STEAD. *The Man Who Loved Children* (1940). New York: Avon Books (P). "It has one quality that, ordinarily, only a great book has: it does a single thing better than any other book has ever done it. . . . If all mankind had been reared in orphan asylums for a thousand years, it could learn to have families again by reading *The Man Who Loved Children.* . . . The book has an almost frightening power of remembrance."—Randall Jarrell, Introduction.

MAX STEELE. *Debby* (1950). Reissued as *The Goblins Must Go Barefoot.* New York: Perennial Library, Harper, 1966

(OP). Harper Prize Novel. "A deeply touching work upon a theme of great humane significance by an extraordinarily gifted author. . . . We are given beauty and indeed a certain joyousness . . . and at the close we are left with a feeling of the greatness of the narrative."—Glenway Wescott.

WILBUR DANIEL STEELE. *Best Stories of Wilbur Daniel Steele.* Garden City, N.Y.: Doubleday & Co., 1946 (OP). "Stories superbly told. Their appearance in one volume fittingly places Steele . . . in the first rank of the American storyteller of his time."—Edith R. Mirrielees, *New York Times.*

JAMES STILL. *On Troublesome Creek.* New York: Viking Press, 1941 (OP). See Bradbury.

FRANK STOCKTON. *The Lady or the Tiger? and Other Stories* (1907). New York: Airmont (P).

T. S. STRIBLING. *The Store* (1932). Part of a trilogy. New York: Bergman (OP). "It is easy to forgive him this preoccupation with white injustice and black resignation, because of the fierce, convincing sincerity which he gives to his novel."— Jonathan Daniels.

HOWARD STURGIS. *Belchamber* (1904). London: Duckworth, 1965 (OP). Introduction, Alan Harris.

ITALO SVEVO. *The Confessions of Zeno* (1923). New York: Vintage, Random House (P).

CHRISTOPHER SYKES. *Character and Situation.* New York: Alfred A. Knopf, 1950 (OP).

HARRY SYLVESTER. *Dayspring.* New York: D. Appleton-Century, 1945 (OP). See Eisinger.

ALLEN TATE. *The Fathers* (1938). Chicago: Swallow Press (P). "The story displays so much imagination and such a profound reflection upon life that it cannot be neglected by anyone interested in contemporary literature."—Edwin Muir.

PETER H. TAYLOR. *A Woman of Means.* New York: Harcourt, Brace, 1950 (OP). "Page by firm page, sentence by animated sentence, this brief novel moves with the quality of the best modern fiction. Quietly it establishes its situations, and then goes on to reveal with an astonishing combination of clarity and subtlety the drives and distortions of its characters."— Paul Engle, *Chicago Sunday Times.*

WALTER TEVIS. *The Man Who Fell to Earth* (1963). New York: Lancer Books (P).

B. TRAVEN. *The Death Ship* (1926). New York: Collier, Macmillan Co. (P). "The finest modern sea story I have ever read." —James Hanley.

LIONEL TRILLING. *The Middle of the Journey* (1947). New York: Avon Books (P). See Eisinger.

JIM TULLY. *Shadows of Men.* Garden City, N.Y.: Doubleday, Doran, 1930 (OP). "A ham-fisted primitive. . . . Genet's pederasts, Burroughs's junkies, and all the minor scarecrows— Selby, Rechy, Schneck, LeRoi Jones—are schoolboys alongside old Tully. And he at least has the virtue of absolute honesty, of innocence."—Gerald Green, *Proletarian Writers of the Thirties.*

AMOS TUTUOLA. *The Palm-Wine Drinkard* (1953). New York: Grove Press (P). "This is the brief, thronged, grisly and bewitching story, written in young English by a West African, about the journey of an expert and devoted palm-wine drinkard through a nightmare of indescribable adventures."— Dylan Thomas.

CARL VAN VECHTEN. *Firecrackers.* New York: Alfred A. Knopf, 1925 (OP). "He has hit upon a world in which his imagination moves easily. He has invented a language which is his and no one else's."—Carl Van Doren.

EDWARD LEWIS WALLANT. *The Tenants of Moonbloom* (1963). New York: Popular Library (P).

FRANK WATERS. *The Man Who Killed the Deer* (1942). Chicago: Swallow Press (P). "Perhaps the best book yet written on the American Indian."—Stephen Vincent Benét.

ROBERT WERNICK. *The Freebooters.* New York: Charles Scribner's Sons, 1949 (OP). "The book succeeds in catching—you can't create them—the myths of war. . . . His is an entertaining

book, over its hard core of bitterness. It never lectures, and
yet the intricacy of the race problem in the Army—which is
not a major theme at all—is presented both humorously and
dramatically, with an unobtrusive force that may not hit you
until you are all through reading."—Vance Bourjaily, *San
Francisco Chronicle.*

ANTHONY C. WEST. *The Native Moment.* New York: McDowell,
Obolensky, 1959 (OP). "A great gift of language always
seems like a kind of magic, and indeed it is. Mr. West's use of
words is not merely wonderfully fresh; it is wonderfully exact.
He is obviously a writer with a mind, and, boldly as he thrusts
out towards the very limits of what language can do, his control rarely falters. His material is the emotions, and skill with
which he can render them is matched by the subtlety with
which he understands them."—Granville Hicks, *Saturday Review.*

DAN WICKENDEN. *The Running of the Deer.* New York: William
Morrow, 1937 (OP). "Mr. Wickenden is quite young and it
seems a shame to afflict him with the word 'promising' when
he has brought off so readable and so engaging a book . . .
there is, for the discerning reader, a special excitement all
through *The Running of the Deer.*"—William Maxwell, *Saturday Review.*

GALE WILHELM. *We Too Are Drifting.* New York: Random
House, 1935 (OP).

JOHN WILLIAMS. *Stoner.* New York: Viking Press, 1965. "Thus
with professional ability does an accomplished author win for
an unappealing hero the ungrudging admiration of his audience; and thus does character unfold with unaccustomed intensity . . . a first-rate piece of work."—*Virginia Quarterly
Review.*

WILLIAM CARLOS WILLIAMS. *White Mule* (1937). Norfolk, Conn.:
New Directions (P). "Open Dr. Williams's book and you are
in a new world of sound. Accents cling to the air. The harmony
is the rough, gravely ironic rhythm of public speech. Like
James Joyce, whose blindness has sharpened his extraordinary
musical ear, Dr. Williams has his characters talk with such a
native freshness that the sound is never obtrusive. It is pure

speech because it is so richly characteristic, and its utter realism is therefore deeper, more meaningful than the violent accuracy of naturalism."—Alfred Kazin, *New York Times*.

HENRY WILLIAMSON. *It Was the Nightingale*. London: Macdonald, 1962 (OP). See Anthony Burgess.

CALDER WILLINGHAM. *Gates of Hell*. New York: Vanguard Press, 1951 (OP).—Tom Wolfe, *American Scholar*, 1970.

WILLIAM E. WILSON. *Yesterday's Son*. New York: Farrar, Rinehart, 1941 (OP).

ANNE GOODWIN WINSLOW. *Winter in Geneva*. Stories. New York: Alfred A. Knopf, 1945 (OP). "There is a passion for clarity here in form, style . . . and for once there is *more* meaning, not less, than meets the eye. Considering all the romantic temptations involved, Mrs. Winslow's reticence, her lightness, her unfashionable accuracy suggest in themselves a lost grandeur."—Marjorie Farber, *Kenyon Review*.

CLARA WINSTON. *The Closest Kin There Is*. London: Victor Gollancz, 1952 (OP).

IRA WOLFERT. *Tucker's People* (1943). New York: Popular Library (P). "The best [novel] to come out of America in four years."—Ernest Hemingway.

BERNARD WOLFE. *The Late Risers, Their Masquerade*. New York: Random House, 1954 (OP). "This book has the bite and sting of a Hogarth cartoon . . . it is moral and memorable." —A. C. Ames, *Chicago Sunday Tribune*.

AUSTIN TAPPAN WRIGHT. *Islandia*. New York: Farrar, Rinehart, 1942 (OP). "I have lived in it (Islandia); and two days ago I met Elmer Davis, a little red-eyed, he said, because he had sat up nights for two weeks fascinatingly reading a book at which he had intended merely to glance."—Lewis Gannett.

PHILIP WYLIE. *Night Unto Night* (1944). New York: Popular Library (P). "His evangelical earnestness and the basic rightness of his dramatic situation have triumphed. Along with the slick and fictional goes a real sense of psychic breadth and depth, and along with too much pretentious talk, intermittent flashes of genuine inner light."—Richard Gorham Davis, *New York Times*.

MARGUERITE YOUNG. *Miss MacIntosh, My Darling* (1965). New York: Signet, New American Library (P). "A mammoth epic, a massive fable, a picaresque journey, a Faustian quest and a work of stunning magnitude and beauty . . . sweeping, swelling and inexhaustibly breeding fiction, which pulls behind it, on and on, page after page, loads and burdens of images proliferating images . . . the book's mysterious readability is effected through enchantment and hypnosis . . . the richest, most expressive, most original and exhaustively revealing passages of prose that this reader has experienced in a long time."—William Goyen, *New York Times*.